f**P**

Mind at Light Speed

A NEW KIND OF INTELLIGENCE

David D. Nolte

THE FREE PRESS   New York   London   Toronto   Sydney   Singapore

THE FREE PRESS
A Division of Simon & Schuster, Inc.
1230 Avenue of the Americas
New York, NY 10020

Designed by Jeanette Olender
Manufactured in the United States of America

1 3 5 7 9 10 8 6 4 2

Library of Congress Cataloging-in-Publication Data

Nolte, David D.
Mind at light speed : a new kind of intelligence / David Nolte.
p. cm.
Includes bibliographical references and index.
1. Optical data processing. 2. Computers, Optical.
3. Artificial intelligence. I. Title.
TA1630 .N65 2001
004—dc21   2001050122

ISBN 0-7432-0501-4

For Nicholas and his mother, a muse finer than Petrarch's

CONTENTS

Light is the quintessential messenger. It travels faster than anything else can travel. It weighs nothing, and costs almost as little to make. A million rays of light carrying a thousand colors can travel along with each other or through each other without interacting, carrying data and commands between millions of locations. This capability is called the parallelism of light, and it represents massive communication and computational power. With it, machines of light will do a million things at once.

Indeed, visual information is streaming into our eyes and hitting our retinas at a rate over a billion bits per second. The need to feed the information-hungry eyes is one of the principal forces driving the exponential growth of information carried by the optical Internet. The desire for ever more sophisticated visual content puts demands on the Internet that can be solved only by using the parallelism of light moving in transparent glass fibers.

The optical revolution that began at the end of the twentieth century was launched by the human eye, but it will move far beyond serving simple human senses. The power of parallelism is the basis of whole new classes of machines of light. These will become ever faster. But faster intelligence is not a revolution—it is just more of the same. The real revolution will come when all-optical intelligence distributes itself over optical networks with light controlling light. The net will have a multiplicity of interconnections that rivals the complexity contained in human minds.

This book is a journey. It begins with the oldest (yet the most sophisticated) machine of light: the human eye. It ends by exploring the quantum optical computers that will be realized late in this new century. To reach that end it will take three generations of machines of light, which I introduce in chapter 2. The first is the Optoelectronic Generation that we are using now, supporting the optical Internet. The second is the All-Optical Generation, when light will control light and images become the units of information. The third and last is the Quantum Optical Generation, when quantum effects that defy classical logic will be used to transport (even teleport) quantum information and perform "uncomputable" computations in the wink of an eye.

What will these machines of light look like? How will they manipulate information? Will they have intelligence? These are some of the questions that I ask when exploring the structure of visual intelligence in chapter 3.

The neural networks of the human eye and brain are the most sophisticated image-processing machines that we know. They provide the starting point for artificial networks in optical machines. Detecting spatial features in a crowded scene is one of the simplest things our eyes and mind can do, yet it is one of the most challenging problems to artificial intelligence. Why? Our neurons are so slow. Our rate of reading is millions of times slower than the processing rates of our simple PCs. How can such slow machines as our minds perform so well? These questions are explored through chapters 4 and 5.

Which raises a tantalizing question: What if machines of light could tap into the parallelism of light without being hampered by human limitations? This is the challenge for the three generations of the machines of light. The Optoelectronic Generation, supporting the bandwidth explosion on the Internet, is described in chapter 6, followed by the migration to optical intelligence, described in chapter 7, when information as light controls light and intelligence on the Internet becomes distributed over more intelligent nodes than there are neurons in the human brain. What kind of intelligence will that represent?

To tap fully the parallelism of light requires that images become the units of information. What if the bit, a simple yes-no, is replaced by an entire image as the "unit" of information? In such machines, one image will tell another image what to do. Chapter 8 describes holographic machines that store information optically inside brilliantly clear crystals and that dream visually.

At the apex of optical evolution driven by parallelism will be the quantum optical computer. Nothing we have ever experienced can prepare us for the astronomical shift that quantum technology represents. What will become possible when quantum neural networks connect together through quantum teleportation across the Quantum Internet? The entire network will become a macroscopic quantum wavefunction. Will it be conscious?

These are questions raised on our journey from hieroglyphics, one of the first optical languages invented at the dawn of civilization, to the holographic quantum computers of the new century. Plug in your eyes.

Mind at Light Speed

1 The Glass Bead Game

Visual Knowledge

THIS SAME ETERNAL IDEA, WHICH FOR US HAS BEEN EMBODIED IN THE
GLASS BEAD GAME, HAS UNDERLAIN EVERY MOVEMENT OF MIND . . .
WITH THE DREAM OF PAIRING THE LIVING BEAUTY OF THOUGHT AND ART
WITH THE MAGICAL EXPRESSIVENESS OF THE EXACT SCIENCES.

Hermann Hesse, *The Glass Bead Game*, 1942

Our lives are filled with images. Every day we see signals, read signs, and learn symbols. We find our way with maps, look for news and bargains in newspapers, calculate our bills and taxes. We turn printed music into wonderful sounds, often without conscious effort. Icons fill our churches, synagogues, and mosques, dot our computer screens, and are sprawled on billboards, on clothing and advertisement pages. Architecture and art conspire to fill our views with meaningful shapes and form. Pictures capture an instant in time, while movies and video entertain us with visual motion. We live in a visual world, full of information transmitted by light.

Writing is the verbal made visual, put into physical form as combinations of letters incised in clay or stone, or on a printed page, or on a computer screen. We understand the words as we see them because the visual impressions on our retinas ultimately connect with the language centers of our human brain. Similar mental processes occur for mathematics and music. Mathematical symbols represent something specific, some thought or quantity, or a relationship between abstract concepts. Notes on a score represent pitch and duration. We see the symbols, visually, and we know what they represent. But how do we know?

More neurons are used to transmit visual sensory information to the brain than for any of the other senses. The retina, the light-sensitive layer at the back of the eye, has a special status above all other sensory organs as a direct extension and outgrowth of the brain itself. In the early fetus, portions of the nascent forebrain extend forward to develop eventually into the eyes and retinas. The mature retina is composed of multiple interconnected layers of neurons that take the images coming into the eye and begin to analyze them for spatial relationships. After the retina performs considerable neural computation, the visual information is coded into electrochemical impulses that are the language of the brain and of intelligence. This all happens before the signals are even transmitted to the visual cortex of the brain. Thus, we already have intelligence in our eyes. Natural selection has driven the evolution of organisms that have sophisticated image acquisition and analysis capabilities because the visual image is an information format with significant advantages for survival. None of the other senses can give the type of explicit spatial information that eye and vision can, especially the ability to provide information about distant predators or prey. What is it about the image that makes it so informative?

A visual image such as a picture is a parallel data structure. That is, all points in the picture or scene either emit, transmit, or reflect light all at the same time—in parallel. A single square centimeter of a picture has well over a million points of light, all emitting together. When the image falls on the retina, a million micron-size receptive fields in the retina process and send information simultaneously to the brain. The parallel data rate on the optic nerve is over 1 megabyte per second—comparable to the data transfer rate of a computer hard drive. By considerable contrast, during oral communication the ear receives words one at a time—that is, serially—at the rate of only a few bytes per second. The parallel processing capability of the eyes, and their highly advanced structure and function, far exceeds the information speed that the serial mode of speech and ears can offer.

Is a picture worth a thousand words? What information is conveyed when a picture is seen compared to when a thousand words are read? Images carry texture and form, and above all provide spatial relationships "at a glance." They present a whole world to which language can only allude. Inevitably, we must ask: How can we better use the advantages of light and image?

THE GLASS BEAD GAME

The search for a universal language of visual symbols that can express the essence and subtleties of all knowledge has had a long and energetic history since the English philosopher Sir Francis Bacon (1561–1626) first suggested such a project. One of the early proponents of universal visual languages was the brilliant and influential German philosopher Gottfried Wilhelm Leibniz (1646–1716), who envisioned a universal "character" that could express all knowledge and act as an instrument of discovery to uncover new concepts and truths. At the time, hints that a universal language might be possible came from the growing awareness of Chinese character writing, as well as the rediscovery of Egyptian hieroglyphic writing. The opening up of the Far East and the growing infatuation with Egyptian artifacts presented European scholars with a treasure of mind-expanding possibilities. There was an impression (albeit false) that the hieroglyphs represented things directly, and were divorced from the peculiarities of the spoken language. The existence of these forms of writing was cited as proof that a universal language was possible, which could impart ideas and concepts directly (visually) through written characters. The difficulty was in finding an efficient means to do this.

Leibniz outlined the goals of the project in his *Dissertatio de arte combinatoria* of 1666. Many of his activities related to the project, even his development of the calculus. He corresponded extensively with Johann Bernoulli (1667–1748), a co-inventor of the calculus, to discuss fine points of notation, striving to find the most consistent and efficient set of visual symbols to express the calculus. The standardized notation we use today for calculus was contributed almost exclusively by Leibniz, superseding the English physicist Isaac Newton's (1643–1727) clumsy notation developed at the same time. But Leibniz was unable to find the time in a busy life to tackle the problem of a more general universal language. Others took up the call.

In the Twentieth Century, the psychologist Carl Jung (1875–1961) strove for universality with his symbols of transformation, and in an altogether different sphere the English logician and philosopher Bertrand Russell (1872–1970) and the English mathematician and logician Alfred North Whitehead (1861–1947) strove for the same thing with the symbolic logic they developed.

Yet the most imaginative picture of the potential of light and image was painted by the twentieth century Nobel Prize winning novelist Hermann Hesse (1877–1962). The novel *Die Glasperlenspiel* (The Glass Bead Game) was the last novel of the author and led to his receiving the Nobel prize in literature in 1946. Hermann Hesse was born in 1877 in the southern German town of Calw by the edge of the Black Forest. As a young man, he developed a voracious appetite for literature as he worked in bookshops in Tübingen and later in Basel, Switzerland. Always a loner and outsider, he immersed himself in books and began a literary career. His first novel, published in 1904 when he was twenty-seven years old, was *Peter Camenzind*. This novel brought the unknown writer rapid fame and won for him the Bauernfeld Prize of Vienna. He married Maria Bernoulli (of the famous mathematical Bernoulli family) the same year. The following years brought more literary success as Hesse explored the inner turmoil of his youth in his literature.

Hesse became acquainted with the theories of Carl Jung, which had a profound influence on his life and writing. In particular, Hesse was fascinated by Jung's ideas concerning dreams and universal symbols. As more novels followed, including *Demian, Siddhartha, Steppenwolf,* and *The Journey to the East*, Hesse's writing progressively looked inward, with increasing emphasis on symbolism and vivid imagery. The culmination of his inward growth appeared in 1942, at the age of sixty-five, with *Das Glasperlenspiel (The Glass Bead Game)*.

The novel describes a utopian intellectual community called the Order, which occupies itself with the study and playing of the Glass Bead Game. This monastic community exists in some future time, in a country named Castilia that is dedicated solely to the purposes of the Order and of the Game. The story of the Game, and in particular of Joseph Knecht, the Master of the Game, known as the Magister Ludi, unfolds through the narrative of a fictitious biographer.

The Game is an idealized version of the universal language envisioned by Leibniz. The narrator tells how the fictitious originator of the Game "invented for the Glass Bead Game the principles of a new language, a language of symbols and formulas, in which mathematics and music played an equal part, so that it became possible to combine astronomical and musical formulas, to reduce mathematics and music to a common denominator." Within this Game, abstract concepts are represented by a set of glass beads, or icons. The visual and spatial arrangement of these beads by players allows all aspects of human knowledge to be related one to another: mathematics to art, music to astronomy, philosophy to architecture, and infinite combinations of these. The winner of the Game was the player who succeeded in weaving the most striking or surprising connections and themes among seemingly disparate concepts. Though fanciful, the Glass Bead Game is a model for the visual representation of knowledge.

A quote from Leibniz in 1678, three centuries before, evokes the spirit of the Game: "The true method should furnish us with an Ariadne's thread, that is to say, with a certain sensible and palpable medium, which will guide the mind as do the lines drawn in geometry and the formulas for operations, which are laid down for the learner in arithmetic." It is easy to imagine Leibniz as the Magister Ludi conducting a sublime Glass Bead Game, the players forming threads of colored glass beads, this one representing a theorem of logic, that one an astronomical observation, and between them a musical theme branching to a mathematical formula—all interrelated, all sharing common forms that span the breadth of human knowledge condensed into symbols.

The importance of the Glass Bead Game is not the physical implementation of a set of rules that defines a game. In fact, Hesse was careful never to describe the actual rules by which the Game was played. Furthermore, it must be admitted that universal language schemes (and there have been many) all have failed by being too cumbersome and naive. However, the profound idea at the heart of the Glass Bead Game is that symbols and rules can be visual and that knowledge can be represented and manipulated visually. The Glass Bead Game is an allegory of a new optical language, the language of light and image needed to run the architecture of the future machines of light. This book explores those machines in which the language of the Glass Bead Game is about to become a reality.

THE HUMAN BOTTLENECK

The measure of any technology is the degree to which we live better by it. This may be posited as the principal thesis of technological humanism. One way that we live better is by reassigning human tasks to alternative agents. James Bailey, in his book *After Thought*, writes about successive stages of reassignment of human tasks. In the first stage, we reassigned our muscle tasks to animals. Horses provided transportation and oxen pulled our carts.

The reassigned work remained on the scale of human effort—one man could drive a few horses. The revolution came after the second stage, when we reassigned our muscle tasks to machines such as power engines and locomotives. This stage spurred the industrial revolution, where the scale of the reassigned work extended far beyond human capability, and the change in society was irreversible. In the third stage, we reassigned our mind tasks to calculators and computers, where the increased scale has been mostly one of speed rather than in ways of thinking. The fourth stage is set to begin when we succeed in reassigning our *conscious* tasks to our mental machines. The way these mental machines think will be the revolution, going beyond mere speed. Some of these machines will be visual.

A goal of early artificial vision systems was the detection of features in an image, such as straight edges in a photograph, or the detection of a unique character in a crowd—like finding the cartoon character named Waldo hidden amongst visual chaos in cartoon books. The machines that perform these image recognition tasks have drawn heavily on the mechanisms of human visual perception as a model of a working visual recognition system. As we see how these machines work, it is possible to envision where machines have a chance to go beyond human capabilities.

Our critical weakness in visual communication is the speed limit on comprehension as we read. The data structure of images allows us to see with speeds comparable to the data rate transferred from a computer hard drive; so why do we read so much more slowly than, say, a scanner can scan a page? For instance, you will spend about two minutes looking at this page of this book, while a laser scanner can scan it in a few seconds, and a digital camera can capture it in one thousandth of a second.

Our limitations were created by evolution. The human brain has "co-evolved" side by side with the evolution of verbal communication. Despite the superior processing speed of the eye and vision over ear and hearing for receiving information, there is no exclusive biological optical equivalent to the vocal chords. We cannot send visual information to another person in a way that utilizes fully the data capacity of the eye. Sign language is certainly one way in which language can be sent visually. This is a highly efficient and expressive manner of communication, possessing favorable qualities that have no equivalent in spoken language. But one of the important findings of the past decades is that the speed of sign language transmission, even among its most adroit practitioners, remains comparable to the speed of spoken words.

The difficulty lies in a bottleneck—that of comprehension. Visual language, such as reading, starts out purely visually, as signs and symbols entering the eye and transmitted as parallel electrical impulses to the visual cortex. Once in the visual cortex, the neural impulses connect to the language comprehension centers of the brain—centers that work primarily serially, a word (or a sentence fragment) at a time. In reading comprehension, the parallel processing by which a visual field of data can be perceived at once, as when we look at a picture, is not available. Visual language (writing, mathematical notation, music scores, sign language, etc.) has always required serial processing in the human mind. That is about to change.

BEYOND ANTHROPOCENTRICITY

Human limitations need not be machine limitations. There is no reason to believe that the specific manner in which we process language is the only possible way. We are free to try new things, to find new ways of interconnecting neurons and nodes in structures that are different from what nature has produced.

With the technologies now becoming available to us, we have an opportunity to explore and test alternative hypotheses as to how intelligence functions. The way a system "thinks" reflects the architecture of the system, which is to say, different structures "think" in different ways. Rather than trying to make computers mimic the way we think, we should find different ways of thinking altogether.

Intelligent model building has already progressed through one stage—the reassignment of mind tasks to machines. This stage started with mechanical calculators, first implemented by the French mathematician Blaise Pascal (1623–1662) and Leibniz in the seventeenth century and by the English mathematician and inventor Charles Babbage (1792–1871) in the nineteenth century. It continued with the greatly improved speed and accuracy of the first electronic calculators in the middle part of the twentieth century. Yet today, our advanced computers remain exceedingly unintelligent, and are still far outstripped in reasoning by the human brain. What is currently demonstrated as artificial intelligence is mostly made possible by the tremendous and ever-increasing computing speed of modern-day computers. The high-speed information-processing abilities of computers make up for lack of insight. They get it right, but primarily by brute force.

Thus, this stage is not the revolution that some make it out to be. Mathematical computation is noticeably sped up by machines, but the calculations themselves remain the same as we would do by hand. The speed of solution has increased beyond human capability, but the structure has not. The real revolution is beginning only now as the reassigned mind tasks evolve beyond human design by using adaptive and genetic algorithms that change their own structure in response to changing inputs, without human intervention. Such algorithms have the potential to evolve into intelligent systems with no human analog—possibly evolving beyond human comprehension.

Part of this revolution in intelligent model building is the current interest in artificial neural networks based loosely on the structures of biological systems. Scientists have analyzed how the functions of the brain are distributed over neurons, and are trying to translate those structures into electronic or photonic models. Networks of nodes and their interconnections mimic some of the structure of biological networks of neurons and their synapses. However, it is an open question whether mimicking the brain's structure is sufficient to produce an "intelligent" system. Biological model building is still in an early stage of development, with significant work ahead. Furthermore, basing intelligence on the biological neurological model may not be the best solution. Newer, non-biological technologies (such as optical technology) may have more to offer.

Optical technology is primed to change intelligent model building. The advantage of the optical computer is its massive parallelism. For a digital computer, the unit of information is the binary unit, known as the "bit." For every tick of the internal clock, only a handful of bits are processed even in the most advanced electronic computers. The bit does not carry much weight: only a "yes" or "no" answer. In some types of optical computer, on the other hand, the unit of information is an image. For every tick of the internal clock, the entire image, with all the information in it, is processed all at once. The parallelism of the image improves the data rate enormously.

If the single advantage of optical computers were in parallel processing, then it would still not be the revolution. Higher data rates may mean more computing power but they do not represent expanded function. Optical computers promise something more. They promise abstract and associative "reasoning," based on images and symbols that exist within a language of spatial and spectral (color) relationships. For an optical computer, a picture may well be worth *more* than a thousand words. A picture may be the program that tells the computer what functions it must perform and what concepts must be employed.

The rudimentary and specialized optical computers built so far in the laboratory are not the flexible, programmable machines that will be able to make conjectures and leaps of imagination. Some of the current limitations have been in materials and in technology. More importantly, a fundamental new architecture must be designed for the next-generation machines of light. The new architecture will need a new language in which to express itself. It must be an optical language, where images are like words and the grammar is made up of visual projections and associations; we will need something akin to the language of the Glass Bead Game.

THE ARCHITECTURE OF LIGHT

Three basic themes are crucial to understanding our own intelligence and how we can go beyond with the next-generation machines of light. First, all manners of human communication, whether audible through speaking and listening, whether visual through writing and reading or the use of sign language by the deaf, or whether tactile through the use of Braille, share a common rate for comprehension that is limited by biological physiology. I call this the Human Comprehension Bottleneck. All communication channels must pass through the same cognitive centers of the brain to provide the ability to make informed decisions.

Second, images and words cannot be equivalent (even when considering the same written and spoken word), because the visual and auditory channels use different media that initially access different parts of the brain. Specifically, the visual channel is a massively parallel data channel which has unique attributes and advantages that far outstrip verbal and serial communication—if only they can be accessed. I call this the Parallel Advantage of Light and Image.

Third, and finally, the biological and physiological limitations underlying the Human Comprehension Bottleneck need not be machine limitations. We can build machines that can perform functions that we cannot. Speed alone is not such an advance. Rather, new machine architectures will utilize information in ways that go beyond human capabilities. This process of searching for new visual architectures based on a visual language of spatial and spectral relationships may allow machines to find new ways of thinking that utilize the Parallel Advantage of Light and Image. That new computational structure will be the Architecture of Light, the guiding principal that shapes the three generations of the machines of light.

2 Three Generations of Machines of Light

The Paradigm

I CAN PROMISE YOU FOUR WORKS, THE FIRST OF WHICH I WILL SOON BE ABLE TO SEND YOU. . . . IT DEALS WITH RADIATION AND THE ENERGY CHARACTERISTICS OF LIGHT AND IS VERY REVOLUTIONARY, AS YOU WILL SEE. . . .

Albert Einstein, 1905

We are already running at light speed. Pick up a telephone and your voice is carried as pulses of light (for at least part of the journey) along delicate strands of glass. The revolution in fiber-optic telecommunications was a rapid one, taking only a little over two decades at the end of the twentieth century to replace most long-haul copper wire with over 100 million kilometers of fiber that, in some places, led all the way to the home. Go to the store, and laser scanners read the universal product code (UPC) and immediately adjust the inventory. Play your CDs, and a tiny laser reads millions of bits that represent full symphonies, reconstructing nearly perfect sound. Watch your DVD movies, and the laser reads billions of bits that are sent to your TV or computer screen, where active pixels modulate light so fast that the separate frames blend into an apparent continuum of motion.

All these activities belong to the first generation of the machines of light, the Optoelectronic Generation (shown in the figure, p. 13), which uses electrons to generate photons, and photons to generate electrons, converting back and forth to use the best advantages of each. We are well into this generation. It began in 1960 with the invention of the laser and later merged with silicon electronics to sustain the Information Age and the Internet's ever-increasing demand for more data at higher speeds. Optical fibers draw ever closer to the home, where video on demand will become commonplace and fibers will enter directly into personal computers. Inside those computers, information will no longer be entirely electronic, but will include optical data streams—first connecting circuit board to circuit board and eventually chip to chip—forming hybrid optoelectronic processors where light and electronics perform separate functions, each using its own talents: electronics for fast logic (still digital), and light for the collection, dispersal, and routing of data.

The second generation of the machines of light is beginning now at the turn of the twenty-first century. This is the All-Optical Generation, which forgoes electronics and uses light to control light. All-optical fiber-optic communication networks will use laser beams to modulate other laser beams, sharing information and directing each other to different destinations depending on the information encoded on the light beams. Information will be stored in three-dimensional volumes as minuscule changes in the optical properties of holographic memory crystals. The vast three-dimensional storage capabilities of such crystals will further enhance our ability to access astronomical amounts of information at the instant we want it. With all this information to sift through, specialized optical computers will go beyond serial digital information and use the Advantage of Light and Image to manipulate and filter information as parallel images at speeds inaccessible to electronics.

The third generation of the machines of light will be the Quantum Optical Generation, which relies on the unusual physics of quanta, the smallest units of mass and energy. This generation will use the quantum nature of the photon to encode quantum bits (called qubits) that have no classical analog. By using qubits, quantum cryptography will make it possible to send information over optical fibers perfectly immune to eavesdropping by third-party information pirates. Harness quantum parallelism to solve problems in minutes that would otherwise occupy classical computers for the age of the universe will make classical cryptography obsolete by using parallelism to factor large prime numbers on which classical encryption is based. Such developments will further drive information transmission and communication into the secure quantum optical regime. Perhaps by the end of the twenty-first century, all information will be in quantum qubits, and the classical bit will be as archaic as a telegraph key is to us today.

These three generations are worthy descendants of the quintessential machine of light born of natural evolution—the eye. The eyes are themselves intelligent. There are more neurons and neural connections within

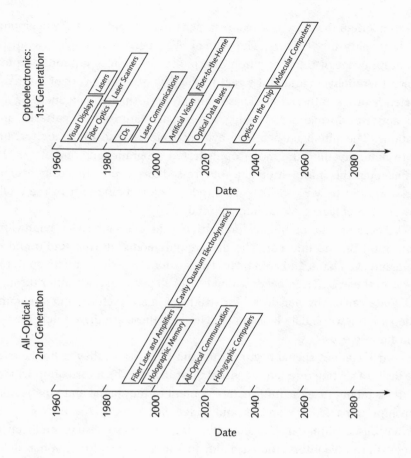
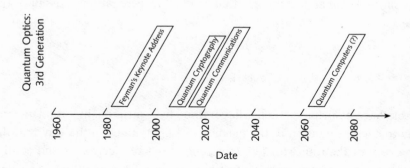

THREE GENERATIONS OF MACHINES OF LIGHT

the retina than there are transistors in personal computers at the beginning of the twenty-first century. The human eye's perception begins with the quantum event of the absorption of a photon of light in a photoreceptor, which then delivers a neural signal to the first of three layers of interconnected neurons in the retina. These neurons perform complex image analyses and transformations, looking for visual features and patterns and motions. The intelligence of the eye recognizes these things better and more naturally than the most sophisticated programmed computers. The retina codes this information in a compressed form, very similar in its compression ratio to MP3 formats used today, before being sent to the really powerful intelligence of the human mind.

The eyes are the dominant force driving the ever-increasing bandwidth (data rate) on the Internet. The data requirements of Web Radio and e-mail, and even bank and credit card transactions, pale in comparison to the needs of the eyes. The slow downloads of Web pages that we suffer through today are caused by our desire for striking visuals. Pictures and streaming video are the worst data hogs on the Net, and these are there solely for our data-hungry eyes.

As artificial net agents begin to surf the Web for us, they will take over the tasks of sorting through the visual information. The information will remain visual because the information content of the spatial and kinetic relationships imparted by images and video far exceeds the capability of textual description. These agents therefore will have visual intelligence. They will receive information as light, and process the information as light, before sending it on to us. The machines inhabited by these agents may ultimately draw from all three generations of the machines of light and from the single seminal technology that made the generations possible—the laser.

LASERS: THE LIGHT FANTASTIC

Lasers have contributed, and will continue to contribute, in a fundamental way to each generation of the machines of light, much in the way that the discovery of the transistor fed later generations of electronics and continues today as the basic unit in electronic circuits. The invention of various types of lasers in several labs during 1960 opened the floodgates to new areas of scientific research and engineering applications. Before that time, light did little more than cast light—passively illuminating the dark. After that time, light has increasingly *done* things, actively participating in optical machines.

The properties of lasers that have drawn popular attention are their brightness and fine focus. Laser beam weapons are a favorite attention-getter of technology reporters. As recently as the Strategic Defense Initiative (also known as "Star Wars"), laser beams were touted as directed energy weapons that would shoot down enemy missiles. However, these popular notions of lasers are neither realistic nor even relevant to their actual unique attributes that have fueled the optics revolution. Lasers have two special properties that are not commonly experienced and that make them truly revolutionary. First, they generate "coherent" light; and second, they are quantum devices.

What is "coherent" light and how is it useful? Coherence is a way of describing how multiple waves add together, such as the addition of one light wave to another. The crowning achievement of electrodynamics in the nineteenth century by the English physicist James Clerk Maxwell (1831–1879) was the realization that light is composed of intimately interlinked electric and magnetic fields that propagate as waves through space. The electric fields in the waves induce magnetic fields that in turn reinduce electric fields. This give-and-take between electric energy and magnetic energy sustains itself as a freely traveling disturbance (wave) that propagates indefinitely (unless it interacts with matter).

Electromagnetic waves can have any wavelength. We use waves with wavelengths of centimeters to heat our food in microwave ovens. We feel the radiated warmth of the Sun as infrared waves with wavelengths of only a fraction of a millimeter. Visible light is composed of electromagnetic waves with wavelengths of about half a micron (1 micron is one millionth of a meter). Ultraviolet light at wavelengths shorter than that burns our skin at the beach, even on overcast days. Doctors and dentists use electromagnetic waves with wavelengths that are a thousand times smaller (or only the size of single atoms) to look through our bodies using X-rays. The furthest reaches of space are measured by astronomers reading the discrete pulses of gamma rays with wavelengths the size of atomic nuclei.

All these waves behave quite differently and interact with matter in seemingly unrelated ways. You cannot feel the "warmth" of X rays, but you feel the warmth of the Sun. You cannot see intense infrared or ultraviolet energy, but you can navigate by dim moonlight. You cannot put metal in a microwave oven without generating sparks, but you use metallic mirrors every day in bright sunlight. The only difference between these very different waves is their wavelength; in all other aspects, the physics of these waves is identical. But let us return to visible light.

We see light in the visible range of the electromagnetic spectrum. The wavelengths that excite the retina in human eyes vary from about 0.4 microns (violet) to 0.7 microns (red). Green light, with a wavelength of around 0.5 microns, is near the center of the visible spectrum. It is no accident that precisely this band of wavelengths from the Sun is most efficiently transmitted through the Earth's atmosphere. Wavelengths longer than red and shorter than violet are attenuated by water vapor or ozone in the air and do not make it down to the Earth's surface in appreciable intensities. Only the visible light makes it through. Our retinas have evolved to be sensitive to the colors that are brightest at the Earth's surface and that form our "rainbow" spectrum.

When we look at light in this visible spectral bandwidth, we see intensity, but we cannot see coherence. For instance, when you look at a red light bulb on a Christmas tree, and compare it with the red laser beam of a checkout laser scanner, they may seem more or less the same. But there is a major difference. And it is one of coherence.

Although it is difficult to illustrate coherent light waves, coherent waves of other kinds are quite common and easily visualized. If you throw a stone into a smooth pond, it generates regular circular wavefronts that propagate outward from the point where the stone disappeared. The wave is composed of several crests separated by troughs with a regular spacing between them. These waves are coherent because all the water molecules on the surface of the pond experience the same regular periodic motion as the wave passes by.

But imagine a lake during a fierce summer squall. The surface of the lake is choppy and chaotic. Crests and troughs abound, but with no regular patterns. Waves are present in all sizes and heights, some as big as a boat, others as small as a drop of rain. All the water molecules experience simultaneous, but unrelated motion. If you watch a navigation buoy or a float on a fishing line in this turmoil, it has no discernible regular pattern of movement. That is incoherence. The light from a light bulb is like storm waves on a lake. The bulb emits many different wavelengths into random directions with random crests and troughs (in the electric or magnetic fields that constitute the light waves). In contrast, light from a laser is coherent, like the ripples across a still pond, with regular and periodic oscillations.

Coherence in a light wave is important because of the way that waves can add together to give strips of bright intensity separated by dark bands. This is called interference, as shown in the Coherent Interference figure. Coherent interference can be either constructive or destructive when waves add together. When crests line up, the interference is constructive and the resultant wave amplitude is larger than the individual waves. When crests line up with troughs, the resultant wave is smaller. In all three generations of the machines of light, the coherence of light, particularly the coherence of laser light, is the key to optical control of light. For instance, simply by changing the distance through which one light beam travels relative to another beam (by changing the position of a mirror, let's say), the waves can be brought from constructive interference (that generates bright fringes) to destructive interference (that produces darkness). This allows the intensity of the observed light to depend on the relative path lengths, and hence allows sensitive control of light intensity.

This is the principle upon which your compact disc (CD) works. On the compact disc there are billions of very small pits that are a digital representation of recorded sound. The depth of the pit is about one quarter of a wavelength of the laser light that is used to read the CD. When laser light

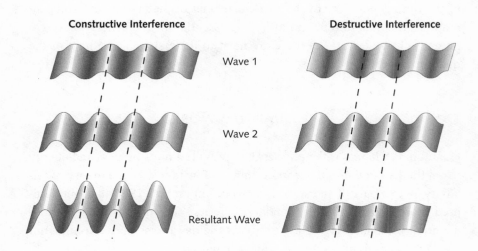

Constructive Interference   Destructive Interference

Wave 1

Wave 2

Resultant Wave

COHERENT INTERFERENCE

shines on the pit, part of the light travels to the bottom of the pit and is reflected back, while part of the light reflects off the surface surrounding the pit. The light that went into the pit and back has a total path length that is a half-wavelength longer than the light that reflected off the surface surrounding the pit. When these two waves are combined, they are exactly out of phase with each other by half a wavelength (the crest of one lines up with the trough of the other). This condition leads to destructive interference of the combined wave (a decrease in the light intensity) that is detected as a drop in intensity by a light detector in the CD player. Successive drops in intensity as the laser beam scans over the pits become ones and zeros that are used to give nearly perfect reconstruction of the initial sound—all based on coherent interference of the laser light.

That is just one example of the importance of coherent interference for optical applications. In virtually all of the machines of light, the coherence of light plays a key role in how the machine functions. In machines of the first generation, the interference is used to control intensities of light. In machines of the second generation, coherence is used to cause one light beam to modulate the intensity or phase of a second light beam, that is, provide a means for light to control light without the need for electronics. In machines of the third generation, coherence is more profound. In quantum optical machines, the coherence regulates the probabilities of detecting photons (quanta of light) in one photodetector over another. But the quantum properties of light are important for more than just the machines of the third generation. Even for the machines of the first and second generations, the quantum nature of light is essential for the generation of coherent light by lasers. We therefore need to understand something of the quantum world.

THE QUANTUM WORLD

Quantum mechanics is the physics of the smallest units of mass and energy (from the Latin *quantum*, meaning "unit"). Together with the theory of relativity, it was part of the scientific revolution around 1900 that one hundred years later is still called "modern physics." The tag has stuck because quantum mechanics is still as strange as the day it was born. No one, not even physicists, is altogether comfortable with it.

When we think of elementary particles, such as the electrons and pro-

tons and neutrons that make up atoms, we must give up the mechanical intuition of our everyday world and consider possibilities that violate our
conceptions of reality. Motion is no longer understandable as a trajectory.
Particles on this scale do not move like a baseball batted into left field. For
an electron in an atom, all trajectories are simultaneously possible. And if
you try to measure which trajectory is actually taken, then you irreversibly
perturb the system so that it no longer has the same condition it had before
you made the observation.

Measuring properties of a quantum particle is like using flamingos as the
croquet mallets in Lewis Carroll's *Alice's Adventures in Wonderland*. No
sooner do you think you have one part of the flamingo in the right shape to
serve as a mallet than it bends somewhere else. Even if you prepare an
electron with the greatest care to be in a very specific state, you may know
precisely where it is, but you will have absolutely no knowledge of which
direction it is moving. And if you try to measure which direction it is moving in, you will disturb the electron in the process, and will no longer know
precisely where it is.

Even beyond these frustrations of quantum physics, there is a fundamentally different way in which physical reality is described in the quantum world. All quantum events are described as probabilities rather than as
actual events with definite outcomes. For a long time, scientists believed it
was necessary for science to make deterministic predictions that did not involve probabilities. That stopped being the case about a century ago. If we
consider a single radioactive nucleus, we cannot tell when the nucleus will
decay. We can state that there is a probability of such-and-such a percent
that it will decay in the next second. But if it survives that second, the
chances of surviving the next second are exactly the same, and the same
beyond that, and so on. Just as many coin flips can land heads-up in a sequence, it is also possible for a nucleus to live much longer than expected.
But if you have just such a nucleus that has lived far longer than expected,
the chances that it will decay in the next second are just the same as for the
second right after the nucleus was born.

This intrinsic unknowability of quantum mechanics has struck many
very smart physicists as a serious flaw. Even Einstein (1879–1955), who
was most responsible for establishing the quantum nature of light, believed
that the inability of quantum mechanics to tell exactly when an event
would take place was the consequence of an incomplete theory rather than
an irreducible uncertainty. In describing how an atom emits a quantum of

light, he said that "(T)he weakness of the theory lies . . . in the fact that it leaves the time and direction of the elementary process to 'chance.' . . ." He strove through much of his life to reconcile this uncertainty with his view of a knowable universe. In the process, he raised some of the most intriguing and challenging paradoxes to quantum theory. Although they all succumbed eventually to explanation, the process of resolving them led to some of the great theoretical discoveries of the twentieth century. One paradox in particular, called the Einstein-Podolsky-Rosen (EPR) paradox, presented in 1935, has provided a basis for the new fields of quantum cryptography and quantum computing.

Despite the apparent paradoxes and non-intuitive behavior of quantum mechanics, it is a powerful theory that has, so far, explained all observed physical phenomena. In nearly one hundred years of intense scientific study on quantum mechanics, there has been no definitive refutation of the predictions of quantum theory. It holds at the coldest temperatures and the highest energies. It holds at the smallest scales of particle interactions and at the broadest reaches of our visible universe. It explains superconductivity and the power of the Sun. It also explains light.

EINSTEIN ON LIGHT

Light played the founding role in the story of quantum mechanics. The first physical theory that required energy to come in discrete lumps or quanta was proposed by the German physicist Max Planck (1858–1947) in Berlin in 1900. He was trying to explain the spectrum (the distribution of colors) of light that emerge from a pinhole in a warm enclosed cavity called a "black body." All the classical approaches failed to explain experimental measurement. The classical approaches used the well-established fact that light is made up of electromagnetic waves. But simple waves, whether coherent or not, could not possibly explain the shape of the spectrum. In a leap of creative insight that may be characterized either as genius or as grasping for straws in exasperation, Planck realized that the spectrum of the black body radiation could be explained if the light was emitted from the walls of the black body only in discrete (or quantized) amounts. This means that the electrons in the walls could change their energy only by jumps or leaps, not continuously.

Planck did a marvelous job describing the experimental data, but there was no physical reason why the oscillating electrons would be restricted to discrete quanta of energy. Planck presented his findings before the German Physical Society in Berlin at a meeting on December 14 in 1900. His feelings of trepidation can only be imagined. What he was proposing was in some sense preposterous. It violated the age-old adage *Natura non facit saltus* (Nature makes no leaps). Despite the radical consequences to physical theory, in that it broke the principle of continuous behavior upon which all classical physics was based, Planck's quantum hypothesis for quantized electronic energy jumps was received with great excitement. There was a sense in the scientific community, even at the very beginning, that something revolutionary was involved.

The physical basis to the quantum hypothesis was provided five years later by Albert Einstein. The year 1905 was Einstein's "miracle year." In the spring he wrote to a friend saying that "I can promise you four works, the first of which I will soon be able to send you. . . . It deals with radiation and the energy characteristics of light and is very revolutionary, as you will see . . ." Among the three other "works" that Einstein was referring to was his famous paper on the special theory of relativity. Relativity is the topic for which he became universally famous in the twentieth century as a common household word and icon, and even at the end of the twentieth century when he was chosen as the "Man of the Century" by *Time* magazine. Yet the relativity paper was not the "revolutionary" work that he was speaking of. Rather, it was his first work on the *Lichtquanten,* or light-quantum, that later became known as the photon.

The revolutionary idea that Einstein proposed was that the energy of light itself must be quantized in discrete units. This idea, though sounding similar to Planck's hypothesis that the electron states could only change their energy by quantized amounts, was radically different. Planck specifically viewed light as classical waves, as had been dramatically demonstrated in the last half of the ninteenth century. It was the *interaction* of these electromagnetic waves with the electrons in the walls of the black body that was discrete. Furthermore, Planck's theory had no physical basis. He had merely noted that the experimental black body spectrum could be explained by discrete interactions; the cause of the interactions remained a mystery. In fact, Planck spent many years trying to reconcile the discrete interaction with classical physics. After all, he was not about to throw away a century of advances in physics simply to explain the properties of thermal light.

But Einstein approached the problem of black body radiation from an entirely different perspective. In his simple paper with the complicated title "On a Heuristic Viewpoint Concerning the Production and Transformation of Light," he made no assumptions about the physical interaction of light with electrons, but instead asked simply what the thermodynamic properties of electromagnetic radiation would be when confined inside a black body cavity. By applying statistics to the problem, he was led to the inescapable conclusion that radiation "behaves with respect to thermal phenomena as if it were composed of independent energy quanta." In other words, his "heuristic viewpoint" was that thermal radiation could be explained if the light were composed of discrete quanta of energy—as if light were composed of quantum particles, which seemed to defy the wave nature of light demonstrated thoroughly in the nineteenth century. The beauty of this early paper, which was published when Einstein was still relatively an unknown, was that it made no assumptions about the interaction of light with matter, as Planck had. Instead, the quantum theory of light was a consequence of simple statistical arguments.

This paper brought Einstein his greatest criticisms as well as his greatest rewards. Planck rejected it outright. For many years, it was considered by the top physicists of the day to be Einstein's greatest blunder. Even so, Einstein remained steadfast in his conviction of the validity of his light-quantum. At the First Solvay Congress, held in Brussels in 1911, Einstein was the first to speak after Planck made his presentation to the gathered scientists. Einstein criticized Planck's application of physical laws that were not necessary if one admitted the existence of the quantum of light. This harsh attack on Planck was returned when Einstein was nominated for a research professorship in the Prussian Academy of Sciences in 1913. Planck wrote: "That he may sometimes have missed the target of his speculations, as for example, in his hypothesis of light quanta, cannot really be held against him." Nonetheless, Planck supported the nomination.

The validity of the quantum theory of light was finally confirmed ten years after Einstein's "revolutionary" paper. The definitive experiments were performed by the American physicist Robert Millikan (1868–1953) on the "photoelectric effect" in 1915. This is an effect where light shining on a metal ejects electrons from the metal surface. In Einstein's 1905 paper, he had specifically used his light-quantum theory to predict that the kinetic energy of the emitted electron would be linearly proportional to the frequency of the light. When Millikan began his experiments, it was ostensibly to put the controversy about Einstein's light-quantum to rest by finally proving the error in Einstein's thinking. Instead, Millikan's experimental data on the photoelectron energy matched perfectly Einstein's theory. Millikan's incredulity was reflected in his words as he described the results of his experiment: "I shall not attempt to present the basis for such an assumption, for as a matter of fact, it had almost none at the time."

In 1921, Einstein won the Nobel Prize in Physics specifically for his quantum theory of light—not for his relativity theory. Although both special and general relativity had been largely accepted by this time, the Nobel Committee was struck most by the far-reaching importance of the quantum theory of light as a revolution in the sciences of mankind that affected photochemistry and photobiology, with potential technological benefits. But perhaps even more important was the effect on physical philosophy with its introduction of the wave/particle duality paradox that has occupied philosophers of science to this day. Planck, though credited as the originator of the quantum hypothesis, could not make a clean break with classical physics; Einstein did. His theory of the light-quantum was the first rigorous quantum theory. It was made at a time when the wave nature of light had been firmly established. To claim that light was a particle was audacious and potentially catastrophic for a young scientist who had not yet made his name. Yet Einstein made his claim and forever altered physical theory. His initial assessment of his "revolutionary" idea indeed proved correct.

HOW LASERS WORK

Einstein had not waited for validation of his 1905 paper to continue work on the quantum theory of light. His most important paper on the topic was published in 1917, only a year after he published his paper on the theory of gravitation. Where his first work on light-quanta was "heuristic," this new work was definitive. It remains a classic in the literature of physics to this day, and also laid the groundwork for the laser. In this paper he described how atoms absorb and emit light. Quantum mechanics comes into play in these processes in several ways.

Because electrons are quantum particles, their energies are restricted to discrete values inside matter. These discrete energies are determined by the wavelike properties of the electrons, and are called energy "states" or energy "levels." When an electron jumps from a higher energy state to a lower energy state, it generates a light quantum or photon. The energy of the photon is exactly equal to the difference in energy between the two energy states that the electron occupies before and after its quantum transition. In a laser, all the atoms are identical, and the electrons in the laser all have the same energy states. Therefore, a photon emitted by any one of the electrons will have exactly the same energy as the photons emitted from other electrons as they jump from the excited states to lower states. So all the photons generated in the material have the same energy, and hence the same wavelength.

Having lots of photons with the same wavelength gives laser light extremely "pure" color, but that alone is not sufficient to make the light coherent. This requires yet another quantum process. When a photon is generated in a laser material, it propagates past other electrons that are in their higher energy states. The photon then stimulates one of these electrons to make a transition from the higher to the lower energy level and emit a photon. This induced photon has the same energy as the first photon. But in addition, this second photon has the special property that it will be exactly in-phase with the first photon. In-phase means that the peaks and troughs of the electric fields from the second photon exactly line up with the peaks and troughs of the first photon, that is, they interfere constructively. These two photons are now coherent with each other, having exactly the same energy and same phase. The process of stimulated emission, introduced by Einstein in his 1917 paper, is clearly a means of getting two photons for one—in other words, a means to amplify light. But there is a fundamental barrier to getting just any collection of atoms to amplify light. This barrier has to do with the way that electrons occupy energy levels when the atoms are in thermal equilibrium.

Thermal equilibrium is a condition of a physical system that is achieved when the system has been allowed to sit unperturbed for a long time. When you put a container of warm tap water in the refrigerator, it takes some time for the temperature of the water to approach the temperature of the inside of the refrigerator. But once it has, its temperature no longer changes. It is said to be in thermal equilibrium. Systems that are in thermal equilibrium are, in some sense, "boring." This is because their properties are in steady state. Nothing is changing—macroscopically. However, on the microscopic level, the molecules of the system are moving and jostling about, colliding with each other at surprising speeds. For instance, the molecules of air surrounding you at this instant are striking your body at an average speed over 1,000 miles per hour. This would seem like a violent attack, if it were not for the light mass of the air molecules. In fact, this incessant bombardment on your skin is nothing other than air pressure.

Despite the microscopic violence, when the air is in thermal equilibrium, even at temperatures much higher than room temperature, most of the molecules are in their lowest energy state, called their ground state. Only a fraction of the electrons in the gas atoms will be in excited states. Therefore, even though a photon might stimulate the emission of a second photon from one atom, both of the photons are likely to be absorbed by the more numerous atoms in their ground states. In thermal equilibrium, the process of absorption wins out over the process of emission, and no amplification of light can occur. This fundamental fact seemed to make the likelihood of a light amplifier highly improbable.

One of the great scientific breakthroughs of the twentieth century was the nearly simultaneous yet independent realization by several researchers around 1951 (by Charles H. Townes (1915–) of Columbia University, by Joseph Weber (1919–2000) of the University of Maryland, and by Alexander M. Prokhorov (1916–) and Nikolai G. Basov (1922–) at the Lebedev Institute in Moscow) that clever techniques and novel apparatuses could be used to produce collections of atoms that had more electrons in excited states than in ground states. Such a situation is called a population inversion. If this situation could be attained, then a single photon would stimulate the emission a second photon, which in turn would stimulate two additional electrons to emit two identical photons to give a total of four photons—and so on. Clearly, this process turns a single photon into a host of photons, all with identical energy and phase.

Charles Townes and his research group were the first to succeed in 1953 in producing a device based on ammonia molecules that could work as an intense source of coherent photons. The initial device did not amplify visible light, but amplified microwave photons that had wavelengths of about 3 centimeters. They called the process "microwave amplification by stimulated emission of radiation," hence the acronym MASER. Despite the significant breakthrough that this invention represented, the devices were very expensive and difficult to operate. The maser did not revolutionize technology, and some even quipped that the acronym stood for "Means of Acquiring Support for Expensive Research." The maser did, however, launch a new field of study, called quantum electronics, that was the direct descendant of Einstein's 1917 paper. Most importantly, the existence and development of the maser became the starting point for a device that could do the same thing for light.

The race to develop an optical maser (later to be called laser, for "light amplification by stimulated emission of radiation") was intense. Many groups actively pursued this holy grail of quantum electronics. Most believed that it was possible, which made its invention merely a matter of time and effort. The race was won by Theodore H. Maiman (1927–) at Hughes Research Laboratory in Malibu, California, in 1960. He used a ruby crystal that was excited into a population inversion by an intense flash tube (like a flash bulb) that had originally been invented for flash photography. His approach was amazingly simple—blast the ruby with a high-intensity pulse of light and see what comes out—which explains why he was the first. Most other groups had been pursuing much more difficult routes because they believed that laser action would be difficult to achieve.

The basic structure of nearly all lasers is the same, from Maiman's first device to the ultra-high-tech lasers found in laboratories today. A laser consists of a laser gain medium placed between two mirrors in a structure called an optical resonantor or an optical cavity. One of the mirrors has perfect reflection, but the other, called the output coupler, transmits a small fraction of light. An external energy source pumps the atoms in the gain medium into a population inversion in their excited states. Photons that are emitted spontaneously in the direction of the mirrors stimulate the emission of additional photons. When the pumping rate is too weak, most photons are lost either through the output coupler or to absorption in the laser medium, and the laser light cannot build up inside the cavity. But once the pumping rate passes a threshold, known as the lasing threshold, the chance of stimulating photons exceeds the chance of losing photons, and the light builds up as the photons bounce back and forth between the mirrors. The intensity of the light coming from a laser as a function of the pumping rate is therefore zero up to the threshold rate, after which it increases extremely rapidly. When the laser is lasing, the light inside the cavity is very intense, and what we see emitted from a laser is only the small fraction allowed out by the output coupler.

Inside the laser cavity, all the photons share the same phase if the wavelength of the photons is equal to an integer number of half-wavelengths. If two different wavelengths satisfy this condition, each wavelength is called a laser mode and represents a resonance of the laser cavity; hence the term laser resonator that is used synonymously with laser cavity. All the photons in a single mode share the same phase, making the laser light coherent from each mode. However, in common lasers, the number of modes can be in the hundreds. The interference of all these modes in the output light defines the coherence properties of the laser light. Such "partial" coherence of common lasers is the origin of many of the interesting and useful properties of laser light. As we shall see, if these different modes can have their phases locked together, then we can make lasers emit extremely short laser pulses that are useful for high-speed telecommunications.

Perhaps the most important aspect of Maiman's discovery was that it demonstrated that laser action was actually much simpler than people anticipated, and that laser action is a fairly common phenomenon. His discovery was quickly repeated by other groups, and then additional laser media were discovered such as helium-neon gas mixtures, argon gas, carbon dioxide gas, garnet lasers, and so on. Within several years, over a dozen different material and gas systems were made to lase, opening up wide new areas of research and development that continue unabated to this day. The birth of the laser was the birth of the optical revolution and the birth of the first generation of the machines of light.

THE OPTICAL REVOLUTION

Not long after the laser was discovered, a pundit was heard to quip that the laser was a solution in search of a problem. The problem with any new technology is that it is hard to commercialize at first because techniques that work in the laboratory are rarely practical when customers simply want to turn a key and have the thing work without knowing how or why. Nevertheless, the laser began making inroads into the marketplace. One of the very first groups to recognize its usefulness were ophthalmologists. At the time, they were already using intense incoherent light sources to reattach detached retinas by literally welding the retina back into place. Light was perfect for this job because the eye is transparent to light, and at the same time it removed the need to cut into the eye invasively with knives. Laser light, because it could be so intense as well as easily focused (compared with ordinary light sources), represented a significant improvement over the existing sources for eye surgery.

Lasers moved relatively quickly into the machining and processing of materials. The high power and fine focus work well for delicate machining that requires high precision, as well as for the more brutish process of welding metals.

The narrow beams of light that lasers emit also work well for alignment purposes, such as surveying. Measuring the time it takes a light pulse to travel to a target and back is an accurate means for range finding. In the early 1970s, one of the Apollo missions to the Moon placed a special laser reflector on the Moon's surface. Laser light directed at the Moon from Earth bounces off this reflector and can be seen with Earth-based telescopes. This has made it possible to track the motion of the Moon with a precision of nearly 1 centimeter relative to the distance of 3.8×10^5 kilometers, representing an accuracy of 1 part in 10 billion. By making observations of the lunar reflector from different continents, the slow rate of continental drift can be measured.

The coherence of laser light also provides unprecedented opportunities for metrology (the science of measurement). Because the wavelength of light is only about half a micron, the coherent interference of laser light as it reflects from surfaces makes it possible to measure surface features with heights down to small fractions of a micron.

In all these initial applications, laser light was being used in traditional roles of illuminating, machining, and measuring. But these uses were not revolutionary. The laser merely replaced older technology to perform the old tasks, albeit perform them better. In the real revolution, the unique properties of the laser created new technologies that had never before been considered. The laser was not just a substitute but a revolutionizing force, driving technology and society in new and unexplored directions—for instance, the revolution in communication.

Moving information over large distances has been one of the technological driving forces behind human history. The invention of writing on clay tablets, the development of semaphore and smoke signals, the invention of the telegraph and radio—all these filled the need in society to move information from one place to another. The search for ever-increasing speed in communication reflected the ever-increasing value of information that was required for the execution of business and politics in societies that have grown ever more complex. We are even today gripped by the search for yet faster speeds of communication.

As the laser-ranging experiments to the Moon demonstrated, laser light, by being so directed and intense, can be transmitted over vast distances— and at the speed of light. But this potential is not enough. The greatest problem in transmitting light through the atmosphere is atmospheric attenuation. For the same reasons that you can barely see a mile on a humid day in the summertime, or even a few feet through dense fog, laser light cannot penetrate further than we can see. What was needed to tap the potential of light for communication was a way of sequestering the light away from atmospheric variability. One approach is to confine light in special pipes—light pipes—that allow the light to travel unimpeded over vast distances. These light pipes are glass fibers.

FIBER OPTICS

Sending light down thin strands of glass is easy because once light is inside a circular fiber of glass, it cannot escape. The light rays experience a process known as total internal reflection. This means that light propagating inside the fiber is completely reflected by the surface rather than being allowed to exit into the surrounding air. Total internal reflection is critical if the light intensity is not to diminish as it moves along the fiber.

Total internal reflection is not limited to light in glass fibers. Anyone spending much time in a swimming pool or snorkeling in a calm lake can experience total internal reflection. It is best observed when wearing swimmer's goggles or a facemask. When you are underwater, look up at the surface of the water and try to look through to the trees standing on the shoreline, or the beach chairs surrounding the swimming pool. You will notice a cone of angles (relative to the vertical) where you can see objects above the water, but beyond those angles you instead see simply a reflection of the underwater. The angle at which you can no longer see past the surface is the critical angle. All light rays traveling at angles beyond that critical angle are totally internally reflected. The same process occurs inside glass fibers. Those light rays that make angles greater than the critical angle are trapped forever to travel down the fiber, making bounce after bounce. Light can travel long distances without losing intensity. Guiding light down a fiber couldn't be easier.

Despite the simple physics of total internal reflection, the early technological challenges were severe. Problems arise from many physical processes that attenuate light intensity. For instance, if the surface of the glass fiber is not perfectly smooth, light can be reflected off the roughness, allowing it to escape. In addition, all glass has impurities that absorb light.

If you look at a thick piece of glass, you will probably notice a greenish color to it. The green color is caused by absorption of red light by impurities in the glass. The roughness of the surface and the absorption severely limit the distances that light can travel down ordinary glass fibers.

In the early days of fiber-optic research, shortly after 1960, scientists could not send light 100 meters without losing nearly all of its intensity. The first breakthrough came in 1966, with the suggestion by researchers in England that a light-guiding core of high-density glass could be surrounded with an outer cladding of lower-density glass. The lower-density cladding still allowed total internal reflection, while shielding the guided light from the rough surface of the fiber. This clad fiber solved one of the impediments to getting light to travel long distances; but there was still the problem of absorption by impurities in glass.

The second breakthrough came in 1970, when researchers at Corning showed that, by using a special fabrication technique called chemical vapor deposition (CVD), the fibers could be made very pure to minimize the absorption. They showed that light intensity in the fiber would drop 99 percent over 1 kilometer. Though this sounds like a big drop in intensity, it was a critical threshold toward which everyone had been working. With this degree of transparency, a fiber system could have a repeater (a photodetector that receives the signal, and a laser that relaunches it down the next segment of fiber) spaced as far as 1–2 kilometers apart. This was a magic number because it was the same repeat distance that was being used by electronic transmission. If it was good enough for telephone wires, it should be good enough for fibers.

In one of the famous coincidences of science and technology, another 1970 breakthrough formed the last critical component in fiber-optic communication systems. Although intense research on fiber-optic communication had been launched in the early 1960s by the invention of the laser, by early 1970 there was still no laser source that could be used in a fiber system. All the reliable lasers at that time were too large and expensive to operate in the many repeater stations that were necessary to regenerate the optical signals every 2 kilometers or so.

Semiconductor lasers, which had been invented in 1963, had the advantage that they were extremely small and inexpensive, but until 1970 they had never operated continuously at room temperature without burning out. As with all the major laser discoveries of the 1960s, a fierce race began to find the right semiconductor structure to achieve continuous laser action at room temperature. Three groups were leading the race: Bell Laboratories, RCA, and the Lebedev Institute in the USSR. The Bell Labs team won the race for the continuously operating room-temperature diode laser during the Memorial Day weekend in late May 1970. They published their results within a month of the Corning announcement of their low-loss fibers. All the components of a complete light wave communication system were now in place. All that remained was development and real-world trials.

The development of fiber-optic communication systems represents one of the fastest R&D tracks in history for taking inventions out of the laboratory and turning them into commercial systems. Within five years, the expected lifetime-to-failure rate of the room-temperature semiconductor lasers had been extended to about a century (compared with the lifetime of only several minutes for the first room-temperature laser). During the same time, advances in fiber technology further reduced the loss of light in fibers. The first field trial was conducted by the Bell System in 1976 in Atlanta, Georgia, and the first commercial systems were put in place separately by GTE and Bell in 1977 in Santa Monica, California, and in Chicago. By 1980, large-scale commercialization of fiber-optic systems was well underway. The time from the first practical components to commercial success had only taken ten years.

Those ten years began a revolution that continues today. Indeed, it proceeds at an ever-increasing rate driven by the machines of light. The first generation of these machines, born with the diode laser and optical fiber, uses electronics and optics together. The second generation dispenses with electronics, and it is just beginning at the dawn of the twenty-first century. The third generation, which harnesses quantum optics, has not quite begun—but it will. The three generations of the machines of light are the technologies that will support the new kind of intelligence based on light. Let's take a closer look at each generation.

THE FIRST GENERATION: OPTOELECTRONICS

Light and electronics are already on intimate terms. Electrons can generate light, and light can be absorbed by electrons. In optoelectronic machines of light, light and electrons perform separate tasks: electrons perform control, while photons carry information. This division of labor is determined by their different physical properties. For instance, each electron has a charge that causes it to strongly attract or repel other charged electrons. This property makes them candidates for control operations. In a field-effect transistor, electrons are the gatekeepers for a channel through which an electric current flows. Change the number of electrons that are in the gate, and this allows or prevents the flow of electrons through that channel. The control of charge by charge is natural and powerful, and it drives the electronics age.

However, the property that makes electrons excellent at control also makes them troublesome messengers. When you want to send information from one place to another, you don't want other pieces of information getting mixed into the signal. If electrons are carrying the information, then other electrons, carrying other messages in the same device, will exert a force on the signal carriers. This leads to a problem known as cross-talk, as on a telephone call when you hear another conversation going on at the same time as your own. With myriads of electrons around (they are constituents of all matter), it is hard to keep them from affecting each other.

Photons, in contrast to electrons, are perfect messengers. Photons have no charge, and pass through each other unaffected. You can take two lasers and cross their intense beams in air, and nothing happens. They travel at the speed of light, and they can travel with a hundred other signals without ever affecting each other. Therefore, fiber optics offers more than just sending information over large distances; the information, when it gets to where it is going, is clear and uncorrupted by electromagnetic interference.

But whereas photons win out over electrons in terms of communication, electrons have the advantage of extremely small size compared to the size of a photon. The photon has a wavelength that is typically around 1 micron, which can roughly be identified with the "size" of the photon. But electrons, when considered as quantum particle waves, have their own characteristic wavelengths less than 1 nanometer—more than a hundred times smaller than light.

The small size of electronic devices directly affects the speed needed for computation. Put simply, smaller electronic devices have smaller distances between them, which take shorter times for signals to travel. The American physicist Richard Feynman (1918–1988) made the point in 1959 that there was plenty of room at the bottom of the size scale to keep pushing the computation rates upward by decreasing the size of the electronic components. After half a century of acceleration in computation rates, there is still room down there.

But being small and fast is not enough to be useful. For logic operations to be insensitive to fluctuations, which can be thought of as static or white noise, strong interactions are needed. Electrons satisfy this requirement and therefore are given the tasks of control and logic in optoelectronic computer chips. In addition, communication among single-electron devices must continue to use electrons as the messengers. At the small scale of 10 nanometers, they are the only possible messenger because the wavelength of light (even short-wavelength ultraviolet light) is around 300 nanometers—thirty times larger. Clearly, light has no role to play at such small scales.

However, a crossover length can be identified that separates the roles of photons from electrons. For distances larger than the crossover length, photons are better than electrons for data communication. Even now, communications between computers are relying more on fiber optics. The length scale for this crossover is currently on the order of a meter; gigabit ethernet is used to connect up system-area networks of separate computers. But the length scale is shrinking as new optical technology opens up areas previously reserved for electrons. Optics will soon be making incursions into the computer boxes themselves to port information back and forth from board to board on the centimeter-length scale. Pushing this trend even farther will bring light onto single computer boards, and eventually into the chips themselves, where light will span millimeter-length scales. Even at this small scale, there appears to be plenty of room at the bottom to push light to work at even smaller distances, possibly even down to the size of the wavelength of light, around 1 micrometer.

At the engineering limit of these kinds of machines, photons and electrons will be inextricably entwined in a three-dimensional optoelectronic architecture. In such machines of the first generation, the distinction between electronics and optics will be blurred. However, electrons will continue to perform the switching functions, while photons will be the fleet-footed messengers. Electrons will generate the messengers and impress information onto the light beams, while light will generate electrons at the appropriate destinations. Light will continue to be used passively to transmit information from one place to another (just as it does in the information systems we have used for millennia—painting, writing, and all manner of body language). The light by itself does not *do* anything, that is, it does not act on other beams of light. The light in these devices is the messenger, but the electrons are in total control. Their reign, however, is about to end.

THE SECOND GENERATION: ALL-OPTICAL

The conversion of electronic energy into light and the inverse conversion of light back into electric energy comes at a cost—a cost of efficiency and a cost of speed. No conversion process can be 100 percent efficient. There are quantum limits in how much energy can be transformed in such processes. For practical optoelectronic devices, the conversion efficiency is about 70 percent. This may sound acceptable, and for many current systems it is, but it means that 30 percent of the energy which should be conveying information is dissipated as useless heat. Furthermore, it takes time for the light energy to be converted to electronic energy, and vice versa. In a fiber-optic electronic repeater, this process becomes a bottleneck. It uses power, and it slows the transmission.

Other optoelectronic elements in fiber-optic systems have their own associated inefficiencies and delays. For instance, there are the routing switches. Every telephone call and every data transfer on the Internet needs to be routed to its destination. The global telecommunications network has grown in complexity to the point where all routing information must be handled locally (and virtually instantaneously) at innumerable routing switches. Currently, these are optoelectronic devices that convert the optical information in the data streams on the fibers into electrical currents, detect the address where the data stream should go, calculate on what trunk line the information should go next, reconvert all the data back into photons, and send them on their way. Once again, a price in efficiency and speed is paid to convert photons into electronics and back again. Why not, if the information is in the optical domain, keep it there for as much of the trip as possible?

There is a simple but daring answer to this problem of conversion. The answer is in the second generation of the machines of light, the All-Optical Generation. For the transmission process (where optics clearly wins over electronics), researchers are devising all-optical devices that amplify and route the optical information without ever needing to convert it into electronics. Already, all-optical amplifiers, known as erbium-doped fiber amplifiers, have been installed in the fiber-optic systems of Lucent and Nortel used by Sprint and AT&T (among others) that require no conversion of light into electronics. In addition, all-optical routers have made their appearance in laboratories around the world and will soon find their way into commercial systems. Light, the messenger, becomes the agent of control in these all-optical devices—light is used to control light.

The beginning of the control of light by light dates back nearly to the invention of the laser in 1960. In 1961, the American physicist Peter Franken, teaching at the University of Michigan in Ann Arbor, transmitted red laser light from one of the very first commercial ruby lasers through a quartz crystal. What emerged from the quartz, in addition to the original red light, was a beam in the ultraviolet. The wavelength of the ultraviolet beam was exactly half of the wavelength of the red light, hence its frequency was double that of the original beam. This new beam was called a second harmonic. It was coherent, just like laser light, and it was generated entirely optically—light had created light inside a non-linear medium.

This first experiment launched the research field of nonlinear optics. The word "non-linear" contrasts with the word "linear." Light is a linear phenomenon in the everyday world that we experience, like taking two flashlight beams and crossing them—nothing happens. Each beam passes through the other without effect. In fact, the linearity of light propagation (inside a linear medium) is one of its greatest strengths as a mode for transmitting information. Two light beams, or more, can propagate together without ever affecting each other as long as the medium they are inside is linear. The information on each beam remains independent of that on all the other beams.

But when you shine laser light through non-linear crystals (if you pick the right crystal and the right lasers), you can generate non-linear *interactions* among the laser beams. Light beams can generate other light beams at either the same or different frequencies. Light beams can exchange photons, sometimes one beam robbing nearly all the photons from another beam if the non-linear properties of the material are strong enough. Light beams can bend or redirect other light beams, something that can allow one beam to control and steer the other. All this occurs through the interaction of light with light inside a non-linear material. In the simplest terms, nonlinear optics is how one light beam alters how another light beam propagates through a non-linear medium. The laser beams are no longer *independent*, but have become *interdependent*.

The technological value of all-optical interaction is clear. Light is controlling light without involving electronics. In some cases, the efficiency of the process approaches 100 percent. And no time is lost, because the light always stays in the form of photons that travel at the speed of light. This may sound too good to be true. If all-optical control is so great, and if non-linear optics was born only a year after the laser, why aren't our systems all-optical today? Why are routing switches still optoelectronic? There are various reasons. Some are economic, while others involve the physics of non-linear optics.

First, electronics is, has been, and will continue to be the fundamental controller in all information and computing systems. The strong electrostatic interactions among electrons will always make them the best choice for control. Second, electronics can be very fast. Just look at the processor speed of your desktop computer. Is it a gigahertz processor? That is pretty fast. And through most of the time of fiber-optic development, telecommunication rates have been traditionally lower than a gigahertz. It is only at the turn of the twenty-first century that the vision-driven hunger for Internet bandwidth is demanding ever higher data rates that outstrip electronic capabilities. Electronic speeds generally die out above 40 gigahertz, while Internet use is demanding terahertz bandwidth. Therefore, it is only in the past few years that the fiber-optical communication rates have needed to push beyond electronic capabilities. The call for all-optical networks is something that arose only in the late 1990s and could never have been foreseen in the 1960s.

Finally, there is the physics of non-linear optics and the challenges faced by the control of light by light. In that first paper in 1961 on second harmonic generation in quartz, the efficiency of the process was about 1 part in 100 million. This number pales in comparison to the 70 percent efficiency for optoelectronic conversion. Admittedly, first tries are never best tries, and today it is possible to achieve nearly 100 percent efficiency for light generation and control through non-linear optics. But again, there is a catch. Achieving these high efficiencies usually requires very high light intensities that can burn or melt a crystal if the beam shines for too long. Applications therefore must use short-lived but intense laser pulses to achieve high instantaneous intensities, but with a lot of dead time between pulses to let things cool.

Researchers in non-linear optics are always dealing with these kinds of trade-offs that allow one type of desired performance to be achieved at the cost of another. But the frustrations of dealing with such trade-offs dissolve before clever engineering. Already, high efficiencies at steady light intensities are already available, and laser intensities in some applications can be weaker than the intensity of light in a dimly lit room, yet still allow strong control of other light beams. These advances, combined with the new need for photonic Internet data rates that outstrip electronic capabilities, are driving the second generation of the machines of light. There is still considerable room for advancement before the all-optical network becomes a reality, but new optical materials are opening up unexpected possibilities. One type of solid medium is particularly amenable to non-linear light interactions: glass. In one of those happy coincidences of technology and physics, optical fibers happen to be ideal media for the interaction of light with light—for several reasons.

First, light can be focused down to very small areas when it is launched into the fiber. For instance, the core of a single-mode fiber is less than 8 microns in diameter. When light is focused down to such a small area, the resultant intensity can be very large, even if the total power is small. The light inside a fiber therefore has surprisingly high intensity—which is just the condition necessary for strong non-linear interactions.

Second, light beams contained in fibers can interact over large distances of 100 kilometers. Even if the optical non-linearities in glass are small, the small interactions between beams can accumulate over the long distances and become large effects. Many types of fiber non-linearities have been studied, and multiple demonstrations have been performed in which light beams control other light beams inside the fiber, even performing operations such as switching, which is one of the critical all-optical logic functions that must be developed for routing and switching in all-optical networks.

Third, fibers can be fabricated containing special impurities, such as atoms of the rare earth element erbium. These fibers are called erbium-doped fibers, and they have an extremely important property: if they are illuminated with light having a wavelength near 1 micron, they will amplify separate beams at wavelengths around 1.5 microns. The 1.5 micron wavelength is a magic wavelength for fiber-optic communications because that is where fibers have their lowest absorption. This combination of low loss with the ability to amplify the light signals has made erbium fiber amplifiers the first all-optical components to make their way into commercial systems that are already in the ground and at the bottom of the ocean carrying telecom signals, including your own Internet browsing.

The all-optical Internet, also called the photonic Internet, will be the first of the All-Optical-Generation of the machines of light. When the Internet goes all-optical, it will need built-in intelligence to direct and route all the information. Now, sophisticated electronic computers perform the complex process of switching and routing information across the Internet, representing a powerful computing resource. As the tasks of these network switches have become more complex, artificial intelligence and neural net algorithms have been added to the control programs to make rapid decisions about optimized routes. When the all-optical Internet takes over, this intelligence will migrate into the optical domain on optical machines. Because the net is distributed, this intelligence will be distributed, spread in parallel over thousands of intelligent nodes. It is the need for this distributed intelligence in the emerging photonic Internet that is driving the development of the second-generation machines that will perform optical logic and computing. But fiber-optic communication is digital, and is therefore fundamentally a serial data transmission process. It takes little advantage of the Parallel Advantage of Light and Image. There is nothing visual about the light coming out of a single fiber.

Therefore, other machines of the All-Optical Generation, for imaging applications, will evolve, in which images become the units of information rather than simply serial messengers. Our visual world is full of images that are better processed in analog form, just as the retina extracts visual features from a scene. As it has made more sense for the optical data in fibers to stay in optical format, it makes more sense in our visual world for images to stay as images. Since much of current artificial intelligence involves image analysis, this is the area where all-image intelligent processors can best utilize the Parallel Advantage of Light and Image. These machines of light will draw from advances in optical computers and holographic neural networks. They will rely on non-linear optics and the interaction of light with light, where the information remains in the image domain without resorting to or benefiting from a conversion to electronic format.

These machines will go far beyond the Human Comprehension Bottleneck and use the full Parallel Advantage of Light and Image. They will also be the primary drivers for the new Architecture of Light. But before these machines establish themselves, a new breed of optical machine will make its appearance. Indeed, the first baby steps of the third generation of the machines of light have already been made. This generation is the last of the three. It is the generation of quantum optical machines that go beyond classical physics and draw from the mysteries of the quantum world to perform feats of intelligence barely within our comprehension.

THE THIRD GENERATION: QUANTUM OPTICAL

Einstein can legitimately be claimed to be the father of quantum mechanics because he made the quantum hypothesis explicit for the first time. Yet as his mental offspring developed through the 1910s and 1920s in the hands of the German physicist Werner Karl Heisenberg (1901–1976) (famous for his uncertainty principle) and the Danish physicist Niels Bohr (1885–1962) (famous for the first quantum model of the hydrogen atom and for his pragmatic approach to the apparent paradoxes of quantum physics), he grew more and more dissatisfied with the direction it took. He was particularly irked by the uncertainty principle that asserted some things in physics were intrinsically unknowable. At the 1927 Solvay Congress, which was the watershed conference for quantum physics at which most of the fundamentals were presented in their complete and modern form, Einstein, father of the field, now found himself its strongest critic. Einstein engaged Bohr in informal arguments in which he proposed a series of increasingly complex "thought experiments" that seemingly violated the interpretation of quantum physics. These paradoxes were simple yet ingenious, and pushed Bohr to the limit of his considerable abilities to respond. Yet, one by one, Bohr was able to see through the apparent paradoxes and to resolve them.

The dialogue between Einstein and Bohr culminated in the now famous "EPR" paradox of 1935, when Einstein published (together with Podolsky and Rosen) a paper that contained a particularly simple and cunning thought experiment. In this paper, not only was quantum mechanics under attack, but so was the concept of reality itself, as reflected in the paper's title, "Can Quantum Mechanical Description of Physical Reality Be Considered Complete?" In this paper, Einstein considered an experiment on *two* quantum particles that had become "entangled" (meaning they interacted) at some time in the past, and then had flown off in opposite directions. By the time their properties are measured, the two particles are widely separated. Two observers each make measurements of certain properties of the particles. For instance, the first observer could choose to measure either the position or the momentum of one particle. The other observer likewise can choose to make either measurement on the second particle. Each measurement is made with perfect accuracy. The two observers then travel to meet and compare their measurements.

So far, this sounds very simple. But then Einstein presented the catch. When the two experimentalists compare their data, they find perfect agreement in their values every time that they had chosen (unbeknownst to each other) to make the same measurement. This agreement occurred either when they both chose to measure position or both chose to measure momentum. It would seem that the state of the particle prior to the second measurement was completely defined by the results of the first measurement. In other words, the second particle is set into a definite state (using quantum mechanical jargon, the state is said to "collapse") the instant that the first measurement is made. This implies that there is instantaneous action at a distance—violating everything that Einstein believed about reality (and violating the law that nothing can travel faster than the speed of light). He had no choice but to consider this conclusion of instantaneous action *to be false,* and therefore that quantum mechanics could not be a complete theory of physical reality; some deeper theory, yet undiscovered, would resolve the paradox.

Bohr, on the other hand, did not hold "reality" so sacred. In his rebuttal to the EPR paper, which he published six months later under the identical title, he rejected Einstein's criterion for reality. He had no problem with the two observers making the same measurements and finding identical answers. Although one measurement may affect the conditions of the second despite their great distance, no information could be transmitted by this dual measurement process, and hence there was no violation of causality (which is the law that no information can travel faster than the speed of light). Bohr's mind-boggling viewpoint was that reality was *non-local,* meaning that in the quantum world, the measurement at one location *does* influence what is measured somewhere else, even at great distance. Einstein could not accept a non-local reality, and thus the battle lines were drawn.

The battle waged for nearly fifty years, carried on by their respective followers long after the original combatants had laid down their verbal swords. Some went so far as to propose alternative theories of the quantum world to answer this paradox, or alternative interpretations of experimental results. These approaches had many variants with intriguing names, such as hidden variables, many universes, consistent histories, among others. The theories were concerned chiefly with interpretation of reality and on the necessity of being either local or non-local, depending on their camp.

All this changed in 1964, when the Irish physicist John Bell, working at the European CERN research center in Geneva, Switzerland, showed that there were quantitative differences in predictions made by conventional quantum theory and the alternatives. The definitive experiments were performed in 1981 by the French physicist Alain Aspect and his research team in Paris by measuring the polarizations of pairs of entangled photons. The measurements were made "on the fly" after the photons were physically separated and could no longer directly interact. The results of Aspect experiments came down firmly on the side of conventional quantum *theory* and against any possible hidden variables buried inside quantum mechanics. It must be added that conventional quantum *interpretation* was non-local, thus supporting instantaneous action at a distance. This conclusion is hard to swallow, not just as it would have been for Einstein, but for most of us, too.

The same year that Aspect published his paper, the colorful physicist Richard Feynman was invited to give a keynote talk at a conference on the physics of computing. The attendance list at the conference reads like a who's-who of theoretical physicists and computer scientists, including Tom Toffoli of Boston University, Ed Fredkin of Carnegie Mellon, and Rolf Landauer of IBM. In his talk, Feynman remarked that certain quantum phenomena could not be computed on classical computers without the computation taking the age of the universe. Yet quantum systems behaved as they did in less than the blink of an eye. What if, Feynman asked, incomputable problems could be mapped onto a quantum system? Then performing the quantum experiment would be tantamount to doing the calculation!

Feynman furthermore pointed out the importance of the Aspect experiment for quantum computers. Although the entangled states had been conceived simply as a thought experiment to illustrate physical principles, these entangled particles would become one of the key resources for quantum communication and computation because they allow a single action on a single particle simultaneously to be shared by all other particles entangled with the first particle.

Feynman's lecture in 1981 opened the door to serious quantum computing. Within a few years, several proposals for quantum computers were made. The information inside such computers is expressed as the quantum equivalent of a bit: a qubit. Qubits are superpositions of quantum states—they hold the answer to a question that can be both "yes" and "no" at the same time without contradiction. The great potential of quantum computers operating on qubits is the massive parallelism represented by quantum mechanics. Because quantum physics can entertain all answers at the same time, doing a quantum computation performs multiple versions of the same calculation simultaneously. This speeds up the computation enormously, and when combined with clever algorithms, can solve classically uncomputable problems—in principle.

These third-generation machines of light are still in the future. Physicists and computer scientists are currently grappling with the Architecture of Light that will be needed to build such machines. The third-generation offspring are coming, and they will change our lives as much as, if not more than, anything yet in human experience.

But before we embark on our tour through the three generations of the machines of light, let us briefly explore the structure of intelligence, and in particular our own visual intelligence that makes up the ground level of the Architecture of Light.

3 The Structure of Visual Intelligence

When a Rose Is a Rose

A SIGN IS SOMETHING WHICH STANDS TO SOMEBODY FOR SOMETHING IN
SOME RESPECT OR CAPACITY. . . .

C. S. Peirce, 1931

WE CAN THEREFORE IMAGINE A SCIENCE THAT WOULD STUDY THE LIFE OF
SIGNS WITHIN SOCIETY. . . . IT WOULD TEACH US WHAT SIGNS CONSIST OF,
WHAT LAWS GOVERN THEM.

Ferdinand de Saussure, 1915

The feature that most distinguishes human intelligence from that of other
animals is our sophisticated manipulation of signs to represent our world.
Above all else, we are signing animals. Almost everything we do: our
words, our drawings, what we read or hear, traffic signals, our thoughts—all
require something (a sign) to represent something else. A word represents
an object or an abstraction; a draftsman's blueprints represent a building
that does not yet exist; a picture of a smoking cigarette with a red slash
across it represents a request or a law. This representational ability is what
sets us apart among animals. We recognize and accept the notion that
scratchings on a piece of paper, or colored points of light on a computer
screen, or smoke rising above the horizon, connect something in our sensory world with something in our conscious mind. One thing can stand for
another; and once that is accepted, then we start on an infinite journey that
removes us from the immediacy of touch and sound, taste and smell and
sight.

The machines of light, as they evolve through their successive generations, will increasingly draw on the ability of abstraction. Holographic and
quantum optical computers will operate at sophisticated levels of concep-

tual sign manipulation. Optical computers in the laboratory have already demonstrated symbolic capabilities in which input image patterns are "associated" with one another and are transformed into new output patterns. Holographic computers have been designed that have neuronlike behavior, with massive cross-connections made between neuronlike nodes inside holographic crystals. These computers are naturals for recognizing and classifying images, processes that are extremely difficult to program into a computer, but that human minds perform almost effortlessly. Furthermore, the optical machines can learn through practice, without needing explicit instructions or algorithms.

Quantum computers will likely go further. The degree of parallelism that is attainable with quantum computers could lead to quantum neural network computers. The massive parallelism achieved through "entangled" photon qubits in these machines may open up our first real chance to approach the multiplicity of neural connections in the human brain. It is an open question whether such a computer can approach our own abilities to manipulate signs and representations, leading ultimately to true intelligence and even to consciousness.

To discuss the structure of visual intelligence, and to understand how this structure is incorporated into the Architecture of Light, we begin with the low-level mechanics and behavior of networks of neurons (both biological and artificial), moving upward in abstraction to semantic networks (networks that relate words in sentences or that parse concepts into hierarchical trees), and finally to semiotics (the science of signs and sign usage) at the highest conceptual level. The present and future machines of light draw from each of these levels.

NEURONS

There is a strong inclination, even a need, to think of mind and reason, those elusive qualities of human intelligence, as ethereal rather than corporeal. Yet human consciousness must ultimately be rooted in the corporeal reality of blood and protein and electrolytes. Mind and reason have certainly resisted the steady onslaught of mechanistic explanation, but is it forever beyond the reach of explanation? By "explanation," I do not mean a reductionist explanation that breaks the process down into parts. Complex systems cannot be deconstructed into their parts. Their collective behavior is fundamentally determined by multiple interactions among all parts. If you dissect the system into its individual constituents, the interactions disappear, and with them any hope of "understanding."

But to reject reductionism is not the same as rejecting a corporeal view. After all, all complex material systems are made of real things—atoms, molecules, gases, liquids, and solids—that interact. You cannot put your hands on these interactions, but you can measure them, just as you can measure the gravitational pull of the Moon by measuring the height of the tides.

In addition, it is necessary to move away from simplistic linear thinking. Any interesting system is never the sum of its parts. No assemblage that interacts non-linearly (a body, a mind, a rain forest, a stock market, a star, even an atom) can be the sum of its parts. And one quintessential assemblage composed of multiple elements, all interacting non-linearly, is a network of neurons.

A biological neuron is a cell with many tendril-like appendages branching off the cell body, shown in the Neuron Structure figure, p. 46. These appendages, called dendrites, receive stimuli from other neurons. Neurons are decision makers. They assess the signals received through their dendrites from neighboring neurons, and then decide whether the information is sufficient to tell their neighbors about it—somewhat like a selective gossip who only passes along the juiciest tidbits. As decision makers, neurons are non-linear. That is, the "decision" implies a change in state—a change of "mind." The new state cannot be just more or less of the former state. It must be something different. Therefore, the output of a decision-making system is *not* simply a sum of its inputs.

A single neuron, either real or artificial, is not just a logic gate. Instead, the neuron response (sequences of voltage spikes) is a continuous, but non-linear, function of the inputs. If the sum of the inputs to a neuron is below a preset threshold, then the neuron gives no output. If the sum of the inputs exceeds the threshold, then the output firing rate is linearly proportional to the excess. Finally, if the inputs are too strong, the neuron fires at its maximum rate, but can go no faster. The non-linear response is an essential feature of the neuron that leads to complex behavior in networks of neurons. It allows the neuron to make decisions—to change its state. This single neural switch therefore constitutes the fundamental building block of extensive networks.

Once the neuron has "made up its mind," it signals its neighbors with a sequence of electrochemical pulses, each with a duration of about 1 millisecond, that propagate down the axon—the neural information highway leading to synaptic contacts with other neurons. The pulse has a peak electrical potential that is constant, diminished neither by distance traveled nor by multiple branching. This aspect of the neuron makes it very different from electrical current in wires, where electrical current is reduced by each branch in the wire, and the voltage drops steadily along a circuit because of resistance to the current flow. The unusual ability of the neural axon to support a pulse that has a constant peak height, independent of distance or branching, is a surprising feat of evolution—but clearly necessary if it is to communicate effectively with distant neurons.

A simple analogy of the propagating neural spike is a line of dominoes with many branches. When the first domino is tipped, it sends a pulse down the line, branching undiminished at each junction until the end of each line is reached. These would need to be unusual dominoes, however, if they are to mimic a neural pulse, because it would be necessary for all the dominoes spontaneously to stand up again after the pulse had passed by. Though this would never happen with dominoes, and would certainly violate several laws of physics (gravity, energy conservation, and entropy, at least), it does happen in a neuron. After the pulse passes by, the axon resets itself in preparation for the next pulse. In the axon, no laws of physics are violated because the axon (unlike a domino) is in constant communication with the chemical energy and information of its surrounding environment.

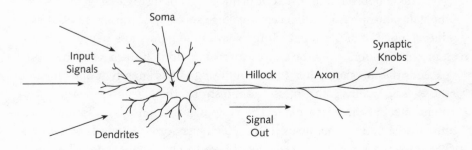

NEURON STRUCTURE

How long does it take a neural impulse to travel from one side of the brain to the other? The physical distance of a neural path across the convoluted geometry of the brain is about a third of a meter. Neural impulses travel at a velocity between 1 to 100 meters per second. If we ignore the time it takes for the signal to jump the 20-nanometer synaptic gap that must be crossed between one neuron and another, then the time it would take a neural impulse to travel a third of a meter is between 3 and 300 milliseconds. It is intriguing that this range of times is involved in many aspects of cognition. For instance, the response time while driving a car is around 300 milliseconds (to see an obstacle and begin to apply the brakes). Similarly, the time it takes a fastball to travel from the pitcher's mound to home plate is about 300 milliseconds—just enough time for a major league batter to change his swing. Another example is the refresh rate needed to prevent flicker on a TV screen or computer monitor. This rate is about 50 hertz, with a refresh time of 20 milliseconds. These times all fall in the range of the neural travel time in the human body.

PLASTIC NETWORKS

There are between 10 billion and 100 billion neurons in the human brain. Each neuron may share as many as 1,000 synapses with other neurons. The number of different ways that this many neurons can make this many synapses is too large for the human mind to "visualize." The number is also too large ever to be simulated on a computer because even a computer could not count all the permutations within a normal human lifetime. In this sense, the brain is beyond the reach of analysis.

It is important to understand that it is the *permutation* of 10 billion neurons over 1,000 synapses that puts the number beyond our grasp. After all, 10 billion is a fairly commonplace number. There will soon be 10 billion people on Earth. There are nearly 10 billion stars in our Milky Way Galaxy. Ten billion years is roughly the age of the universe. There are many businesses in this country whose worth is greater than $10 billion—and $10 billion is significantly smaller than the national debt. So the number of neurons in the brain is something that many of us can grasp, both conceptually and in practice. But what we cannot grasp is the number of permutations that are possible with 10 billion neurons making 1,000 synapses each.

Nevertheless in the developing brain of a fetus, nearly 2 million neurons are formed per minute from neural stem cells throughout prenatal life to establish the 10 billion neurons in the brain at birth. During the early part of fetal development, billions of neurons migrate in an orderly manner to locations predetermined by genes. Many stable synapses are formed at precise locations on the cell membranes of target neurons, and these do not change through the continuing development of the brain. Such hardwiring leads to behavior associated with instincts—which for humans includes the language instinct. On the other hand, other connections are plastic and transitory, and strengthen or atrophy in response to both chemical and physical stimuli. This part of development is the basis of learning.

Many more early neurons and synapses are created than are needed in an adult. A strong weeding-out process occurs over a period of the first couple of years of life, in which neurons and synapses that are not used are removed. After the weeding-out period, the number of surviving neurons stays more or less constant for the remainder of the life of the individual. Nonetheless, though the number of neurons remains relatively constant, the interconnections among them continue to change with life's experiences. What we experience as memory—what seems "stored" semipermanently in our heads—is patterns of millions of new synapses that are either formed for the first time, or older synapses that have been strengthened or weakened, all in response to experience. These neural synapses continue to change with the addition of memories upon memories throughout life.

But if we are to model all these changing connections, it is far easier to start from the other end of the problem, by studying small collections of neurons in simple artificial networks. What emerges from this study is the identification of common units and responses which become building blocks that are used to construct the more complicated networks and activities of the brain. This approach is quite helpful, though it is like trying to understand the Taj Mahal by studying the carbonate crystallites in its marble bricks.

Artificial neural networks represent one of the main branches in the field of artificial intelligence. These so-called neural networks bear little resemblance to natural neurons; the model networks are simply mathematical relationships that are most often implemented on computers as software algorithms. The origin of their name is by analogy: mathematical neural networks are networks of nodes that "receive" signals from and send signals to other nodes by connections that have specified weights that are "learned" as the networks adapt to their "environments." These parallel computational models are simulated on ordinary computers that operate one operation at a time. Nonetheless, these software models have become increasingly adept at recognizing fingerprints, faces, and text characters at speeds competitive with humans.

Artificial neural networks have been studied in various forms since the 1940s. The seminal paper that launched this field was entitled "A Logical Calculus of the Ideas Immanent in Nervous Activity," by the neurophysiologist Warren McCulloch of the University of Illinois and the mathematician Walter Pitts, of the University of Chicago published in 1943. They showed that very simple networks of model neurons (in their case, simple binary switches) could implement the AND, OR, and NOT logic gates. Since any universal computer (or Turing machine, which is the most general class of computing machine) can be built out of these gates, the implication was that more complicated networks of model neurons could compute anything—perhaps even the functions of the brain itself.

The first networks that were systematically studied were termed *perceptrons* because it seemed they might represent the most fundamental mechanisms for perception. These perception networks were arranged in two "layers": an input layer and an output layer connected by synaptic weights. Perceptrons could implement several general responses like edge detection, as well as some logic gate functions, that initially made them look like attractive analogs of natural neural networks. However, the exuberance of the field was dampened when Marvin Minsky, the artificial intelligence (AI) maven of MIT, pointed out in 1969 in a book with Seymour Papert that the perceptron could not implement the exclusive OR (XOR) logic gate. This is a two-input gate, which gives a single output equal to "1" only if one or the other, but not both, of the inputs are equal to "1." That such a basic and simple gate could not be constructed by the perceptron was a near fatal blow.

The simple perceptron failed because the limit to two layers of neurons was too severe. In the early 1980s, researchers added hidden layers of nodes between the input and output nodes that removed the perceptron limitations. It was initially not clear how to assign the synaptic weights efficiently between the nodes of the more complicated networks. Then, in 1986, several groups developed a technique called error back propagation that solved this problem. Soon after, layered networks with any number of nodes and any number of layers could be constructed. Furthermore, it was proven that only three layers, shown in the Three-Layer Network figure, were sufficient to simulate any arbitrary function. For instance, the problematic XOR function is easily implemented with a single hidden neuron. These breakthroughs initiated a furious pace of neural network research.

Mathematical neural networks naturally mimic some functions of the brain, especially the processes of association and classification, which are perhaps the most common. In the process of association, a stimulus (a sound, a smell, an image) elicits an associated response, either the recall of a memory or the initiation of a physical response. All manner of things can be associated. The elicited response might be a "completion" of a partial stimulus, as when a partial image of a face elicits the memory of the entire face. Or it can recall entire life events. A photograph may elicit memories of the taste and smell of a cookout over a log fire. A quotation from Shakespeare may recall a whole passage or scene. A phrase from a diary may transport its writer back in time with a rush of emotion. Association also can be less direct. Smoke rising above the horizon is associated with a fire burning out of sight. The fall of leaves in autumn is associated with oncom-

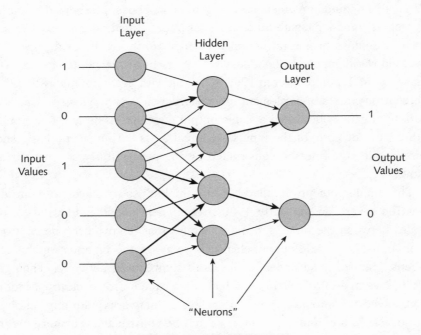

THREE-LAYER NETWORK

ing winter. The muted wail of a horn and a low rumble on a silent night is associated with the passing of a distant train.

Moving from simple association to higher functions of the brain, we find the ability to classify objects—even objects that have never been seen before. For instance, everyone has a sense of the class of Trees. Trees are plants with limbs and leaves. But every tree is different, and some can deviate significantly from the ideal form of their species. However, this poses no difficulty for us. We can see a warped and damaged tree for the first time and still know that it is a tree because it has attributes that we know go together with "Treeness." The example may seem trivial, but it is extremely difficult to program a digital computer using rules to classify trees, especially if the task is to differentiate between trees and bushes.

Neural networks eliminate altogether the explicit programming. This was the revolutionary step. A computer could never perform an operation that a human programmer had not originally conceived of and put into place. A network, on the other hand, "learns" to perform certain tasks; it is not programmed.

A basic model for learning and adjustment of synaptic weights among neurons was put forward in 1949 by the physiological psychologist Donald Hebb (1904–1985) of McGill University in Canada in a book entitled *The Organization of Behavior.* In Hebbian learning, an initially untrained network consists of many neurons with many synapses having random synaptic weights. During learning, a synapse between two neurons is strengthened when both the presynaptic and postsynaptic neurons are firing simultaneously. In this model, it is essential that each neuron makes many synaptic contacts with other neurons because it requires many input neurons acting in concert to trigger the output neuron. In this way, synapses are strengthened when there is collective action among the neurons. The synaptic strengths are therefore altered through a form of self-organization. A collective response of the network strengthens all those synapses that are responsible for the response, while other synapses, that do not contribute, atrophy. Despite the simplicity of this model, it has been surprisingly robust, standing up as a general principle. It remains one of the training techniques used today to teach artificial neural networks.

Learning in artificial neural networks can be supervised or unsupervised. In supervised learning, the network is trained with a stimulus and an associated (known) correct response. The synapses of the network that were active when the network gives the correct global response are reinforced, while the others are weakened, as in Hebbian learning. Supervised learning requires prior understanding by a teacher of the correct responses.

In unsupervised learning, only the stimuli are known. In this case, the network organizes itself in response to the stimuli. For instance, if it is shown a random set of photographs of trees and dogs, it internally adjusts its synaptic weights in response to the similarities among the features of trees on one hand contrasted with those of dogs on the other. When it is later shown a new photo of a tree that was *not* in the training set, the network (if trained well) gives a strong TREE response and almost no DOG response. This is one of the most important features of neural networks—that they can generalize—which seems nearly humanlike.

But trees and dogs share no common properties. Other examples reflect the ambiguity that abounds in the world. Is a tomato a fruit or a vegetable? Is a cedar a tree or a bush? There may be scientifically explicit classifications that put these in their correct pigeonhole, but few people know the difference. After a training session on trees and bushes, a network may respond ambiguously to an input. It may not be able to "decide" whether the plant is a tree or a bush. In this case, both the TREE and BUSH outputs will be activated. The degree to which a tree looks like a bush or a bush looks like a tree would be reflected in the relative values of the activations. Such an ambiguous response is valuable in a gray-scale world. Part of adaptability is flexibility in the interpretation of stimuli. Neural networks have this attribute.

For instance, let's put aside the example of trees and bushes, and use the case of cancerous cells versus normal cells. Because of the catastrophic effects of making a wrong diagnosis, either in a false positive or a false negative, it is important to have an intelligent system that places odds on the results. If in one sample there were several suspicious-looking cells that were not clearly cancerous, then the output of the expert system should reflect this fact. Rather than simply mailing the patient a "yes" or a "no," the system can mail the doctor a probability. Depending on this probability, the doctor can decide to take further biopsies immediately, or elect to have the patient return after a judicious amount of time. Neural networks can take such ambiguity and respond in a measured way that safeguards the physical and mental state of the patient.

The different learning strategies of artificial neural networks (supervised or unsupervised learning) find analogies in biological systems. Supervised learning is similar to trial and error. When an individual tries something that provides a global reward, such as food, this behavior is reinforced (i.e., the synapses that successfully participated in obtaining the reward are strengthened), whereas if there is a personal penalty, such as pain by putting a hand in fire, then those synapses that were firing when the pain occurred will be weakened.

This type of learning leads to the notion of "selfish" neurons that care little for the overall wellness of the system, but alter their synaptic strengths to maximize their own ability to fire. However, there is a global benefit to the organism that arises from the selfish acts of individual neurons, much in the manner that enlightened self-interest benefits society (a healthier society brings greater rewards to the individual).

Unsupervised learning, on the other hand, has no global reward or penalty process, but instead relies on internal competition among neurons through excitatory synapses that compete with inhibitory synapses (synapses that suppress the postsynaptic potential). This process gives rise to local groups of neurons that respond in similar ways to similar stimuli. These groups form spontaneously in a collective and self-organized manner. This competition is thought to produce much of the microstructure of the brain. For instance, spatially localized groups of neurons in the primary visual cortex of a cat respond similarly to a common feature in an image, such as a line of specific orientation, like a horizontal line. Groups of neurons nearby respond to visual lines of slightly different orientation; and so on. This local structure is thought to arise through competition among neurons that excite neighbors, but inhibit the response of more distant neurons.

The structure of local excitation versus distant inhibition is common among biological neurons and is found in many parts of the nervous system. In the retina, which is a neural network that senses light and prepares the visual information for transmission to the visual cortex of the brain, this is the dominant structure. The structure is especially important for the retina because the competition among neurons makes the structure highly sensitive to edges in an image, and edge detection is one of the most important aspects of visual cognition.

Unsupervised competitive learning is a Darwinian process of natural selection, in which populations of successful synapses are strengthened or are cloned to form new synapses, while populations of unsuccessful synapses are weakened or removed. One extreme case of Darwinian selec-

tion is a winner-take-all process. If a group of neurons has inhibitory connections among them, then the neuron with the strongest output suppresses all the others, and it alone continues firing. Winner-take-all is a
useful strategy when a group of neurons needs a unanimous output. As
opposed to the fuzziness of classification where ambiguity is possibly helpful, sometimes it is necessary to make a definitive decision in order for the
system to take action. Artificial neural networks implemented by optics
often adopt winner-take-all strategies. "Recognition" rates in these artificial optical systems one day may far exceed human recognition rates. Possible applications of such systems include quality assurance systems in
manufacturing that can spot faulty products on an assembly line.

Examples of artificial neural networks performing visual tasks abound.
Neural networks are currently being etched into silicon to form devices
called neuromorphic processors. A silicon integrated circuit designed by
Carver Mead's group at CalTech can function as a rudimentary silicon
retina that "sees" patterns in complex images. One particular silicon retina
has specialized neural responses to sharp edges in pictures, mimicking biological retinal responses. It ignores broad expanses of constant illumination, facilitating image compression.

An increasing number of research efforts are using very large-scale inte-
gration (VLSI) to make massively parallel neural chips in silicon. For instance, the Advanced Telecommunications Research (ATR) Laboratory in
Kyoto, Japan, was developing a billion-transistor electronic neural network,
containing 1 to 10 percent as many neurons as the human brain, while operating at speeds approaching a gigahertz—far in excess of the speed of
natural neurons.

Moving beyond silicon, optoelectronic neural network computers have
been demonstrated in the laboratory. The neurons are again integrated
circuits in silicon, but the complex interconnections are made through
free-space optical communication links. Because light beams pass through
each other, the massive interconnections that are necessary to build neural
networks are implemented much more easily using straight beams of inter-
crossing light than using electrical wires, which would resemble unappetiz-
ing spaghetti.

In the second generation of the machines of light, holographic optical
computers bring us into a domain that uses optical beams and devices
without need for electronics. Optical beams again provide the ability for

extensive interconnections, but the role of artificial neurons is played by holograms formed from alterations in the optical properties of optical crystals. The impressive feature of these holographic neural networks is that the neurons and their interconnections form by themselves, and are constantly changing as the system learns and adapts. Such dynamic "rewiring" and changing morphology would not be possible with permanent neurons etched into silicon. This adaptability of optical neural networks gives them an air of intelligence that is lacking in the electronic forms.

Understanding neural networks helps us understand the structure of visual intelligence at the level of the "nuts and bolts." The local excitatory and inhibitory behavior of individual neurons is simple to describe and model, and complex behavior emerges from the interactions of many neurons connected in networks. But intelligence works on higher planes than mere voltage spikes coursing down axons, or even in the complex behavior that emerges from collections of neurons.

There is a higher level to intelligence where the many "global" behaviors of neural networks are generalized. For instance, it is often possible to construct relations among categories of network responses. In many cases, it is possible to represent these relations as a hierarchical tree relating higher-level behavior to lower-level, or deeper, behavior.

DEEP THOUGHT

Through the first half of the twentieth century American experimental psychology was dominated by a school of thought called behaviorism. In behaviorism, all mental functions were deemed inaccessible to scientific verification, and behaviorists believed that patterns of behavior could be understood solely through the processes of stimulus, response, and reinforcement. In reaction to this extreme viewpoint, an increasing number of researchers (including D. O. Hebb) in the mid-1940s and through the 1950s pursued cognitive experiments that attempted to explain the workings of the brain based on physical structure. They faced sharp criticism from the behaviorists, who looked dimly on mechanistic models of the mind. At the same time, the behaviorists applied their dogma ever more broadly to an increasing range of human behavior and finally went too far—they attempted to explain human language in behaviorist terms. This tactical error opened a long-sought chink in the behaviorists' armor, a gap that would lead to the death blow that toppled the behaviorist dominance.

In 1957, B. F. Skinner (1904–1990), a behaviorism extremist, published a book called *Verbal Behavior*. In it he expounded the acquired aspects of language and attempted to explain language behavior in terms of reinforcement—Pavlovian response, so to speak, with children mimicking their parents' language and receiving reinforcement when they spoke "correctly." This book was reviewed in 1959 in the journal *Language* by Noam Chomsky (1928–), a linguist from MIT. Chomsky took off the gloves in a scathing review in which he stated that "the magnitude of the failure of [Skinner's] attempt to account for verbal behavior serves as a kind of measure of the importance of the factors omitted from consideration." Chomsky went on to add that Skinner's use of terminology "creates the illusion of a rigorous scientific theory [but] is no more scientific than the traditional approaches to this subject matter, and rarely as clear and careful."

This single book review has been credited with much influence. Some say that it marks the birth date of the field of cognitive psychology that flourishes today. Others point to it as the end of behaviorism. It has been called revolutionary by some, causing a major paradigm shift in experimental psychology, and evolutionary by others, simply defining the viewpoint of the cognitive minority that had been gaining ground through the decade. No matter which view is true, the important point is that the review received wide *notice*. Chomsky's attack was the child saying the emperor had no clothes. Many had known or felt the same way for some time, but no one with sufficient stature dared say it. After Chomsky's review, others took up the battle cry. Discussions and arguments continued, as they always should in science, but cognitive psychology was now an acceptable field of study. Language provided the decisive battleground for these arguments because it is simultaneously a learned phenomenon and an instinct unique to human beings. Where behaviorists ascribed to the brain complete plasticity in which all behavior is learned, cognitive approaches ascribed to the brain inherited structure that influenced how the brain functioned.

In addition to his review, Chomsky's impact on cognitive psychology stems from his postulate of a "surface structure" of language (sounds, gestures, written marks) that is connected to a "deep structure" (conceptual meaning) through transformational rules. The different modes of expression for the nearly five thousand different languages in the world are surface structures that implement language. Sounds and marks and visual motion provide a means of creating a series of differing elements (signs) that can be perceived and understood by others. But meaning is not in the elements. The elements arise from a deep structure rooted in mental function, and it is in the deep structure that the meaning resides. The process that translates the meaning in the deep structure into the surface implementation is called transformational grammar.

Transformational grammar is expressed through tree diagrams known as semantic networks. In the derivation of a tree diagram, one starts with the surface structure sentence, then breaks it apart into smaller and smaller segments according to a few rules. These rules break sentences (S) down into noun phrases (NP) and verb phrases (VP). Noun phrases need the noun as well as determiners (Det) such as the articles "a" or "the" or adjectives. Verb phrases are further broken down into verbs, more noun phrases, and prepositional phrases (PP). Even the verb is broken down into an auxiliary and verb, while the auxiliary (Aux) can at times be broken down into a tense and modal verb. If all this sounds confusing, there are actually only about seven phrase structures. Once all the phrase structures of a sentence are identified, one uses transformational rules that arrange them into the word order of the expressed sentence.

As an example, let's perform the transformational derivation on the following sentence:

The linguist has sent his review to the journal

which you can see in the adjacent Semantic Network figure. At the bottom of the tree diagram we find most of the words from the original sentence, but the word order is unusual, and there are extra elements, such as "past" denoting past tense of the verb "send." This derivation (or deconstruction) makes it possible to identify common principles by which languages are put together. Many different languages share tree features in common. The elements of change, which cause languages to evolve and diverge, act on the rules that transform deep structure into surface structure in a specific language; but the deep structure often remains invariant. The distinction between surface and deep structure also makes it clear why all language signs are fundamentally arbitrary, since the meaning resides not in the symbol it-self, but in what element of deep structure the sign signifies through trans-formational grammar. This puts all modes of expression, whether writing, speech, or sign language, on nearly equal footing.

The important distinction between the surface structure (which exists in the physical world, composed of sounds or gestures or written characters) and the deep structure (which exists only as an abstraction or as a general-ization of brain network behavior) can be extended to cover a broader range of sign usage that includes non-language visual communication. The question for those interested in a new kind of light-based machine intelli-gence is whether visual communication carries with it something above and beyond language capability, and especially whether it carries *more* in-formation than mere words can convey. More specifically, can a visual sign have a greater significance than a sign of speech? To answer that question, we need to explore the distinction between icons and symbols, between motivated images (that share some visual resemblance to what they repre-

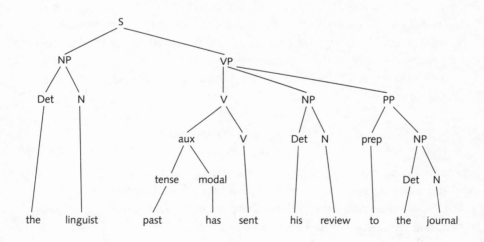

S = sentence
NP = noun phrase
N = noun
Det = determinative

VP = verb phrase
V = verb
aux = auxiliary verb
modal = modal verb

PP = prepositional phrase
prep = preposition

SEMANTIC NETWORK

sent) and arbitrary images (like written letters). To do this, we need to look at the rather overgrown field of semiotics.

SEMIOTICS: A USER'S GUIDE TO THE LIFE OF SIGNS

When the poet Gertrude Stein wrote that "A rose is a rose is a rose" in the early part of the twentieth century, she could have been describing a semiotic chain that translates a physical rose into a symbol of the rose into a conceptual image in the mind. This chain of translation is a simple example of the process by which "something is represented to someone by something else," also known as the semiotic process, or semiosis.

Semiotics is the study of signs and sign-using behavior. It attempts to explain what constitutes a sign, how signs are used, and what role they play in perception, communication, language, and thought. The breadth of semiotic study is immense, far exceeding issues in linguistics. Any situation in which something acts in the place of something else to elicit a reaction in any system can broadly be included as a semiotic process. Such a wide net catches most of the processes at the foundations of perception, whether human perception, animal perception, or machine perception. Semiotics provides a formal theory with tools to analyze communication processes.

The term *semiotics* was first coined by the English philosopher John Locke (1632–1704) in *An Essay Concerning Human Understanding* (1690). "The third branch [of science] may be called Σημειωτικη, or, the doctrine of signs, the most usual whereof being words . . . the business whereof is to consider the nature of signs the mind makes use of for the understanding of things, or conveying its knowledge to others."

Although Locke introduced semiotics in the seventeenth century, the subject only gained widespread acceptance through the writings of the American mathematician and logician Charles Sanders Peirce (1839–1914) and the French linguist Ferdinand de Saussure (1857–1913). Through the work of these two men, semiotics (alternatively semiology) became a branch of natural philosophy and linguistics. Though they took two different approaches, providing a dual perspective for the budding field, each man introduced terms and classifications that proved enlightening and fruitful for discovering and explaining complicated and subtle semiotic processes.

Peirce defined three different types of signs that serve as categories that are used almost universally today. These sign types are Icons, Indexes, and Symbols. An Icon most closely resembles the Object. For instance, a picture of a church on a road sign is an icon for a nearby place of worship. An Index is indicative of the Object, but does not directly express all the qualities of the Object. For instance, smoke is an index of fire, being one of several properties of fire. As another example, in the popular movie *Jurassic Park* in the early 1990s, the distant thud accompanied by the vibration of the water in the glass is an index of the approaching *Tyrannosaurus rex*. The third sign, Symbol, is a conventional sign, meaning that it is agreed upon by a semiotic group (of people or components of a communication system) to stand for the Object. A Symbol may have no obvious connection to the Object other than the agreed-upon convention, such as the combination of visual letters "tree" referring to a tree.

Saussure, on his part, contributed one of the principal tenets of semiotic theory—that of the arbitrariness of the sign. He made this point one of the keystones of his modern theory of linguistics, which contradicted earlier arguments, some of which proposed motivated beginnings of language. "Motivated" means an iconic connection between something and the sign used to represent that thing. For instance, the word "swish" is onomonopeic; the sound of the word in English is reminiscent of the sound it represents. Likewise, the name of the popular Japanese dish called *shabu shabu* is derived from the sound of shaking thin slices of beef in broth using chopsticks. These examples are simple and obvious. But onomatopoeic origins miss the inherent ability of the human mind to accept arbitrary representations—surface structure of any shape or form—including purely visual forms.

The expression "arbitrary" is perhaps misleading. "Arbitrary" carries with it a connotation that it is not fixed or permanent, but is haphazard. Words are not so much arbitrary as they are conventional, i.e., mutually agreed-upon by some group. Therefore, in the semiotic sense, "arbitrary" is accepted to denote those signs which Peirce called Symbols, which carry no causal relationship with that which is signified. There is no need for onomatopoeic origins of words—humans simply invent words (surface structure) when necessary. As long as the group accepts the invention, the word is used and becomes part of that group's convention of language.

The origin of writing has elicited some controversy concerning arbitrary versus motivated origins. In this case, however, the "motivated" camp has seemingly more ammunition in the archeological record. The first Sumerian clay tablets, dated to the fourth millennium B.C. and used for accounting purposes, consist almost exclusively of motivated visual symbols. A sheaf of grain, a mat, an arrow—these images were pressed into clay to represent objects stored, traded, or given in tribute or taxes. But here again, the human facility for abstract representation is also clearly present in the writing of numbers. While it is easy to see the motivated origin of simple slashes to represent units, i.e., three strokes of a stylus represents the numeral 3, the early scribes were not about to make a thousand strokes for a thousand sheaves of grain. Therefore, even in these earliest of all recorded writings, single abstract symbols were adopted for the representation of large numbers.

The human talent for abstraction is further manifested in the relatively rapid evolution of Sumerian cuneiform from motivated images to arbitrary cuneiform. Although motivated origins of many cuneiform symbols can certainly be found, once the symbols were established, they become in some sense arbitrary—once a symbol becomes conventionalized, the motivated origin becomes irrelevant, and the forces of change allow the symbols to evolve into forms that have no apparent relation to the original image. The reasons for change can be as simple as a need for efficiency or a change in the writing instrument. This is startlingly and clearly demonstrated in cuneiform writing around the third millennium B.C. when the symbols were rotated by 90 degrees to facilitate the process of writing with the newly invented stylus. By this time, the motivated origin of the symbols had been forgotten, or was not needed, and the symbol could just as easily stand for something when it is on its side as when standing straight up.

In addition, all writing relies on abstract aspects of the medium of writing or printing. For instance, the connection that appears obvious between writing and verbal language is not a simple one-to-one relationship. Written letters and words take on a life of their own through creative typography, which often can express relationships that have no analog in audible speech, such as juxtapositions of words or letters with images on posters or Web pages, or transformations of letters into images that are often highly effective in advertisements or announcements. This is because the communication channel of writing is visual, not auditory-vocal. The auditory-vocal channel is strictly one-dimensional or serial (sounds arrive one at a time); the visual communication channel is two-dimensional (or even three-dimensional, if perspective plays a role in the writing medium). It is therefore possible to do things with the written word that are impossible with verbal speech. This fact is heavily relied upon in visual advertisements to give impact to a presentation.

American Sign Language is a key to understanding visual communication. Sign language is commonly and erroneously confused with manual spelling, but it is in fact the single best example of a truly visual language that has absolutely no reliance on or connection with any spoken language. The symbols and visual syntax of sign language stand as a fully expressive language, capable of expressing any human thought or emotion. More important, the visual medium lends itself to unique ways of expression that have no analog in auditory-vocal languages. Sign poetry, for example, uses space and motion to give the poetry different dimensions than are possible with the written word. The silent poet is using the Advantage of Light and Image.

Yet the visual communication rates of both reading and sign language turn out to be nearly identical to the rate of spoken language. What, then, has happened to the advantages of optical communication when language is involved? They are thwarted by the Human Comprehension Bottleneck. Written letters and signed signs are all surface structures of the same language instinct.

So, what isn't surface structure of language? What visual system of signs has nothing to do with language, yet still communicates, still signifies to the mind? This question is where "visual" and "verbal" part company. Visual representation is best for communicating the external properties of reality, properties such as size and position, color and texture and lighting. Put even more simply, vision provides the answer to the questions of "what?" and "where?" These two simple questions are answered in physiologically distinct regions of the brain that receive their information from the lower visual pathways of the visual cortex (described in the next chapter).

Our eyes draw on visual intelligence even as we do nothing more complicated than to look around ourselves. Suppose we look at a box in shadow: the sides of the box are unevenly illuminated, and a number of the sides are not even in view. Despite the non-ideal viewing conditions, our eyes and mind construct visual "constants" that make the box appear as if the individual sides had constant intensity. Furthermore, even if the box is large enough that parallax makes parallel edges converge at a vanishing point, we still "see" a box with edges at right angles. In other words, we can apprehend an object that has little to recommend it as an ideal geometric form, and yet our minds abstract the object as an element of the ideal class of boxes. This type of visual abstraction produces many of the "constancies" of vision in which objects are perceived as being much more perfect and considerably less ambiguous than they would appear if viewed as simple pixels on a digital camera. Such visual intelligence goes beyond simple feature detection in the retina, but draws from the higher functions of the mind. This visual abstraction is purely non-verbal intelligence.

Going beyond visual abstraction, geometric and mechanical reasoning are uniquely human traits of intelligence. Much of this intelligence draws from spatial and temporal information obtained mostly visually. It resides primarily in the right frontal lobe of the human cortex and is responsible for our ability to shape tools and rearrange the elements in our environment into useful or pleasing configurations. Using this type of intelligence, we can also solve mechanical problems with the help of ramps and levers, ropes and pulleys.

More impressive than mechanical problem solving is the logic used in the mathematics of geometry. Here we come again to visual signs, only this time the signs (circles, angles, arcs, squares, etc.) are clearly ideal abstractions from the external properties of "reality," for rarely does anything in the real world come close to the ideal forms represented by these geometric signs. What is the semiotic function of a circle? Is a circle an icon, an index, or a symbol? An argument can be made for each. It is an icon because it resembles what it represents—an idealized circle. It is an index because its "circleness" is one property of the idealized form. It is a symbol because a circle exists only as an abstraction, and the symbol is manipulated only through its symbolic relationship to other geometric symbols.

Moreover, if a circle is some kind of visual communication element, and if a geometric proof showing the angles of a triangle add up to 180 degrees is a kind of visual communication sentence, does human visual communication happen at the same rate, or faster than verbal communication? This is the central question concerning the Human Comprehension Bottleneck. Can visual communication using the Parallel Advantage of Light and Image get around the bottleneck?

Why shouldn't visual communication be faster? If a picture speaks a thousand words, why isn't the image of a circle quicker at communicating the idea of a circle than the word "circle"? Certainly, it does. Visual abstraction benefits directly from the Parallel Advantage of Light and Image and clips along at amazing speed. But to understand intelligence, especially if we are to endow intelligence on our machines of light, we need to know something more about the speeds of comprehension. Though measuring the speed of high-level visual manipulation, as in a geometric proof, is not easy, simple geometric tasks can be accurately measured and compared against verbal information rates. We will see that purely visual tasks that are unrelated to language have approximately the same speed as language when they require a subject to successively choose between two alternatives. The common speed of "choosing," regardless of whether the input is verbal or visual, is the Human Comprehension Bottleneck.

But such high-level comparisons that draw on the cognitive functions of the brain must come after a closer look at the intelligence that operates first in our eyes. This intelligence is versatile and fast—far faster than any decision making the brain can muster. In the structure of visual intelligence, the eyes (specifically the retinas) are the front end where the parallel nature of the image is used to full effect. They are the best model upon which to base elements of future machines of light.

4 Mechanisms of Vision

From the Retina to the Brain

THE VISUAL CORTEX IS PERHAPS THE BEST-UNDERSTOOD PART OF THE BRAIN TODAY AND IS CERTAINLY THE BEST-KNOWN PART OF THE CEREBRAL CORTEX. [BUT] WE ARE FAR FROM UNDERSTANDING THE PERCEPTION OF OBJECTS, EVEN SUCH COMPARATIVELY SIMPLE ONES AS A CIRCLE, A TRIANGLE, OR THE LETTER A.

David H. Hubel, 1995

Leonardo da Vinci viewed the eye as the window to the soul. Although sight is only one of the five senses through which the mind and soul of man apprehend the world, Leonardo gave the sense of sight paramount importance over the others. He felt that it is through the eye that human understanding has its most complete view of the infinite works of God. During his anatomical dissections of the human skull and brain, he clearly observed and recorded the physiology of the eye and keenly noted its tight connection to the brain through the impressive optic nerve. The eye and the optic nerve were obviously the conduit between the man and his perceived reality.

LEONARDO'S BOILED EYES

Leonardo lived in one of the confluences of history when great powers of intellect and politics converged. During his lifetime between 1452 and 1519, he crossed paths and words with Michelangelo, Raphael, Machiavelli, and Cesare Borgia. Along with Leonardo, each of these personalities shines among the most notable contributors to the Italian Renaissance. The

65

coincidence of Leonardo's life with theirs could not fail to mold and affect his mind as well as his fortunes.

Despite his reputation today as a polymath inventor, scientist, architect, and painter, Leonardo identified himself principally as an artist. All his prodigious intellectual activities served his art, even activities that today appear as fundamental science. Visual art at that time was undergoing a revolution as it increasingly drew its physical foundations from mathematics and science. The artist Filippo Brunelleschi at the beginning of the century had extensively studied mathematics and discovered some of the mathematical laws of perspective, including the concept of the vanishing point, which had been known by the Greeks and Romans but had been lost. These efforts on perspective by Brunelleschi and later by Leon Batista Alberti helped to ground art and science as two facets of the same tangible world. Leonardo seized on this idea and amplified it. When he was nearly forty, he conceived of developing a comprehensive "science of painting." He launched into many fundamental scientific investigations because he felt that the artist's faithful representation of the perceived world required complete comprehension of the form and function of all subjects, living and non-living. He produced a treatise on painting, a treatise on architecture, a book on mechanics, and a broad outline on anatomy.

In the course of writing notebooks filled with his studies of the science of art, Leonardo developed a visual record in which scientific illustration took precedence over written text. He was guided by a conviction that artists were uniquely qualified to derive and record new knowledge because of their special ability to perceive visually and to render that knowledge pictorially. The illustration was, for him, the most unambiguous and direct "language" in which to convey understanding. In his notebooks, contrary to the contemporary scientific traditions that used verbal description almost exclusively, Leonardo used illustration as the primary record and words mostly for annotation. His techniques were the predecessors of modern scientific illustration.

By Leonardo's own admission, he dissected as many as thirty human corpses during his lifetime, giving him firsthand knowledge of unprecedented depth concerning human anatomy. Despite the number of dissections, it appears that he never quite got used to the process. He wrote in one of his later notebooks: "And though you have a love for such things, you will perhaps be impeded by your stomach, and if this does not impede you, you will perhaps be impeded by the fear of living through the night hours in the company of quartered and flayed corpses fearful to behold."

Particularly fascinated by the structure of the human eye and its connection to the brain through the optic nerve, he traced the nerve to specific parts of the brain, which he identified as the "seat of the soul," where apprehension of the visual image turned into comprehension and consciousness. In the process, Leonardo discovered the structure where the two optic nerves from each of the eyes crossed. This is today termed the *optic chiasm,* and Leonardo was the first to identify it. His discovery took place while he was investigating aspects of binocular vision, and he took the convergence of the two optic nerves in the chiasm as proof of the dual use of the images of both eyes to form a single mental image.

Dissections of the human eye presented unexpected problems for Leonardo, especially in observing the shape of the internal structure of the eye. When the eye of a newly deceased corpse was cut, the aqueous humor that fills the eye behind the cornea would leak away, deforming the eye before he could note the shape of its internal structure. As a result, many of his early drawings of the shape of the lens are incorrect, which misled him in his theory of image formation in the eye. In a later notebook, he devised a characteristically ingenious technique of preserving the eye's shape by first boiling it in egg white. After the hardened mass was removed from the water, the white and eye could be dissected together, with the hardened white providing support for the sliced eye.

Leonardo was the first to appreciate fully the role played by the iris in regulating the intensity of light allowed into the eye. In his notebooks, he clearly depicted the analogy of the eye to *camera obscura,* a technique for forming images without lenses by making a small hole in a wall of an otherwise darkened room (hence the Latin name, which means "darkened chamber"). Illuminated objects outside the room will cast their image on the wall opposite the small hole. This technique was known in antiquity, and was revived in the fifteenth century as an aid to creating perspective drawings. It continued to be used up to the nineteenth century in the form of small black boxes with frosted glass opposite to the pinhole. The invention of the modern camera required only the simple substitution of a light-sensitive plate for the frosted glass.

The analogy of the eye as a camera obscura is a good one, but it caused an apparent problem. The camera obscura projects an inverted image on the far wall, and Leonardo could not reconcile the inverted image of the camera obscura with the "upright" perception of the world in the mind. This difficulty was compounded by his troubles dissecting the eye, in which he incorrectly characterized the lens as spherical. A spherical lens behind the iris seemingly solved his problem of the inverted image, because it would in fact reinvert an image to right side up. But in this respect, he was incorrect. The lens of the eye does not reinvert the image, and in fact the image *is* projected upside down on the retina. We know now that the eye is not so much a "window" as it is a translator. An upside-down image causes no problem for the brain. It is merely the first distortion in the process of seeing.

THE DISTORTING EYE

What is at the bottom of the mystery of the eye? In many ways, it is a straightforward optical instrument. It projects an image onto the light-sensitive layer at its rear called the retina. The retina, in turn, is a transducer, that is, a translator that takes the patterns of lightness, darkness, and color that constitute the image and converts them into the language of the brain—electrical impulses that travel along the optic nerve. The eye is contained within a roughly spherical lining composed of the sclera—the white of the eye, which connects continuously with the protruding cornea.

The image-forming components of the eye—starting from the outside— are the cornea, the iris, and the crystalline lens. The crystalline lens, despite its name, is not the primary focusing element in the eye. In fact, 70 percent of the focusing power of the eye comes from the cornea. This is because focusing power is strongly dependent on differences in the optical density at the interface between two transparent media. The difference in density between air and the cornea is about three times larger than the difference in density between the crystalline lens and the liquid surrounding it. On the other hand, the crystalline lens exclusively controls the focus to see near or far as muscles increase or decrease the tension on the lens, slightly changing its curvature.

The eye is a specialized organ with specialized tissue unlike any other in the human body. For instance, the transparent cornea is composed of the same material as the opaque white of the eye, to which it is a contiguous part. Both materials contain collagen fibers, but while in the cornea these fibers are all aligned, in the sclera the fibers are randomly oriented. This simple difference in fiber distribution causes the difference between opacity and transparency.

Yet the best example of a uniquely specialized layer in the eye is the retina. The retina is the light-sensitive layer of neurons that lines the inside of the eyeball. The light-sensitivity of the retina is not uniform, but has varying sensitivity depending on the location relative to the visual axis, shown in The Eye figure. At the far posterior end of the visual axis lies the fovea. This is where an image is focused when you concentrate your vision on a point straight ahead. The retina here is highly sensitive to color, and is able to resolve fine spatial features. Farther off the visual axis, the retina responds mostly to intensity, independent of color. The place where the retina attaches to the optic nerve is the blind spot. No receptors are present at this location.

The most important aspect of the retina is that it is composed of neurons that have many similarities to neurons found in the brain. Indeed, the

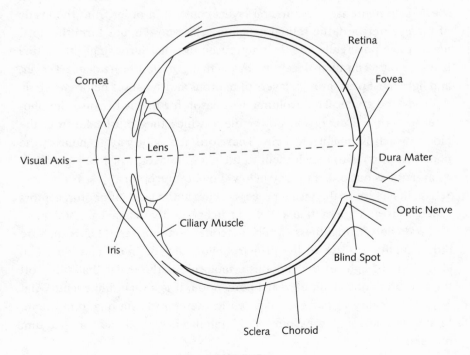

THE EYE

retina in a human fetus is initially formed as an appendage of the brain, which only later moves forward in the skull and differentiates into the specialized light-sensing organ of the fully developed child. Furthermore, the sclera is physiologically a continuation of the *dura mater,* the outer covering of the brain. Therefore, the eyes are not just connected to the brain, but are part of it. The next time you look at the whites of your eyes in the mirror, remind yourself that you are looking at the covering of your brain poking out the front of your head.

Leonardo was correct about the intimate connection of the eye and brain. He saw and comprehended their similar tissues and structures. But in his mistaken conclusion of an inverted image on the back of the eye, Leonardo could not know of the adaptive processing power of the neural networks in the retina and brain. He was correct to identify the optic nerve as the conduit that passes visual information from the eyes to the seat of the soul, the conscious self; but he could not know that all vision is projected to the brain in a coded form that is created by the image compression functions of the retina.

The retina is made up of three distinct neural layers, each containing specialized neurons. These neural layers contain, in order from the inside of the eye outward, the retinal ganglion cells whose axons form the optic nerve, the bipolar cells, and the photoreceptor cells. Surprisingly, the retina is inside out. The photoreceptors are actually buried in its deepest layer, and light must pass through layers of neurons and synapses before reaching the rods and cones. The evolutionary reason for this is because the photoreceptors need energy to power them, which they must take from the blood, which is opaque to light. Therefore, the only way to nourish the photoreceptors is to attach them to the choroid layer, which is highly vascular, but lies out of light's way below the photoreceptors.

The first stage of the visual process occurs in the layer of photoreceptors called rods and cones that carry the light-sensitive chemical rhodopsin. The rods detect brightness, while the cones come in three kinds that are differentially sensitive to the primary colors of red, green, and blue. The absorption of light in the rhodopsin molecule is the event that starts off the neurosemiotic chain of visual perception. It is a quantum event. What we see as reality in our everyday world therefore has a quantum origin. In this fundamental way, our visual intelligence is already a quantum process.

THE QUANTUM ORIGIN OF PERCEPTION

All measurements of the quanta of light begin with atoms and molecules. All atoms and molecules absorb light one photon at a time because a molecule is itself a quantum mechanical object. It has internal energy states that are quantized. When a photon has a quantum of energy that is precisely equal to the difference between two energies in the molecule, the molecule can absorb the photon and be triggered into this specific 'excited state.'

Excited states of atoms and molecules are the beginning of chemical reactions. If an atom is in an excited state, it has an extra amount of energy that it can give to another atom or molecule. Or it can change chemical bonds by combining with other atoms, or separating a larger molecule into smaller chemical parts. This is what happens when rhodopsin absorbs a photon of light and is excited into a higher energy level. The absorbed energy starts a chain of events that ultimately launches an electrical impulse up the optic nerve to the visual processing centers of the brain. This is how we know light. Our eyes are quantum photoreceivers that measure quanta of light energy. Sufficient light stimulation of many molecules of rhodopsin in the receptor eventually triggers the photoreceptor axon that excites the neural synapses of the next layer of neurons in the retina, the bipolar cells.

A single bipolar cell collects the excitations of many photoreceptors, forming complicated interconnections that cross the interface between the two layers. This is the first stage of neural interconnections, which starts the process of information extraction and compression as the image falling on the retina is turned into a succinct code for transmission to the brain. The interconnections become even more complicated when bipolar cells make connections with retinal ganglion cells. The retinal ganglion cells are the final neural step in the retina, and their axons are what comprise the optic nerve that passes from the eye and brings the "image" to the higher visual pathways of the brain. By this stage, the image has been condensed, compressed, and even accentuated into a representation that would be hard to recognize as coming from the original image—hard to recognize, that is, by an outside observer. For the brain, it is the most natural and efficient representation.

STREAMING MEDIA FOR THE EYES

The human retina contains about 120 million rods and about 6 million cones, but only about 1 million ganglion cells send signals to the brain. Therefore, on average, the light information falling on 126 photoreceptors produces only a single signal in one ganglion cell axon. Where has all the information gone?

To understand how the brain "sees," it is first necessary to ask specific questions about what it means for an image to have an information content. At the simplest level, an image can be thought to consist of a collection of pixels. A pixel is the smallest independent area in an imaging system. In photographic film, a pixel is a grain of silver halide crystal. On your computer screen, a pixel is a bright point of light. In a digital camera or video, a pixel is a small silicon photosensor. There are typically about 10 million pixels per square centimeter in a photograph, about 100,000 pixels per square centimeter in a digital camera, and around 2,000 pixels per square centimeter on a high-resolution computer screen. Clearly, the photograph wins over the electronic technology in terms of the fineness of detail it can capture, although the electronic technology is gaining.

In all these examples, each pixel is purely a *local* function of light intensity. There is no influence that would cause one pixel to respond differently depending on how its neighbors are responding. Each pixel is fully independent, and gives a unique measure of local information. Therefore, a digital camera that has $1,000 \times 1,000$ pixels, where each pixel can respond to 12 bits of intensity (4,096 different gray-scale levels), produces an information output of 12 million bits. This information is a straight point-by-point representation of the image. It can be stored electronically, and used to reconstruct the image on a display device. The process is simple and direct, but extremely inefficient.

When you look at a picture, what do you really care about? If there is a featureless blue sky in a photograph, do you need to know which and exactly how many pixels are blue? Aren't you much more interested in how the blue sky is terminated by the spectacular profile of a snow-capped mountain range? The edges are where the interest lies.

Have you ever wanted to photograph something beautiful set in shade when the background is in full sunshine? Your eye can see all parts of the scene clearly, the fine details and subtle shades and hues. Yet when you have the film developed and expect an award winner, you find the object black and featureless in the print, and the background overexposed. No photographic film, or even a video camera, can do what the eyes do when extracting features from a scene with very large differences in brightness. This is because the eyes do more than just respond locally to intensity. The magic of vision, in all vertebrates, arises because what one ganglion cell "sees" and tells the brain depends on what its neighbors see. The brightness and color of everything you see depends on what surrounds it because information is not just a local property.

The transformation of the signals from 126 million receptors into 1 million axons in the optic nerve is called information convergence. This is approximately how much the information in a typical image can be reduced to its basic "interesting" components. The retina achieves information convergence by responding only to changes in space or changes in time, that is, the retina detects spatial and temporal features while simply ignoring the lack of features. It is a feature detector. To measure a change in something—for instance, a spatial change from light to dark, or an object moving from one place to another—requires that light detected at one location be compared against light detected at a different location or at a different time. What is happening somewhere else needs to be compared with what is happening locally. Because feature detection requires comparisons among neighboring pixels, feature detection in an image is a *non-local* process that requires lateral connections among the pixels, that is, among the ganglion neural cells.

Lateral connections are made when one bipolar cell connects to many photoreceptors, or when many ganglion cells connect to many bipolar cells, producing an increasing hierarchy of complexity as the optical signal moves up through the retinal neural network to the optic nerve. In addition, there are special neurons that reside exclusively within a synaptic layer, facilitating and augmenting the lateral connections. The terminology of the differing neurons in the retina is pleasantly descriptive. Horizontal cells come in forms called mop, brush, flat-topped, midget, and centrifugal varieties. The ganglion cells also come in assorted types such as parasol, shrub, garland, and diffuse varieties. While descriptive of the form of the cells, the names offer no hint about their functions. These functions, in fact, are still being sorted out.

But, much is known. The lateral connections made in the synaptic layers produce feature detectors. The most common feature detectors found in the retina are edge detectors. These can be constructed in a very simple way using an architecture of neural connections mentioned above, called "center-surround." In the center-surround configuration, photoreceptors in the center of the ganglion receptive field produce a direct excitatory response to light stimulus, while the photoreceptors in the surrounding part of the receptive field inhibit the ganglion response. For a uniform illumination of the full receptive field, the two effects cancel out, and the firing rate of the ganglion cell is unaffected. Uniform illumination—a lack of any feature or information—produces no ganglion response.

On the other hand, an edge feature in an image that is caused by a change in lighting or color *will* produce a ganglion response. For instance, if the left part of the surround is in the dark, but the rest of the receptive field is in light, then the excitation from the center cannot be balanced by the left-hand surround, and the ganglion cell will be excited. Conversely, if only the left-hand surround is illuminated, then the ganglion cell will be inhibited. Therefore, as an edge passes through a center-surround receptive field, the ganglion will first be quiescent when it is uniformly illuminated, then will be inhibited, then will be excited, and finally will become quiescent once more when the edge has passed and the field is again uniformly illuminated.

The center-surround receptive field is only one of many types. In addition to the on-center surround field, there are also off-center surround fields in which the center of the field inhibits the ganglion, while the surround excites it. There are also orientation-sensitive edge detectors that respond differently if the edge is a step up or a step down in intensity, or if it is oriented vertically, horizontally, or at any other angle. All these examples are of spatial feature detection. In addition, there are receptive fields that can respond to motion, and can sense the direction of motion.

Despite the complex neural circuitry contained in the retina, and the wide variety of visual functions it supports, it represents only the "front end" of a visual cognition system. The ability to recognize edges and features and specific movements is necessary for any functioning visual system, but not sufficient. It is primarily an information compression and editing process, much like the compression that you use when you view streaming video off the Internet. The compression ratio of 126:1 of the retina is surprisingly similar to the standard compression techniques, such as MP3, used for the Internet. However, this is just the beginning. The compressed information must still move to the higher visual pathways in the brain in order for *cognition* to occur, that is, in order for us to know what we are looking at.

DECONSTRUCTING THE IMAGE

The recent rapid advances in functional imaging of the brain using magnetic resonance imaging (MRI) and positron emission tomography (PET) make it possible to perform highly controlled experiments that show where brain activity is heightened during specific tasks, or in response to specific visual stimuli. However, an understanding of the human visual pathways remains largely incomplete because of the understandably limited opportunities to perform invasive experiments. Old World and New World monkeys do not have the benefit of such protection and have contributed in a substantial way to the understanding of the visual pathways of primates in general. Of the different species of monkeys used in vision research, the unfortunate macaque monkey has borne the brunt because PET shows strong similarities between human and macaque cortical structure. Therefore, most of what is known of our visual processing has come from primate research.

The work on the monkeys (and to a lesser extent on cats) has taught us that the first stop in the visual pathway, on the road to the higher cortical areas, is the lateral geniculate nucleus (LGN). On the way to the LGN, the optic nerves split in two, with half the information from each eye directed to opposite LGNs on the right and left sides of the brain. In the LGN, the ganglions from the left and right visual fields terminate in a sandwich structure, with six layers that alternate between left and right. This is the first stage of interleaving that ensures binocular perception in the brain. It also is a process that pulls both images apart and scrambles them.

Another important differentiation which is first noted at the LGN, but which is maintained far into the higher visual processing centers, is that almost all of the ganglion receptive fields can be classified into two general types, known as the "what" and "where" ganglions. "What" ganglions respond to features such as shape and color, while "where" ganglions respond to motion as well as to form caused by motion. Most of the ganglions are "what" ganglions—about 80 percent. The "where" ganglions make up about 10 percent, with the remainder made up of ganglions that cannot be so easily classified. The unequal division between "what" and "where" reflects the more difficult task of ascertaining *what* something is relative to the easy task of simply telling *where* it is. These "what" and "where" ganglions terminate in segregated layers in the LGN, where they retain the specific topographic arrangement that their receptive fields had in the retina. In this way, each LGN contains two mappings of the spatial relationships. One mapping is of the "what" fields and the other is of the "where" fields. However, it is important to keep clear that the distribution of neurons in the LGN is not an "image" map, but consists of the feature code signaled by the retinal ganglion cells.

The interleaved left and right layers of the LGN connect to the primary visual cortex through neural axons that make up a structure in the brain called the optic radiation. The optic radiation terminates in a special layer in the visual cortex called the 4C layer, where neurons respond to the basic center-surround fields of the retinal ganglion cells. The primary visual cortex is also known as the striate cortex, or as the *aria striata,* because it was found that the brain in this area is made up of minute striations parallel to the surface of the cortex. The regularity of the layering of the striate cortex differentiates it markedly from every other part of the cerebral cortex, perhaps reflecting the regularity in the division of the visual field into definable elements, such as line orientations and lengths, direction of movement, curvature, and so on. The striations are therefore external manifestations of an internal complex layering of neurons that respond to stimuli coming from the LGN (and ultimately from the retina) in very specific ways.

One of the significant cognitive discoveries of the twentieth century pertaining to visual perception in the brain was made by David Hubel (1926–) and Torsten Wiesel (1924–) working at Johns Hopkins University in the 1970s, for which they received the Nobel Prize in 1981. They inserted electrodes into the brains of cats who were shown specific shapes, for instance, simple lines with varying orientations. Electrodes that penetrated neural cells in a single layer (or column) of the striate cortex would respond only when a line with a specific orientation was shown, but not for other orientations. An electrode in an adjacent column would respond to a line orientation that differed only by a few degrees from the columns on either side. In this way, they found that a sequence of columns was responding to successive line orientations. This represents the first level of complexity in visual perception above the simple center-surround architecture of the retina. Specific shapes are being "recognized" by specific columns of the striate cortex.

Such detectable organization of the cortex, insofar as it is understood today, mostly stops here. As the neurons of the visual cortex connect to the higher visual pathways, the complexity of the features that are "recognized" increases dramatically, and it has been difficult to define the organization of the higher visual regions with the same specificity as for the visual cortex. Adding to the complexity of the interconnections, some neurons in the higher visual areas reproject back onto earlier areas in the visual pathway, creating feedback circuits that allow the brain to dynamically and adaptively adjust its internal neural signals in the visual recognition process.

There has been a long-standing half-joke among visual cognitive researchers, who posit the existence of a "grandmother" cell. This fictional grandmother cell would be a cell in one of the higher visual areas of the brain that responded only when the image of the subject's grandmother appeared in the visual field. The joke is that no one believes any cell could exist that had such specificity to a visual stimulus. On the other hand, the reason it is only half a joke is because primates are extremely good at recognizing members of their family. This might reflect some sort of "hardwiring" in the brain for this specific function, which had evolutionary advantages for the survival of the individual.

At a somewhat less absurd level of the specificity of neural response, although still strongly controversial, is the hypothesis of a visual alphabet. It states that the higher visual areas respond to a discrete and finite number (although possibly a very large number) of archetypal forms into which all images can be deconstructed. Some evidence has accumulated to support this hypothesis, but it is widely viewed as overly simplistic. Almost all evidence suggests that the brain responds fundamentally as a distributed network in which information and responses are associatively spread over many neurons. The response to complex stimuli, like the grandmother's face, is therefore better viewed as a collective response of many neurons, rather than as the response of specialized individual cells. Similarly, the visual alphabet is not likely to be so specific, nor are images likely to be so regularly deconstructed into elemental parts that stimulate only one or a small group of cells. On the other hand, it is also clear from the experimental evidence that as the image moves farther and farther up the visual path-

way, there is a rapid increase of physically distinct cells that respond to ever
more elaborate combinations of visual stimuli. Maybe buried deep in the
mind there *is* a grandmother cell. Who can say?

What can be said with some certainty is that visual information can be
mapped in broad generality to higher cortical areas retaining the "what"
and "where" pathways that began in the LGN. For instance, object vision
maps to the inferior temporal lobe, spatial location to the posterior parietal lobe, spatial memory to the dorsolateral frontal lobe, and object memory to the inferior convexity. These locations (as well as the names) are
vague and largely unhelpful in understanding how we finally come to the
moment of "aha," when we recognize something or someone. At some instant, through the ever-increasing complexity of the neural connections,
and the ever more subtle ability to recognize more and more intricate features, we finally arrive at cognition.

Putting it all together—explaining how the brain knows what is out
there—has actually been a process of taking it all apart. At each stage in
the visual pathway—starting at the photoreceptors in the eye, moving
through the preprocessing layers of the retina, then the transmission of the
compressed visual information to the lateral geniculate nucleus, which first
interweaves left-and-right and then transmits the information to the
columns of the *aria striata,* which is the staging area for the dissemination
of the information into the higher visual cortex—the information becomes
less and less identifiable as it is deconstructed and distributed across the
brain's neural network. In the end, the original image has diffused into un-
recognizability as its bits and pieces disappear into the myriad folds of the
cerebral cortex.

But this deconstruction of the image is what the brain needs to put it all
together. The original image came from tangible reality, where the laws of
physics determine what things are possible and how they behave. Yet what
we ultimately experience as visual reality is coded as oscillations and
waves of neural excitation that wash back and forth across our brains.
These neural dynamics are part of what we call consciousness. Our brains
take sensory information and turn it into a conscious awareness of what's
out there. Exactly how we put that awareness together remains one of the
continuing mysteries of life and science.

Fortunately, in our mission to understand the basic properties and advantages of visual language and so to build machines that use it more effectively than we can, we can ask specific questions that have experimentally

measurable answers. Such as: How fast can we recognize an object? And how fast can we read? What is the data rate of human communication in general, including spoken language, sign language, or just reading? What limits the rate? Are there visual information formats that can convey more information faster than verbal language? These are all questions that can lead to quantitative answers. They are the kinds of questions the engineers of the next kind of intelligence ask.

5 The Speed of Seeing

Rates of Human Visual Perception

> . . . INFORMATION IN COMMUNICATION THEORY RELATES NOT SO MUCH
> TO WHAT YOU DO SAY, AS TO WHAT YOU COULD SAY. THAT IS,
> INFORMATION IS A MEASURE OF ONE'S FREEDOM OF CHOICE WHEN ONE
> SELECTS A MESSAGE.
>
> *Warren Weaver, 1949*

Putting our thoughts into writing can take some time. Before Gutenberg, a single manuscript could take a medieval scribe a year to complete. Even after Gutenberg, setting the type for a single page of a book could take several days. Of course, once the type was set, hundreds of pages could be printed in a run. The speed of putting things into print is simply a matter of technology. But once the graphic medium is before our eyes, the speed at which we comprehend a text or diagram is dictated by human physiology. In the preceding chapters, I have talked about the Parallel Advantage of Light and Image that is based on the two-dimensional information structure of an image. All points of light enter the eye at the same time, hitting millions of photoreceptors in the retina simultaneously. I have discussed the tremendous data rates that this represents. Now it is time to put numbers to the words. What constitutes visual "information," and how do we quantify it? And most importantly, how fast do we see?

THE MEASURE OF INFORMATION

In the late 1940s, as an outgrowth of the work on communication systems during the war years, a breakthrough concept was introduced by an American systems engineer at Bell Telephone Laboratories named Claude Shannon (1916–2001). Shannon believed that language and other types of communication could be quantitatively measured. For years there had been attempts to subject the living chaos of human language to a rigorous analysis. Intuitively, this made sense—in the human communication process, one can easily feel that there is a rate of information transfer. But the hard part was putting numbers to this feeling.

Claude Shannon was the first to put rigorous numbers on the quantity of information transferred and its rate of transfer, building on the property that language and communication followed surprisingly accurate and constant statistical probabilities. These probabilities could be easily tabulated from written text, and could answer such questions as: How much more frequently is the letter E used in a given language than the letter Q? In English, for instance, E is the letter most commonly used, and occurs 108 times more frequently (on average) than Q. Tables of probabilities can be constructed simply by counting the occurrences of each of the letters in any text. For modern English, the probability table is shown below. What Shannon realized was that these probabilities could be put into a quantitative theory using analytical equations that accurately specified how much information was being conveyed. As a result, information could be measured for the first time. But first, his theory requires a definition of what a "unit" of information is.

There can be no single definition of a unit of information because information takes on so many different forms. A typed letter could be a unit of information for which (in English) there are twenty-six possible choices from A to Z. There are even more choices if we include spaces and punctuation. A numeral can be a unit of information. In the Hindu-Arabic numeral system, this unit of information can take on ten different values from 0 to 9. This is also the number of fingers we have, or the number of toes. The Babylonians liked units that were one sixtieth of a whole. These are all examples of digital systems—the elements of the systems are discrete and finite in number.

Because there are so many different ways of thinking about a unit of information, it is important to settle on a single definition that can act as a standard to which all forms of information can be compared. The simplest choice of a unit of information is a pair of opposites: yes or no; on or off; white or black; Yin or Yang; 1 or 0. In computing or information theory, a

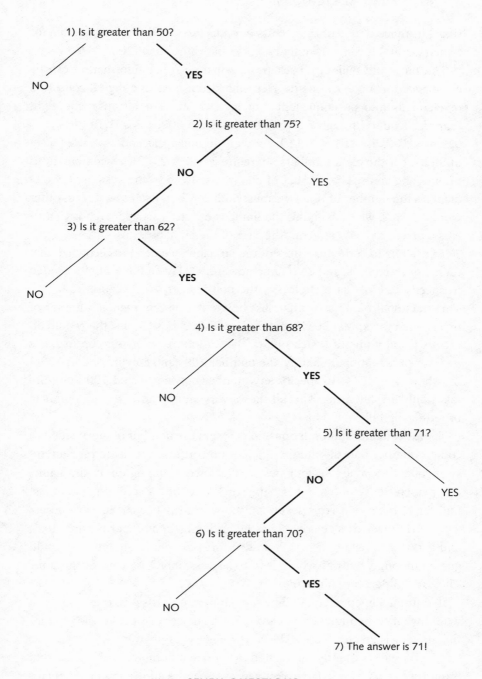

1) Is it greater than 50?

NO

YES

2) Is it greater than 75?

NO

YES

3) Is it greater than 62?

NO

YES

4) Is it greater than 68?

NO

YES

5) Is it greater than 71?

NO

YES

6) Is it greater than 70?

NO

YES

7) The answer is 71!

SEVEN QUESTIONS

single instance of one of these pairs of opposites is called a bit, standing for "binary unit." It can have only two possible values or states.

The bit is the building block from which all other information can be constructed. A code can be devised which translates any digital collection of elements into an equivalent sequence of bits. For instance, the eight numbers from 0 through 7 can be coded as $0 = 000, 1 = 001, 2 = 010, 3 = 011, 4 = 100, 5 = 101, 6 = 110, 7 = 111$. To make this code, we used a set of 3 bits. For the eight numbers, there are $2 \times 2 \times 2 = 2^3 = 8$ combinations of ones and zeros. The number of bits we use to code any system of N elements is the number of times we must multiply 2 by itself to get N. In other words, $2^b = N$, where b equals the number of bits. This approach is clear if N is a power of 2. What about the case of the alphabet?

To use bits to code the letters of the alphabet, we need to recognize that there are 26 choices, and 26 is not a power of 2. The number of bits needed to specify one of these choices is the non-integer 4.7, because $26 = 2^{4.7}$. This fractional number of bits must be viewed as the *average* number of bits needed to express 26 characters. But if we choose 5 bits, this would allow us to fully identify each one of the 26 letters with some options left over for punctuation. Similarly, the number 100 can be expressed as $100 = 2^b$, where $b = 6.644$. To specify any number between 1 and 100 therefore takes only a 7-bit string. This all shows very simply how to code numbers or letters digitally.

There is an important relationship between the number of bits needed to code a number and the number of questions it takes to search for an answer. Take the game "Seven Questions" shown in the figure. In this game, one person thinks of a number between 1 and 100. A second person must find the number by asking seven questions or less. The chances of success are clearly low if the guesser starts by asking if the number is equal to 1, and if not then asking if it is 2, and so forth. Similarly, the guesser could guess randomly, but this would lead to success only 7 percent of the time. That is a 93 percent failure rate.

If your life depended on finding the number in only seven questions, you would want to be much more clever. For instance, you could ask whether the number is greater than 50. When you get your answer, either "yes" or "no," you have instantly eliminated 50 possible numbers. Let us say that the answer was "yes." Then you can ask whether the number is greater than 75. Regardless of the answer, you have now eliminated an additional

25 numbers. If the answer was "no," you could ask if the number is greater than 62. Now you have eliminated 12 additional numbers. This has only been three questions, and you have ruled out 87 of the 100 initial possible numbers. You will notice in the figure that you are dividing the open possibilities by a factor of 2 each time. By the time you ask seven questions, you will almost certainly have found the correct number.

This game illustrates the importance and efficiency of what is known as a binary search tree, shown in the Binary Search Tree figure for five levels. As the tree is descended, looking for the number 13 out of 32 choices, say, the number is reached by taking a left branch, two rights, a left, and a right, giving 13 = LRRLR. In binary notation, 13 = 01101. Each branch in the tree corresponds to a single question. The number of levels in the tree corresponds to the number of binary questions that have been asked. The answer to each binary question corresponds to a single bit of information.

To illustrate how a sequential search becomes exponentially more difficult as the number of bits increases, consider playing "Twenty Questions." A sequential search in this case would take on average half of 2^{20} = 1,048,576 guesses compared to only 20 guesses using the binary search method—clearly a dramatic saving in time and effort.

Descending decision trees is an important way of representing the exercise of intelligence. An intelligent mind makes informed judgments by descending a decision tree one bit at a time, similar to the way we saw language descend a tree of transformational grammar. How fast does the mind descend such information trees? And how much information is contained in an actual sentence of English?

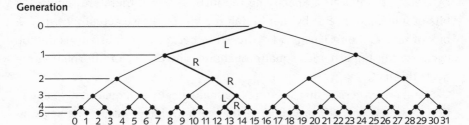

BINARY SEARCH TREE

INFORMATION THEORY

The key to quantifying information is to recognize that, in a meaningful information exchange, not all possible messages are equally likely. It is the surprise that tells us something new. One way of illustrating this point is to consider data sequences that carry no information. For instance, completing the sequence

$$1001001001\_$$

can be done with near certainty . . . the sequence consists of a repeating segment of 100, and the next number is almost certainly 0. Therefore, although we have added a bit to the sequence, that bit carries no "information." If the extra bit does nothing to change our expectations, then that bit tells us nothing new. In a quantitative definition of information, something carrying a 100 percent probability counts as carrying no information at all.

Using examples from English, the missing letter in

$$EXPLICI\_$$

carries no information, given the existing letters, because T is the only choice that gives an English word. However, the missing letter in

$$P\_N$$

carries somewhat more information because there are four possibilities: PAN, PEN, PIN, and PUN. Specifying the missing vowel therefore requires 2 bits of information. But by identifying the vowel, do we actually *convey* 2 bits of information? This is a key question because the four words do not occur within English with equal probability. The theory of information reflects this fact.

Shannon expressed these features mathematically in a quantitative equation that used only the probabilities that certain signals occur. The key was not merely to count how many bits were needed to form a complete code (as in our examples above, where we decided that it took 4.7 bits to code the English alphabet). Rather, it suffices to find the probability of occurrence of each letter, and use the probabilities to weight the average number of bits to code a message.

For random sequences of letters from the English alphabet, if all the letters are equally likely to occur, the weights are all equal and the information content is simply 4.7 bits per letter, which is just what we got before when we asked how many bits we needed to code the 26 letters. At that time, the fractional number of bits was a little troublesome, because it is hard to think in terms of a fraction of a "1" or "0." In this new definition, the fractional bit is not a problem, because we now view the information content as a statistical average. It takes 4.7 bits of information, *on average,* to send or read the alphabet (when all the letters are equally likely to occur).

On the other hand, when the letters are not equally likely to occur (which is always the case in practice), the information content is smaller than the number of bits needed to code the message. To see this, consider a four-letter alphabet given by A, B, C, and D. We know that it will take 2 bits to code this alphabet ($2^2 = 4$). But let us say that the relative probabilities for these letters to occur in my language are given by

Letter	Probability	Binary Code	Efficient Code
A	0.6	00	0
B	0.24	01	1
C	0.10	10	10
D	0.06	11	11
		2 bits	1.5 bits

The information content of a series of sentences using this language would be equal to 1.5 bits. Clearly, we have a lower information content than the 2 bits needed to code the language. In an efficient code, I can vary the number of bits needed to code a symbol. Because A occurs most frequently, I can code it with a single bit, and similarly for B. Only when I get to C do I need to use 2 bits to code it. In this way, I only use an average of 1.5 bits to code my limited language, which is equal to the information content. This is an efficient code with no redundancy.

As a more realistic example, we can consider the letter frequency of English orthography. (Orthography is the aspect of language concerned with letters and their sequences in words.) We gave the relative letter frequencies in this chapter in the table on page 89. Using these frequencies as probabilities, the information content of modern English orthography is found to be 4.14 bits per letter. Therefore, in English we convey only 4.14 bits of information per letter, while using on average 4.71 bits per letter to code the language. We seem to have an inefficient language.

Examples of efficient coding have been in use for over a hundred years. One of the earliest attempts at efficient coding is the Morse Code, developed by the American painter Samuel Morse (1791–1872) for transmitting messages on telegraph lines. Morse ascertained the relative frequencies of letters in English by counting the quantities of type in a printer's office, and then assigned sequences of long and short dashes to the letters, with the shortest sequences assigned to the most frequent letters. In his original code, the letter frequencies are efficiently coded. Thus, the letter E, which is the most frequent letter, required only a single short dash. Morse's original code included both long and short dashes in addition to spaces. The ease of transmitting and decoding was later improved upon by removing the spaces and relying only on dashes and dots, and the short dash of the letter E became the "dot." The economic use of coding from Morse has been retained to a large degree in the modern form.

Is it always a good idea to have an efficient code? Efficiency also means that there is little room for error. One misplaced or miscoded bit, or a bit obscured by noise, and information is lost. In a highly efficient code, the missing information may not even be noticed, or if it is noticed, may not be correctable. Such an error-intolerant code is very unlike ordinary human language. We rarely hear every sound that is being uttered, yet we can usually collect all the transmitted information. Our world is filled with extraneous noises that threaten to drown out meaning—on busy streets, in crowded lunch rooms, around working machinery—all potentially louder than the voice we are listening to, yet we are able to follow conversations with great detail and little miscomprehension. Why? The answer is a combination of context and redundancy.

THE BIG PICTURE

Context and redundancy can be viewed as a language's built-in error correction facility. Without context and redundancy, we would be able to glean very little from communications in the real world because people actually hear a lot less than they think. Much of what we "hear" is pieced together as guesses—albeit educated guesses based on what words have gone before. In this sense, sound perception is not unlike visual perception in that much of what we perceive is actually constructed by the brain.

Context is the process by which previous information influences the an-

Rank	Letter	Probability
1	E	0.13105
2	T	0.10468
3	A	0.08151
4	O	0.07995
5	N	0.07098
6	R	0.06882
7	I	0.06345
8	S	0.06101
9	H	0.05259
10	D	0.03788
11	L	0.03389
12	F	0.02924
13	C	0.02758
14	M	0.02536
15	U	0.02459
16	G	0.01994
17	Y	0.01982
18	P	0.01982
19	W	0.01539
20	B	0.01440
21	V	0.00919
22	K	0.00420
23	X	0.00166
24	J	0.00132
25	Q	0.00121
26	Z	0.00077

LETTER FREQUENCIES OF MODERN ENGLISH

ticipation and interpretation of succeeding sounds or words. It is much easier to guess what a word will be, or guess what a misheard word is, if we know what the topic of conversation is.

Redundancy is a repetitiveness that ensures that a word is understood, just as repeating a word several times improves the chances that it will be understood. But redundancy in human language is more subtle than sheer repetition. Drawing from a previous example, the missing T in EXPLICI_ carries no information because the only letter that will complete the English word is T. By the time the other letters have been written, the T has become redundant through the context of prior information. It may seem useless in that case to complete the word. Why not use abbreviations when letters have become redundant? But that is true only in a noise-free environment. In real-world situations, such as human communication in a noisy environment, every letter can count when the environmental noise is severe. That missing T may be the difference between comprehension and misunderstanding, and in a particularly hostile world, the missing letter may be the difference between life and death. In such cases, the natural redundancy of human language may be a life saver.

Both context and redundancy are aspects of higher-order properties of language. By specifying the probabilities by which individual letters occur, as we did in the table on page 89, we did not exhaust the statistical description of language. In all languages, what follows is influenced by what precedes. Letters do not occur statistically independently, but are linked by higher-order probabilities that govern how likely pairs of letters occur (called digrams), or triplets of letters (called trigrams), and so on.

To get a good feel for the importance of various levels of statistical probabilities, one can construct fictitious words and sentences based on the statistical properties of a language. Claude Shannon constructed the following illustrations based upon increasing orders of statistics:

1. Zero-order approximation (symbols independent and equi-probable, including the space):

XFOML RXKHRJFFJUJ ZLPWCFWKCYJFFJEYVKCQSGHYD QPAAMKBZAACIBZLHJQD.

This sentence has no similarity with English. Other than using the Roman alphabet, there is nothing remotely reminiscent of a sensible language.

2. First-order approximation (symbols and space independent but with the frequencies of English text):

OCRO HLI RGWR NMIELWIS EU LL NBNESEBYA TH EEI ALHENHTTPA OOBTTVA NAH BRL.

At this low level at least the lengths of the words are not unreasonable.

3. Second-order approximation (digram probabilities of English):

ON IE ANTSOUTINYS ARE T INCTORE ST BE S DEAMY ACHIN D ILONASIVE TUCOOWE AT TEASONARE FUSO TIZIN ANDY TOBE SEACE CTISBE.

Already by this level there are collections of letters that are actually English words, such as ON, ARE, BE, and AT, as well as a proper name, ANDY. Even some of the words that are not accepted as English are acceptable as candidates for our language, such as DEAMY and maybe ILONASIVE. (Perhaps the DEAMY teenager is being ILONASIVE.)

4. Third-order approximation (trigram probabilities of English):

IN NO IST LAT WHEY CRATICT FROURE BIRS GROCID PONDENOME OF DEMONSTURES OF THE REPTAGIN IS REGOACTIONA OF CRE.

Trigram probabilities continue the process of forming letter sequences that are familiar, but do nothing to improve any sense of meaning, or even reliably produce English words.

Where, then, is redundancy and context? While context is still certainly missing, redundancy has already appeared in these examples. We know that redundancy exists in these passages because we "feel" that many of the words *could* be English, although certainly they would be obscure ones that we were never taught.

Rather than continuing with higher-order statistics of letters above trigram probabilities, Shannon continued the illustration by picking words randomly according to their statistical frequencies.

5. First-order word approximation (words chosen independently with the probabilities as in English text):

REPRESENTING AND SPEEDILY IS AN GOOD APT OR COME CAN DIFFERENT NATURAL HERE HE THE A IN CAME THE TO OF TO EXPERT GRAY COME TO FURNISHES THE LINE MESSAGE HAD BE THESE.

6. Second-order word approximation (di-word probabilities of English):

THE HEAD AND IN FRONTAL ATTACK ON AN ENGLISH WRITER THAT THE CHARACTER OF THIS POINT IS THERE-FORE ANOTHER METHOD FOR THE LETTERS THAT THE TIME OF WHO EVER TOLD THE PROBLEM FOR AN UNEX-PECTED.

This is not exactly literary quality, but it may be recognizable as something related to English.

How are higher-order statistics of language, which in principle can extend to arbitrarily large order, included in the definition of information theory? What is the true information content of language, when considering all orders of statistics?

The redundancy of English can be quantified by comparing the actual information content with the theoretical maximum. If we take 2.5 bits as the limiting information for the orthography of the English language on a letter basis, then it turns out that English is 40 percent redundant. Forty percent of what is written is redundant? What would your freshman writing teacher say? As a simple experiment to verify this number, you could take a text of English and randomly remove about three or four out of every ten letters:

Ths pocss ay ak a wil, lie dcihein a cde mesae, bt te ifomaio cotet
i al thre. ha is isin, an wht mke th deiperen difiul, is edndnc.

For the first word or two, you may find it difficult to follow the meaning. But after several words, you begin to get a strong sense of the context. Armed with this information, you go back and refine your expectations of the previous words, reiterating until you have extracted nearly 100 percent of the meaning of the text.

In this example of redundancy, we have considered only the statistics of letter sequences. But redundancy in language also uses word statistics. Therefore, Shannon went further and included first-order word statistics, as well as experimental techniques that obtained even higher-order word statistics. Using these values, he was able to estimate that the information content of English orthography approached 1.5 bits/letter, with a redundancy of 68 percent, when all levels of statistics are included.

The high redundancy of English (and of virtually all other languages) and the low information per letter makes language look highly ineffective at communicating. But remember that each bit of information is eliminating fully half of all remaining possible choices of letters. In a single line of this book, there are approximately 60 letters and therefore 90 bits of information. This means that a single line of text chooses among $2^{90} = 10^{27}$ possible alternative meanings in a binary decision tree. That is an astonishingly large number of alternatives—over a trillion trillions for a single line. Then considering that there are 10,000 lines in this book . . . I don't even want to think how many alternatives you will have eliminated by the time you get to the end.

Fortunately, we don't *have* to think about it. Reading is a natural and easy process. We might even remember most of the several hundred points that a book makes. The intelligence of our minds handles the task of reading with great facility, without having to worry about alternatives (the vast majority of alternative choices of letters are meaningless anyway). The important point of information theory is that language can be accurately quantified. And now that we have a firm quantitative measure of the information content of English, seemingly all we need to do to define an information rate for verbal processes is to see how fast people talk and listen. And if we want to compare that with visual communication, first as reading, and then in a pure visual communication mode unrelated to language, we simply need to see how fast we do each of those things. But that is easier said than done. When it comes to the eye, it is not an easy matter to see how all the eye motions relate to the information rate incident on the retina. But there are imaginative experimental approaches that can truly get to the absolute measure of communication rates. This brings us to the field of psychophysics.

PSYCHOPHYSICS

As the naive physicist, with the usual disdain toward the *soft* sciences, I had always been suspicious of the term *psychophysics*. It struck me as a bit of an oxymoron, or perhaps as a synonym for *psychobabble*. The notion that physics could be applied to psychology did not seem to me to be very likely. Or if it were, that it could not be applied in a rigorous (i.e., mathematically quantifiable) manner. I have found such conceit toward psychology is unwarranted. Psychophysics concerns the quantitative measurement of cognitive processes. It accurately measures quantities and rates of perception and cognition. In its methodology and precision, it matches anything a physicist can muster.

One of the principal tools of visual psychophysics is a venerable gadget called a tachistoscope. A tachistoscope is a device that can present to a subject a specified image of a specified radiance, for a specified amount of time. It is highly accurate and versatile, making pictures, diagrams, words, or patterns visible to subjects. Its beginning as a tool for psychophysics goes back before the turn of the previous century, when physicists were still fumbling around with the ether and had not even thought of relativity or quantum mechanics. The first recorded use of a tachistoscope was by the American psychologist James McKeen Cattell (1860–1944), who published in 1885 an article entitled "Uber die Zeit der Erkennung und Benennung von Schriftzeichen, Bildern und Farben" (On the Time for Comprehension and Naming of Letters, Pictures and Colors) in a German scientific journal. Cattell published in German as many did at that time, especially in psychological fields.

Cattell devised a shuttered projector that showed pictures, letters, and colors to subjects. The subjects, after very brief exposures, were asked to name the objects that had been presented. The time it took them to respond, as well as the percentage of correct answers, was noted as a function of exposure time and intensity. He found that from a 40-millisecond tachistoscopic exposure, subjects could identify 3.7 random letters and 2.0 random words (comprised of 9.3 letters). The important feature of this study was the increase of the number of correctly identified letters from 3.7 for random letters to 9.3 when the letters were contained in English words. Clearly, the letters in the words were not as "random" as the letters. This is the role played by redundancy in the English language that we just discussed. The tachistoscope had uncovered the role of redundancy (although it was not called that at the time) long before Shannon's theories.

Because of its quantitative capabilities, the tachistoscope quickly became a mainstay of perceptual studies. Already by 1908 it was fully established as a means of measuring reading rates. It also became useful in much more fundamental studies of non-conceptual perception, such as how fast a light can flicker before we no longer see it flickering. The rate at which flicker fuses into a constant illumination is called the flicker fusion frequency. Flicker fusion is what allows us to see movies projected on a screen, or video on a computer monitor, without flicker. This is another example of how our physiology (the rate at which our eyes respond to flicker) guides *perceived* reality, as separate from *actual* reality.

The human critical flicker frequency is an important parameter for measuring the rate of visual information perception. Flicker sets the lower limit on the time to perceive visual information. Unlike the studies in which letters or images are flashed on a tachistoscope, flicker studies are much more basic. They simply ask subjects whether they can perceive flickering or continuous intensity in a small point of light. The experiment can be performed psychophysically (asking the subjects if they see flicker), or neurologically (by implanting electrodes directly into the retina to measure the action potential of the photoreceptors). The results of the experiments vary little from subject to subject.

The critical frequency above which flicker is not discernible increases as a function of brightness. In very weak light in a dark room, it can be as low as 1 flash per second. In nominally bright light, it is typically 30 flashes per second, while in extremely bright light it can be as high as 60 flashes per second. It is interesting to note that the frame rate in a movie theater is 24 frames per second. Under bright illumination, this frame rate would make the screen seem to flicker. However, under the dim conditions of most movie theaters (both the subjects and projector are relatively far from the screen, and intensity falls off with increasing distance), 24 frames per second are well above the critical frequency, and the movie looks fine.

In the discussion of human visual information rates, it is therefore always necessary to state the level of adaptation of the eye. The eye has a tremendous range for detecting intensity, covering nearly fifteen orders of magnitude from the detection of light in the darkest of rooms, to the saturation of the photoreceptors under the brightest lights. This is perhaps the largest adaptive dynamic range of any biological sensor system. So, what we perceive has a lot to do with how bright it is. In our discussions of visual information rates, we will adopt a *typical* critical flicker frequency (under nominal illumination) of about 20 flashes per second. This frequency means that if a light is flickering 25 milliseconds on and 25 milliseconds off, we can just barely perceive it as flickering.

The choice of a 25- or 30-millisecond flash for the nominal time associated with the perception of temporal variations in intensity is consistent with uses of the tachistoscope to present visual information. It was discovered early in the use of the apparatus that 30 milliseconds was a sort of break-even exposure time. If simple images were projected for less than that time, the subject would have difficulty identifying the objects correctly. However, if the image was presented for 30 milliseconds or longer, then the percentage of correct identifications would be nearly 100 percent. This was in spite of the fact that it would take the subject from between 200 milliseconds to 500 milliseconds actually to *give* the correct identification. This extra time needed by the subject to make the identification is related to the process of *comprehension,* which certainly involves thinking. But the psychophysical time *to register* the stimulus is the 30-millisecond exposure time.

THE NERVOUS EYE

The image that is cast upon your retina, the image of this word-filled page, is right now washing back and forth across your retina at amazing speed. Your eyeball has a high-frequency tremor that jitters the image back and forth at a rate faster than the frame rate of a movie screen. In addition to this, the image is drifting, even if you fix your gaze at a specific spot on the page. Finally, as you read this line of text, your eye jumps rapidly from one fixed spot to the next, rather than moving smoothly. These involuntary motions are separate from the motions of the eye that you cause knowingly. Even when you force yourself to focus on a spot, these involuntary motions continue without your being aware of them.

The image moves so much on your retina—even for the relaxed process of reading a line of text—that it seems a miracle that you can see at all. With all this motion going on, why doesn't the world look as though it is careening around at breakneck speed? Why don't you get motion sickness or vertigo? Or why isn't our sight a steady blur? The answer is that your brain *constructs* visual perception. Though the image is indeed moving and jerking and trembling (in a seemingly chaotic manner), the muscles that are causing the shakes in your eyes are transmitting the information to the brain. These motor signals are combined by the brain with sensations of the inner ears, which sense balance and motion, to construct the perception of a stable world.

Based on our earlier discussion of the functions of the retina in the previous chapter, this ceaseless and involuntary motion of the eyeball actually makes sense. Above all else, the neural networks of the retina are sensors of variable illumination. Variable illumination is the primary stimulus that sends signals up the optic nerve. Spatial variability in illumination excites the common center-surround receptive fields discussed earlier. Temporal variability in illumination is just as important, and the nervous eye provides a source of temporal change in illumination.

Using a specialized image projection apparatus, scientists are able to cause an image on the retina to stand perfectly still, despite the continuing involuntary motion of the eye. This is achieved using sensitive feedback that tracks the high-speed motions of the eye, and causes the projected image to exactly match the eye's motion. This means that the image on the retina can be made truly stationary—without the jitters imposed by the natural eye motions. When this is done, a subject will report that an image is initially visible when it is presented, but then fades away in one to three seconds. After three seconds, although the image is still present and stationary on the retina, the subject reports no sensation of vision. So, a perfectly stationary image on the retina will cause no excitation of the ganglion cells, and therefore no signals to the brain. This experiment provides dramatic proof that the eye is a detector of transients, and cannot detect steady-state images. This motion sensing (or novelty sensing) allows the eye to ignore parts of an image that are not changing in time, just as the center-surround receptive fields allowed the retina to ignore broad expanses of uniform lighting. It is a means for image compression that is part of the 126:1 convergence of the number of photoreceptors in the eye to the number of ganglion axons that form the optic nerve.

The involuntary motions of the eye therefore provide an extremely important function. Even when the gaze is fixed on a single spot, the constant motion of the eye sweeps the image back and forth across the retina. This process turns a fixed projection into a moving image on the retina. The motion on the retina causes temporal changes that are detected as transients, which are sent to the visual cortex. In short, the chaotic and involuntary motion of the eyes prevents the visual world from washing out and disappearing if you let your gaze fix on a spot for too long. Think of times when you were attempting to focus on an extremely fine detail of a picture, or a miniature model, or the mechanisms of a mechanical watch. Think how frustrating it would be if the harder you concentrated to see fine detail, the faster it faded and vanished from sight. You would only be able to see things you weren't concentrating on. What you most wanted to find would become invisible to you.

These useful motions of the eye are divided into three types: tremors, drifts, and saccades. The high-frequency vibrations are called tremors. The eye oscillates back and forth with small excursions at frequencies in the range of 50–100 times per second (50–100 Hz), with an oscillation period of only 10–20 milliseconds. The slow drift that occurs when the eyes are fixed at a single spot (called a fixation) occurs over a time of about one fifth of a second, which is about 200 milliseconds. The rapid and large jumps that the eye makes when it moves quickly from one fixation to the next are called saccades (from the French *saccade,* which means "jerk"), which take only about 30 milliseconds from start to finish.

As you read this line of text, your eyes jump to a position on the page; they stay roughly fixed at that point for about 200 milliseconds, during which time the eye experiences fast tremors and slow drift, then jumps rapidly to the next fixation, and the process continues as before. For relatively simple text (when the content is easy to understand), a typical reader will make about five fixations per line of text. This corresponds to a single fixation for every two words. In reading more difficult text (maybe like the one you are reading right now), you will make up to ten fixations per line, or about one fixation per word. Regardless of the difficulty, you make a fairly constant five fixations per second. If a difficult text takes more fixations per line, then it takes more time to read the text.

It is satisfying to realize that the tremors and saccades occur on time scales that are somewhat smaller than the critical flicker time. This guarantees that we are unable to "see" the effects of tremors and drifts. It is also interesting that the minimum time for visual *perception,* which is the time it takes a subject to register that a visual event has occurred, is about the time of a fixation of 200 to 300 milliseconds. Therefore, a "good look" is the time of a single fixation; it is the time it takes the brain to construct visual perception leading to comprehension.

Here, then, is the rate at which visual information is sensed by the eyes. We can make use of tachistoscopes and eye motion to put together an average visual perception rate for the human brain. And most important, we can finally look at how this human visual information rate compares with the actual information content of an image.

VISUAL INFORMATION RATES

How much information enters the eye during a "good look"? The answer is a function of the physics of light and of the physiology of the eye. The aperture of the eye is the iris. The diameter of its circular opening changes in response to the brightness of illumination. Under very intense light, the diameter can be as small as half a millimeter, while in the limit of extremely dim light is can be as large as 4 millimeters. Although this aperture is over a thousand times larger than a wavelength of light, the wave nature of light still limits the finest details that you can see through such an aperture. Light is composed of different wavelengths for different colors. In the green, which is where sunlight is most intense, light has a wavelength of around 0.5 microns. It is a property of all waves that when they pass through an aperture they are diffracted into a range of angles. This spread in the waves after passing through an aperture smears out the image of a point into a blurred spot on the retina. The diameter of the spot is easily calculated from the physics of diffraction to be about 5 microns. It should come as no surprise that the average separation between cones in the retina is also about 5 microns in the fovea. In other words, the process of evolution has converged on an optimal distribution of photoreceptors (cones) in which one photoreceptor will detect the light from one point source diffracting through the iris.

The size of a "pixel" for an image entering the eye is therefore set by the distance between cones. There are approximately 5 million cones in the human retina, with as many as 40,000 cones within a central 0.5-millimeter diameter in the fovea, where vision is most acute. From tachistoscopic evidence, we know that the minimum time needed to excite the photoreceptors in the retina is about 30 milliseconds. Therefore, approximately 5 million receptors detect light in a 30-millisecond snapshot, or frame. In addition, the eye detects about 100 levels of gray scale corresponding to about 7 bits. The data rate is therefore 7 bits of gray scale times 5 million receptors divided by 30 milliseconds, giving a bit rate of over 1 billion bits per second *incident on the retina*. This bit rate is the upper limit set by the laws of physical diffraction and neural physiology. However, this high bit rate is not the most relevant information rate for human visual communication. We need to ask a more careful question about how much information is actually sent up the optic nerve to the brain, and then compare this with the ability of the brain to perceive the information.

To put conservative numbers on the information rates in the eye, consider only the 200,000 ganglion receptive fields associated with the area in and around the fovea. Also, the 30-millisecond frame is not of any use to the brain if a different image is presented to the retina every 30 milliseconds. The 200-millisecond fixation time is more appropriate to give the brain time to perceive and comprehend the stimulus. Therefore, the practical information rate traveling up the optic nerve to the visual cortex would be 7 bits of gray scale times 200,000 ganglions divided by 200 milliseconds. This gives 7 million bits per second. Such a data rate is comparable to the data transfer rate of a computer hard drive.

This is a tremendously fast rate. All the text in this book that you are reading right now can be represented using only about 1 million bits of information. That number is obtained by taking the 100,000 words in this book, and efficiently coding them. We could code that amount of information visually on a single page by creating a dense array of black and white square pixels. A typical book page has an area of 12 cm × 19 cm = 228 cm². To support 1 million pixels in this area, each pixel would need to be about 150 microns on a side. A fairly low-end 300 dpi (dots per inch) laser printer can print feature sizes down to 80 microns on a side, which is sufficient to print out the appropriate pixels. Therefore, all the information in this book, using an efficient code, could be printed as black and white pixels on a single page of paper using a common laser printer. In principle, you could "see" the entire information content of this book in a single glance. Unfortunately, that is clearly nonsense!

Let's estimate how long it will take you to read this entire book. At one word per fixation, that is about three to four words per second. This book contains about 100,000 words, which will take you approximately nine hours to read (not counting time thinking, looking at pictures, and also omitting the time spent rereading text to understand it, all of which extends the reading time to something over twelve hours). Clearly, the information rate at which you comprehend this text is much slower than the 7 million bits per second information rate streaming up your optic nerve. Where is the bottleneck?

The bottleneck is in the brain. Specifically, it is in the process of language comprehension. To get a firm grasp on this bottleneck, we can combine tachistoscopic evidence with the information content of English discussed at the beginning of this chapter. The tachistoscopic measurements of reading rates performed by James McKeen Cattell over a hundred years ago have been repeated with more modern equipment, but the basic findings remain the same.

When random letters are presented, subjects can correctly recognize about five letters in a single exposure. The information content of random letters is 4.7 bits. The information content of five letters is then about 24 bits. After a 30-millisecond tachistoscopic exposure, it takes the subject about a second to comprehend. The total data rate is therefore about 24 bits per second.

When random *words* are presented, subjects can correctly recognize about two in a single exposure. The information content of letters in words is lower, at about 2.5 bits per letter, because of redundancy in English words. At nearly five letters per word, this corresponds to about 25 bits that are recognized in one second—the same data rate as for random letter recognition.

When sequences of words are presented in which the words are part of meaningful sentences that have context, subjects can correctly recognize about five words in a single exposure. Redundancy per letter in the case of meaningful English text reduces the information content per letter to nearly 1 bit. A sentence segment of five words with an average of five letters per word therefore gives an information content of about 25 bits—again equal to the data rates for random letters as well as random words.

These experiments give strong evidence (psychophysical evidence based on information theory and precise measurements) that the capacity of the human information channel for recognizing English is a sluggish 25 bits per second. This is a snail's pace compared to the 7 million bits per second that are streaming up the optic nerve to the visual cortex. Why is there such a huge mismatch in information rates?

When a tachistoscope presents a black-and-white word to a subject in a 30-millisecond flash, 1 million receptive fields receive illumination. However, all those receptive fields are actually only responding to about five black letters. Each of the letters is chosen out of only twenty-six possibilities. Therefore, while the *structural* image consists of 1 million bits (or pixels) of information, the *semantic* (or meaningful) information content of the image is only about 25 bits. It is this semantic information that taps into human comprehension, into knowledge or understanding, and this comprehension rate is slow—a mere 25 bits per second. That is the human comprehension rate—the Comprehension Bottleneck noted in the introductory chapter. It is our physiology, and we are stuck with it.

Still, there is the intuitive feeling that images convey more information faster than the written word. After all, it feels as though an image is perceived "at a glance." Furthermore, written words are merely another form of surface structure used to implement the deep structure of spoken language. Writing and reading are no different than spoken language. Any surface structure will do, whether it is auditory, visual, or even tactile (Braille). They all tap into the deep structure of language. But what about a form of communication that has no verbal counterpart? A form of communication that arises entirely within the visual domain without ever hearing verbal language? Take, for instance, the sign languages of the deaf, with their complex use of space and motion in intricate dynamic signs. Might not these pure visual languages use the Parallel Advantage of Light and Image?

"PURE" VISUAL LANGUAGE

Sign languages of the deaf are possibly the purest form of human visual language. It is important to be clear what is meant by this. Natural sign languages, referred to as "Sign," are conceptual languages in which semantic propositions are depicted by using surface structure consisting of gestures of the hand, face, and body. The natural sign languages that have evolved spontaneously among the many deaf communities across the world have no relationship to specific verbal languages. American Sign Language (ASL) has virtually nothing in common with spoken English. Signs in ASL are generally arbitrary. While there is strong evidence that many early signs in ASL had iconic origins that were motivated from the events or actions being signified, these signs slowly evolved into arbitrary form under the same influences of language change that affect verbal languages, such as the influence that caused French to evolve from Latin and English from Anglo-Saxon. Some iconicity persists today in signs that signify particularly concrete objects or actions. However, ASL is as full of abstract concepts and propositions as any language, and no iconicity can be identified in these more numerous signs. ASL is therefore neither a manual reflection of spoken language nor merely iconic gestures. It is a fully functional and fluent means of communication that carries with it all the nuances of meaning possessed by any spoken language.

As with any human language, the signs of ASL are governed by their own firm grammatical rules of the use of position and time to convey meaning. But the visual grammar of ASL carries with it an added potential that is missing in verbal languages. The use of motion and location of signs, and the continuous blending of one sign into another, provides an additional dimension to ASL that cannot be used in verbal language. This added potential for meaning is purely visual, using three-dimensional space, as well as motion through that space, to signify nuances of meaning that pertain to actions, or feelings, or intentions. The position of a gesture—whether far forward or close to the chest, whether higher or lower on the body—can carry specific meaning. Repetitions of signs, the speed of signs, the fluid or abrupt articulation of a sign, all carry grammatical meanings that take the role of the inflexions, tenses, and pronouns that occur in spoken language.

ASL is also dynamically creative. In the course of a monologue, a signer can "reserve" a location in space for a specific person or item that recurs in a story. By pointing to that location, or moving a gesture toward that location, the signer can use the location as a pronoun, or as the subject or object of an action. The choice of location can change each time the same story is told, but in a single telling, that location is constant. In addition, ASL has art forms as well as poetry and puns. Just as calligraphy can add artistic value to a written letter, signs can be embellished or modified to be visually pleasing. Signs can also be presented in novel ways that mimic other signs or concepts, giving the sign a poetic depth that can be interpreted on several levels, or they can allow a single sign simultaneously to have multiple meanings. Plays on signs are common, producing visual jokes that could never be translated into English. The pun or joke can rest completely in the visual similarities among signs for which there can be no spoken analog.

These visual aspects of ASL make use of the parallelism of the image. Since many signs use the face and body as well as both hands, many signifying features are presented simultaneously, that is, in parallel. The signs are presented inside an image space that is somewhat like an imaginary bubble surrounding the signer. To the three dimensions of space is added the fourth dimension of time because nearly all signs have motion. This motion across the visual field adds a temporal aspect to the image. The process of signing therefore presents to the viewer a sophisticated tableau of features and motion, treating him or her to a complex visual dance of meaning.

Given the radically different mode of expression, is the information rate of sign language different from written language? Since the medium taps into the Parallel Advantage of Light and Image, shouldn't the parallelism unique to visual communication be active in this purely visual language?

In the 1970s, researchers began to study sign language in earnest. Before that time, ASL was largely ignored by linguists. The neglect was partly due to prejudicial societal misconceptions about the legitimacy of sign language, but also to the lack of appropriate equipment. It was only in the 1960s that video equipment became available that allowed for detailed visual analysis of sign languages. This equipment was essential because so much of the meaning of sign language is in the nuances of very transitory components of gestures. Also, the very parallelism that gives ASL its unique expressiveness made it difficult simultaneously to capture and assess. With the new equipment, the full structure of ASL could finally be captured and subjected to exhaustive analysis.

A comparison of the rate of speaking and signing was reported in 1972 by Ursula Bellugi and her co-workers. The questions they wished to answer were simple enough: How fast can signers sign compared with how fast speakers can speak? What they did not anticipate was how difficult it would be to make such a comparison. Spoken language and ASL are such different modalities of communication that literal translation is not possible. English sentences cannot be translated "word for word" into ASL without adding specific contributed signs that are not part of the natural sign vocabulary, and ASL cannot be translated literally into English without appearing to be sparse. For such different modes of human communication, finding common ground was not obvious. Defining common communication rates was also not easy. Part of the difficulty was with the literal translation. English and ASL are like fruits and vegetables. What fruit is equivalent to the artichoke—a pineapple?

The solution to this problem was provided by fluent bilingual subjects who were the speaking children of deaf parents. For these children, ASL was learned in the home at the same time that English was learned from older siblings or from children on the street. Such children are especially fluent as translators for their parents, translating back and forth between ASL and English. The fluency goes so far that many can speak and sign simultaneously as they communicate to a mixed crowd of speaking and deaf members.

One of the first steps in finding common ground between ASL and English communication rates was simply to measure the rate at which a story was told in words by a fluent subject, then comparing it to the rate at which the same subject told the same story in ASL. Different subjects were asked to either start with the spoken version, or start with the signed version, then switch. The measured rates were not dependent on what mode was used first, and were also relatively constant between subjects.

For the spoken stories, the subjects used approximately 4.7 words per second. This is in close agreement with the reading rate that gives about 25 bits per second. For the signed stories, the rate of the use of signs was significantly slower, presenting only about 2.3 signs per second. There appeared to be a significant difference between the speaking and signing rates. It certainly took more time to "articulate" a sign than to articulate a word. On the other hand, 210 words were used in the spoken version of a story, while only 122 signs were used to tell the same story. Both stories were told in about the same amount of time.

Two possibilities emerged from this study. Either the signed version eliminates some information to make up for the slower expression of signs, or else the fewer signs provided more information per sign than the information per word. To test the first possibility (that ASL eliminates information to help speed up communication), the researchers had a bilingual subject translate an English story into ASL that was observed by a second bilingual subject. The second subject could only see the resultant signs, not the English text. The second subject was then asked to retranslate the signed story back into English. The dramatic result of this experiment was that the retranslated story was virtually identical to the original English text, even though about half as many signs were used as words. Nothing important was lost in translation. Even pronouns and articles that were not explicitly signed reappeared in the final English retranslation. This proved that the expressive capabilities of ASL were fully equal to all the grammatical nuances of inflection and tense possessed by English.

This result left only the second possibility, that there is more information per sign than per word, as the likely explanation to the differing rates of speaking and signing. As the researchers learned more about the expressive capabilities of ASL that used the advantages of parallelism, they began to understand that isolated signs could not be compared with English words. By gaining a deeper understanding of the semantic use of space and motion, they were able to break down a story into semantic propositions that were somewhat equivalent to noun-phrase and verb-phrase elements in the deep structure of language. When they made this conversion, they found that spoken stories expressed approximately 1.3 propositions per second, while signed stories expressed an equivalent 1.5 propositions per second. Given statistical uncertainty, and differences among subjects, these two rates are virtually identical. Finally, since spoken language proceeds at approximately 25 bits per second, and signed language rates are equivalent to spoken language rates, we can assign an information rate of the same 25 bits per second to sign language.

This result is significant for an understanding of both the advantages and disadvantages of visual communication. On the positive side, signs do indeed use the parallelism of the image. Each sign is generally more expressive than a word because it can tap into the parallel nature of images, allowing more than one semantic element to be expressed at the same time. Only the eye can do this—attend to information that is present simultaneously (in parallel) at different parts of the visual field. On the negative side, the added visual meaning to a sign was needed to compensate for the overall slower expression of signs. So what had been gained through parallelism was immediately lost by the slower rate.

This understanding further confirms that there is a fundamental rate of human language expression and comprehension that proceeds at about 25 bits per second. This rate is essentially independent of the surface structure of language, whether auditory or visual. And when in the visual mode, it does not matter whether the visual expression parallels verbal language (writing), or whether it expresses itself in a purely visual medium (signing). In all these cases, language is being used. All these forms of expression, no matter how alien they are to each other—for instance, the fact that there can be no verbal analogs of visual puns, and vice versa—are all just the surface structure created by the deep structure of the human language instinct. And the language instinct chugs along at the rate of about 25 bits per second, regardless of the surface structure.

But let us not stop here. We may have shown that human language manipulation has intrinsic rates that are surprisingly constant; but visual language is not the only form of visual communication. What about purely geometric communication? What about the rate at which we see visual forms that have no language analog? The challenge in getting to the limiting rate of human visual communication is to disassociate the visual test completely from any aspect of language. By presenting visual information that has only graphical content, is a different rate of human information processing possible?

BACK TO THE BOTTLENECK

Studies of the human response to non-verbal visual stimuli measure the time it takes a subject to respond. The stimulus is often a light bulb that flashes, or a set of light bulbs, some of which flash and some that do not, to create different patterns. The subject is to respond appropriately to the flashes, perhaps by identifying which of several alternative patterns was presented. Because the light bulbs simply present patterns, there is no verbal content whatsoever in the stimulus. Responding to such stimuli certainly does not look like reading, or speaking, or signing. So, how fast do typical human subjects recognize the patterns?

Response time experiments on human subjects have been performed for about as long as accurate time instruments have been available. However, the meaning of a response time is not a simple thing. For instance, once subjects know that they want to react, or know how to react, it still takes some time for them to actually respond. The response may either be to speak the answer, or else to move a hand to hit a button. In either case, neural transmissions to the appropriate muscles must take place. In addition, it takes time to move a hand across a fixed distance. On top of these uncertainties, there is simply the time it takes to know that a stimulus has been seen, let alone trying to decide how to react to it. All of these different response times compound to create a total response time. These in turn complicate the question of how fast the mind sees.

One solution is to break the response time apart into its different constituents. Measuring how long it takes to complete a particular movement is easy. The subjects may be required to hold down a "start" button before a stimulus is presented. Once the subjects know how they want to respond to the stimulus, they remove their fingers from the start button to hit the appropriate response button. The time between letting up on the start and hitting the target buttons is the movement time. If this time for movement is subtracted from the overall response time, a reaction time remains. But even that reaction time is still made up of two components: the time merely to register the fact that a stimulus has occurred, and the time to decide what action to take.

The beauty of using arrangements of flashed light bulbs is that the information content can be precisely measured. If only two light bulbs can flash, there will be exactly four possible patterns: both off; the left on and the right off; the right on and the left off; or both on. Two lights give 2 bits of information. Three lights have nine possible patterns and represent 3 bits, and so on. The subject has to decide which specific pattern has been flashed, then hit an appropriate button. By doing so, the subject is making binary decisions.

When the reaction time is measured in experiments like these, a nearly universal reaction time is observed for typical subjects. First, there is the time it takes to simply react to 0 bits. Zero bits is easy to implement—it is a single light that always goes on to indicate the stimulus. If it always goes on, then there is no information—0 bits. But it still takes time for a subject to react, about 300 milliseconds. This is about the same time as a visual fixation when looking at an image, which is also about 10 frames (30 milliseconds per frame). Although a single frame can elicit a response, that response will not come for about 300 milliseconds—a factor of 10 longer than the stimulus. It therefore looks as though the brain needs the full time of the fixation to "register" the event. This tells us something fundamental about cognition.

To transmit more information, additional bulbs are added. For instance, 1 bit can be used, where a single light may or may not go off during the stimulus. Or two lights, or three, and on up. The number of lights that may or may not go off is equal to the number of bits because the number of alternative patterns is given by the number 2 raised to the number of bulbs. When these more complicated patterns are used, and the subject must respond correctly to the pattern, the reaction time gets longer. It gets longer by about 30 milliseconds for each additional bit of information that is presented. This time of 30 milliseconds per bit, when inverted, gives about 30 bits per second. This data rate for non-verbal information is virtually the same as the 25-bit-per-second rate for language comprehension. Perhaps it is a bit faster, but not by much.

This seems like a coincidence—that the binary decision rate for visual information, expressed in bits per second, is virtually the same as the information rate of human language exchange. What are the chances that verbal communication rates and abstract visual communication rates are connected? If they are connected, why do two such different modes of communication have such similar data rates? Language is a specific skill, very different from reacting to flashed lights. But these results make it seem that choosing alternatives among arbitrary stimuli is somehow similar to the language process.

We have seen that making choices among alternatives is the same as playing the game "Seven Questions," where the number of guesses is equal to the number of bits it takes to express the largest number in the allowable range. The game can be described as a binary tree as choices are made between two alternatives at each step. Although "Seven Questions" is a *conscious* game, might the human mind operate *subconsciously* on binary decision trees? If it takes a fixed amount of time per binary decision (perhaps 30 milliseconds), then we would get precisely what is measured—that it takes 30 milliseconds per bit to decide an issue.

We can therefore say with certainty that there is a limit to human cognitive capabilities: a comprehension speed limit. If a picture is worth a thousand words, it may very well take as many visual fixations on the picture as it takes to read a thousand words—at least if we are going to use the information to take action. On the other hand, there are still ways that we can use the parallel attributes of our vision. If we do not need to make a decision, at least not right away, then perhaps the massive parallelism of the image can still implant itself somewhere in the brain. After all, there are about 7 megabits per second of information traveling up the optic nerve. Are we to believe that all this information is cast away, and only the trickle of 25 bits per second gets through? It is not likely. But where the information goes, and how useful it is, is an open question. In any case, the Advantage of Light and Image appears to be mostly lost on us. Evolution has not found a way to help us use the parallelism of the image to good effect.

But human limitations need not be limitations of our constructed machines of light. Our physiology may be limited, but the parallelism of light remains available if we can find the right way to manipulate it. This advantage may not be used in a biological mind, yet it may be used in a "mind" of light, made by human ingenuity to perform beyond human capability. When we do this, we have done more than reassign mind tasks from people to machines. We have started a revolution. This is the optical revolution of the machines of light.

6 Communicating at the Speed of Light

The Optical Internet

I HAVE HEARD A RAY OF SUN LAUGH AND COUGH AND SING. I HAVE BEEN
ABLE TO HEAR A SHADOW, AND I HAVE EVEN PERCEIVED BY EAR THE
PASSING OF A CLOUD ACROSS THE SUN'S DISK.
Alexander Graham Bell, 1880

At the dawn of the third millennium, the world is wrapped in a fabric of
glass fiber. A tightly textured mesh covers some continents, while others
are ringed by only a single thread. But the fabric is whole, connected by a
fiber strand that circles the globe. This glass mesh was woven at incredible
speed: the oldest threads are barely a quarter-century old. The first few
trunk lines established the initial warps from which later threads spread out
over the countryside, linking up. The weaving grew finer, moving into sub-
urban areas, then towns, drawing ever closer to the home. Meanwhile,
fiber-optic local area networks grew spontaneously inside businesses and
across campuses, primed to tie into the global fiber network.

The force driving this growth is the potential for instant and unlimited
information provided over the Internet. Everyone around the world seems
to want more information faster. Ultimately, Movies-on-Demand will allow
you to see any movie ever made any time that you want to see it. And similarly for audio. Shopping-on-Demand would bring to your fingertips every
product for sale anywhere. Knowledge-on-Demand would link you to
every database storing everything ever learned or discovered.

The data rate that will be needed to supply all these "on-demands," to
all the people who want them, will significantly exceed 1,000 billion bits
per second, known as a terabit per second, on the trunk lines that feed local areas. The only technology with the potential to deliver this data rate
over long terrestrial distances is optical fiber. Fiber working at lower data

rates is already out there, and is coming closer to the home. Fiber-to-the-curb (FTTC), where the fiber comes to an optoelectronic switch that converts the information to electric signals that come into the home, will be followed by fiber-to-the-home (FTTH), and eventually by fiber-to-the-box (FTTB), where the optical connections are made directly into household appliances. The homes themselves become computers, networked intelligently to control all the household appliances, such as the oven and refrigerator and air conditioner. And of course the household Internet appliance (the appliance that will replace what separately used to be called the TV and the PC) will be connected to the household network—all optically.

But it won't stop there. Inside the "box," optics will also be making increasing inroads into the functioning of computers. Already we use optical discs for memory. In the future, moving information around will become increasingly difficult for electronics as the processor speeds continue to rise. Porting information optically inside the box from board to board or chip to chip will have the same advantages that fiber transmission has over copper and electronic signals, allowing extremely high data rates without electromagnetic interference.

Optics inside the box will always be restricted to "long-distance" transmission because the wavelength of light is so much larger than electronic switches in silicon; but the definition of "long-distance" is relative. Compared to the micron distances between electronic gates on a computer chip, centimeters or perhaps even millimeters will look "long-distance." As the processing speeds grow faster, the crossover length above which optics is used and below which electronics is used will shrink, and optics will become an inseparable element inside hybrid optoelectronic computers. The optics in the box ultimately will connect seamlessly with the optical network. Every computer will become an intelligent node on the intelligent optical fabric that drapes the world.

THE FIBERS OF THE NETWORK

Among machines of the first generation, the Optoelectronic Generation, the ongoing optical revolution is being driven by several technologies. The two most notable technologies are optical compact discs (optical memory) and optical fibers (optical communication). Optical communication presents significant challenges, and requires a steady sequence of breakthroughs to feed the ever-growing appetite for increased data rate. The demand for data rate is also the principal force that will push optical technology beyond optoelectronic machines and into the second All-Optical Generation of the machines of light.

Central to optical communication is the optical fiber. There are many types. In thirty years of research and development, scientists and engineers have devised an astounding variety of ways to confine light inside threads of glass. The simplest type of fiber has a central core of silica glass that is typically only 4 to 8 microns in diameter. Silica is a special form of silicon dioxide that has crystal-like properties while remaining an amorphous material that can be drawn into fine threads when heated. It has a notably higher melting point than ordinary glass and also has extremely good clarity and transparency—crucial properties for transporting light over long distances. This silica core is surrounded by a cladding layer in an annulus that is typically 60 microns thick. The cladding is also silica glass, but of a different kind, in which the speed of light is slightly faster than in the core. This difference in light velocity causes the total internal reflection described previously that keeps the light energy from leaking out of the fiber core. The cladding also isolates the central information-carrying core from humidity and mechanical stresses.

The cladding and core make up the working part of the fiber and have a total diameter of only 125 microns. To put the size of the fiber into perspective, a typical human hair has a diameter of around 75 microns. Yet this fine strand of glass can carry a data rate that exceeds a terabit per second—a data rate that can transmit 20,000 volumes of an encyclopedia in only one second. Imagine surfing the World Wide Web if you have this much bandwidth (data rate) coming directly into your computer. The World Wide Wait will be a distant memory.

To be useful, fiber core and cladding need to be flawless. Fabricating such exquisite objects is a fine industrial art. The process begins with a high-purity silica glass rod called a preform that is several centimeters thick and a meter long, coated by a layer of the high-velocity material. This preform is loaded at the top of a drawing tower several stories high, where it is melted. As molten glass is drawn away from the molten tip, it cools in air, and the drawn fiber is coiled directly onto spools.

The chief property of the final fiber that most affects how it will perform is how much it attenuates light. For instance, even a "perfect" fiber of the highest attainable purity will attenuate light that travels many kilometers.

The attenuation comes from fundamental physical processes associated with silica glass that cannot be circumvented. Because silica is a glass rather than a perfect crystal, frozen-in density fluctuations scatter light out of the core guiding region. This effect is known as Rayleigh scattering and is the same mechanism that makes the sky look blue. Rayleigh scattering is much stronger for shorter wavelengths, which is why the blue part of sunlight is scattered more effectively by density fluctuations in the atmosphere. Likewise in a fiber, wavelengths shorter than a micron are strongly scattered. Working with wavelengths larger than a micron improves the transparency up to a wavelength of about 1.55 microns, when another attenuation mechanism starts to dominate as the oxygen and silicon atoms in the glass absorb energy by converting the light energy into mechanical vibrations of the atoms. Therefore, there is a window of transparency for transmitting wavelengths between 1.3 microns and 1.6 microns, between where Rayleigh scattering falls off and the infrared absorption turns on.

However, there is trouble even within this window. While great pains are taken to make silica preforms that are virtually impurity-free, it is impossible to make all of the chemical bonds perfect because of the amorphous nature of glass. Some bonds are available to bind impurities, such as simple water, creating a hydroxide chemical bond. This impurity complex absorbs infrared light with wavelengths around 1.4 microns. This impurity absorption splits the transparency window into two bands, one centered on 1.3 microns and another centered on 1.55 microns. These two wavelength bands define the working wavelengths for long-distance transmission through fibers.

The transparency of glass at these wavelengths is measured in terms of the attenuation, which is expressed in units of decibels per kilometer (dB/km). Decibels are an insidious invention by engineers that challenge general intuition, but that turn out to be a useful way to describe how much signal comes out of a communication system. An attenuation of 20 dB, for instance, represents an output power that is only 1 percent of the input power; in other words, 99 percent of the light is lost. Attenuation is defined as the number of decibels of power lost per length of fiber.

In the transparency window of silica fibers, the attenuation gets as low as 0.16 dB/km at a wavelength of 1.55 microns. For transmission through 140 kilometers (87 miles) of fiber, this would give a total attenuation of 22 dB, or a reduction of the optical intensity by a factor of almost 200. This means that more than 99 percent of the light would be lost simply by transmitting from Philadelphia to New York City. Given this seemingly low efficiency, how does anyone send an optical signal across the country, or across the Pacific Ocean?

The answer implemented in first-generation fiber systems was to place optoelectronic repeater stations every 140 kilometers. Repeater stations are optoelectronic relays which have a photodetector that absorbs the signal photons and converts them into electrons. Once the signal is in the electronic domain, electronic circuits amplify the signal to drive a laser transmitter that converts electric current back into photons sent downstream to the next repeater station. During this optoelectronic regeneration, the optical pulses are reamplified, reshaped, and retimed in a process called 3R regeneration. 3R regeneration is a critical aspect of the optoelectronic repeaters because optical pulses traveling down a fiber suffer more than simple attenuation. They also become distorted and are either delayed or advanced, depending on mechanical or thermal stresses on the fiber.

Because repeater stations use electronics to perform 3R regeneration, they require electric power. In terrestrial lines, the power is usually taken from local utilities, while in submarine fiber-optic cables the electricity is supplied by copper that runs the full length of the cable. Even in fiber systems installed terrestrially, conventional copper wires still carry information about the performance of the repeaters, as well as information about routing of the signals. The elaborate electronic control protocol for managing the information on fiber-optic networks is called SONET, which stands for synchronous optical network. These conventional SONET systems are members of the first generation of the machines of light, using light for transmission but electronics for control and intelligence.

The data rate that can be placed on a single fiber has been increasing exponentially ever since the first fiber systems were installed in 1980. Exponential growth is an exhilarating type of expansion that takes one's breath away. Like compound interest, a small number quickly grows to unexpected proportions as it accumulates over time. This type of growth is usually characterized in terms of the number of years it takes for the amount of something to double. Exponential growth has been a long-standing part of the electronics industry. The number of transistors per chip has been doubling every eighteen months. This growth rate has been going on since the mid-1960s, and has acquired the name of Moore's Law. Gordon Moore (1929–) is one of the founders of Intel Corporation. In 1965 he predicted that the doubling rate would hold steady for some years to come. His scant data at the time was hardly sufficient to merit projecting the trend thirty years into the future, yet the rate continued to stay relatively constant over many years, extending into decades. After awhile his observation became an expectation, and later a mission that has taken on almost a religious fervor. Maintaining Moore's Law has become a principal driving force in Silicon Valley.

Fiber-optic systems are now experiencing the same kind of exponential growth. The data rates of fiber systems have been doubling steadily every eighteen months for the past twenty years; this equals the doubling rate of Moore's Law. To predict the future, it makes sense to look at the fastest data rates that are being achieved in research laboratories because improvements in the laboratory have typically moved into commercial use with a lag time of only three to seven years. Laboratory demonstrations have already exceeded many terabits per second, so these will be in the ground supporting Internet traffic by around the year 2005. At least this much growth can be expected to continue into the future.

But there is an exciting new trend coming out of the research laboratories. Over the past six years, the doubling time for data rates has decreased noticeably, to almost a year. If the commercial systems continue to follow the laboratory trends, as they have for the last twenty years, this means that data rates for the Internet may start to double every twelve months instead of eighteen. This would allow Internet usage to grow by a factor of 200 in only five years. Putting this another way, if a network company installs a new fiber system in the ground today that initially operates at only 10 percent of maximum capacity, by the end of only two years the cable will be fully saturated. To prevent loss of revenue share, the company would need to install a new cable every year—at a prohibitive cost.

To avoid this cost, intense research is being supported by the large network companies to find ways of increasing the data rates on fibers already in the ground. In parallel with this activity, scientists and engineers are working toward a concept called an all-optical network, in which the light pulses making up the optical data would stay as light pulses between the source and the destination and never need to be turned into electrons. An all-optical fiber system would ideally be independent of the actual data rate traveling down a fiber, meaning that a fiber system would need to be installed only once. Data rates would be increased at the sending and receiving end by changing the optoelectronic systems that feed the fiber; but no new fibers would need to be put into the ground, considerably cutting the costs usually associated with higher data rates.

Although the technical challenges for an all-optical Internet are extreme, advances are being made, and the first components that will lead the way to all-optical systems are now being introduced by the telecom companies. How high can data rates ultimately go on these fibers? Fundamental limits dictated by physics give an upper speed limit for data rates on a single fiber of about 30 trillion bits per second.

DATA RATES AND BANDWIDTHS

The word "bandwidth" has become a mantra to those who telecommunicate or who surf the Web. Everyone wants bandwidth, and telecommunication companies that can deliver "broadband" services hope to make killings in the stock market. Where did this word "bandwidth" come from? How broad is "broadband"? And most importantly, how does data rate use up bandwidth? Why is the maximum data rate 30 terabits per second?

Let us look again at the transparency windows for fiber optics. Transparency minimums represent communication "bands," just like radio stations, that are used for optical communications, and they exist at 350 terahetz, 240 terahertz, and 180 terahertz (corresponding to the primary communication wavelengths of 850 nanometers, 1.3 microns, and 1.55 microns). The three bands have widths of about 20 terahertz each. The specific question of data rate and bandwidth is this: What is the highest data rate that can be sent down a fiber, given the useful widths of these communication bands?

I have emphasized that optics is excellent for information transmission *because light beams travel through each other without affecting the information on either beam.* If this is true, then what stops us from using as many different light frequencies as we want within this transparency bandwidth? Changing the frequency of the light carrying the information is like changing the channel on a radio. If the data rate on each signal is fast enough, what stops us from having an arbitrarily large data rate by using an arbitrarily large number of channels? The answer has to do with the physics that connects the data rate of a channel to the frequency bandwidth of the channel. These two properties of a data signal are not independent. We might think that a pure channel frequency is perfectly distinguishable from a neighboring channel frequency. This is *not* the case. For instance, the shorter an optical pulse duration (to get more bits per second), the more waves are needed to generate the pulse. This means that higher data rates with shorter pulses need larger bandwidths.

Simple wave addition leads to an inverse relationship between the pulse duration and the bandwidth that makes up the pulse. A long pulse has a small bandwidth with relatively pure color. A very short pulse has a broad bandwidth. This inverse relationship between pulse duration and bandwidth is closely related to the Heisenberg uncertainty relationship mentioned in chapter 2. This type of time-bandwidth relationship is quite general for any wave phenomenon. Since optics concerns light waves and quantum mechanics concerns matter waves, they share this aspect in common.

What has the frequency bandwidth to do with the data rate of a sequence of pulses? Not surprisingly, the bit rate in units of bits per second, is equal to the bandwidth of the signal in units of Hertz. This is the simple answer to our question of how much bandwidth is used up by a given data rate.

Let us look at the details for a moment. The transparency window around the wavelength of 1.55 microns has a bandwidth of about 30 terahertz. If we create a pulse out of this bandwidth, the pulse will have a duration of only 33 femtoseconds. Conversely, pulses of 33 femtosecond duration can carry 30 terabits per second of information. This is the ultimate data rate that a silica fiber can carry within the 1.55-micron band. It is the speed limit for this technology, based on fundamental physics of waves (how they are put together to form pulses) and on the absorbing hydroxide impurities in the silica glass.

But is it attainable in practice? For instance, a pulse duration of 33 femtoseconds is an incredibly short time. While short pulses are created by the addition of innumerable waves of slightly different wavelengths, the phase relationships among all these waves must be delicately balanced to maintain the short pulse duration. What happens if the balance is upset? Can such a short pulse, supposing we could even make one, propagate without distortion over the 100 kilometers that are necessary between repeater stations? This question alludes to an important physical property of optical fibers that we have not discussed up to now. It is the property known as dispersion.

THE SECRET OF SUN DOGS

Dispersion dictates how different frequencies of light travel with different velocities through a transparent material like glass or water. Dispersion is a general property that occurs in all materials and is the basis of beautiful optical effects and demonstrations. Indeed, the most dramatic atmospheric displays of color arise from dispersion, such as rainbows and glories, moon rings and sun dogs. Whether in a raindrop or a glass prism or a cut diamond, dispersion breaks sunlight down into its spectrum of colors any time that a ray of light is refracted at the surface of a dispersive material. Larger dispersion causes larger separation of the constituent colors of light. It is because diamond has greater dispersion than glass in the visible range of light that diamonds acquire their valued brilliance. Sunlight is broken apart into the colors of the rainbow when it refracts at each of the many facets of the cut diamond.

Dispersion is a common property of all materials for the simple reason that electrons have charge and mass. All the optical properties of a material are based on the forces that the electric fields (making up light waves) exert on charged electrons in the material, and how the electrons respond to the forces. An electron in matter is not free, but is connected to the nucleus of an atom through the Coulomb force that attracts the negatively charged electron to the positively charged nucleus. This attractive force can be represented as a spring (under appropriate conditions that usually hold for optical properties) that connects the electron to the nucleus.

When an electron experiences a force caused by a steady electric field, it is pulled slightly away from the nucleus to a distance established by a balance of the force of the field against the attractive force of the spring. This displacement of the electron is what constitutes the property called atomic polarization. Atomic polarization can also be viewed as the field pulling on an originally spherical atom and elongating it into a slight football shape along the direction of the field. When the atoms are part of a solid material, this collection of polarized atoms produces a macroscopic material polarization.

For a steady electric field, the electronic polarization is proportional to the strength of the field. But the electric field of a wave of light is oscillating in time, not static. At typical optical frequencies (in the many hundreds of terahertz), the electron has very little time to respond because of its inertia (its mass). Therefore, the magnitude of the polarization will not be the same as for a static field, and there is often a time lag or delay in the motion of the electron responding to the oscillating field. These effects cause the electronic polarization to be different for different frequencies.

The velocity at which a light wave travels through a medium is determined by the interaction of the wave with the bound electrons on the atoms. The propagating wave is a superposition of the original wave with new waves that are radiated by the oscillating electrons (which are responding to the original wave). There is a time lag between the original wave and the radiated wave because of the inertia of the electrons. Mathematically, the velocity of the resultant wave propagating through the medium is directly linked to the magnitude and lag of the polarization induced by the wave. Because the polarization is different for different frequencies, the velocity is different for different frequencies.

This frequency-dependent wave velocity, dependent on the polarization properties of the electrons, is the material dispersion. Different materials have different configurations of bound electrons and therefore different optical dispersions that relate back to the chemical composition and structure of the material. The unique curve relating the velocity of light to the frequency of light for each material may be viewed as the material's optical "fingerprint."

However, material dispersion is not the only cause of dispersion in optical fibers. Optical fibers have a strongly restricted geometry. As we saw earlier, the inner core of a fiber is only 4 to 8 microns in diameter, which is comparable to the wavelength of infrared light (around 1 micron). The wave is therefore restricted to a small volume, reflecting back and forth (through total internal reflection) between one edge of the core and the other. For a given wavelength of light, there is only one angle of reflection in the fiber that allows the wave to propagate down the fiber without destructive interference. Rays of light reflecting at other angles eventually produce destructive interference that prevents the wave from propagating.

Because there is only one allowed angle of reflection for a given wavelength, these types of fibers are called single-mode fibers. It is possible to make thicker fibers that allow two or more reflection angles for a given wavelength, producing what is known as a multimode fiber. But multimode fibers are not appropriate for long-distance fiber-optical communication because the rays reflecting at the different angles travel at different velocities, mixing up the signal at the output of the fiber. Even for single-mode fibers, which are the fibers currently used for long-distance optical communication, different wavelengths have different angles of reflection. The angle of reflection changes continuously with the wavelength of the light. This changing angle causes the different wavelengths to travel with different velocities, producing what is known as waveguide dispersion.

In an optical fiber, the material dispersion of the silica and the waveguide dispersion combine to cause different frequencies to travel with different velocities. As we saw earlier, a signal at any given data rate assumes a frequency bandwidth equal to the data rate. Therefore, in the presence of dispersion, the different wavelengths making up the data pulses travel at different velocities. This has important consequences for the transmission of data.

The most dramatic effect is that a pulse of light broadens as it propagates. Imagine a pulse made by adding up waves of different frequencies such that they all produce constructive interference within the pulse, and destructive interference outside the pulse. But this happens only when all the waves line up at the center of the pulse. When that pulse travels down a fiber, the different frequencies travel at different velocities, and the perfect lineup is removed. This takes away the perfect destructive interference outside the pulse, and the pulse becomes broader. The farther the pulse travels, the more the different waves shift off of the perfect lineup and the broader the pulse becomes. Dispersion (both material and waveguide dispersion) therefore causes pulses to broaden as they propagate.

The effect of dispersion on a pulse at the 0.850-micron band is drastic. Consider a pulse that originally could support a data rate of 1 terabit per second; after only 10 kilometers, the data rate will be 200 times smaller. If a data rate any faster than 500 megabits per second were to be used, then the pulses representing the bits of the signal would spread out and overlap with each other, causing neighboring bits to interfere and introduce errors in transmission. Therefore, dispersion in glass fibers causes serious difficulty for high data rates, even if the transport distances are as small as a few kilometers. This example is extreme, because the dispersion at the 0.850-micron band is large. However, it serves to demonstrate how dispersion in optical fibers produces optical bottlenecks to data bandwidth.

It also demonstrates how length scales become connected with data rates. For instance, inside a computer, the transmission lengths between boards may only be 10 centimeters. The spreading of the pulse over this short distance is only 20 femtoseconds, which is negligible for a 1-picosecond pulse. Therefore, the wavelength band around 0.850 microns can support a data rate of many terabits per second if the distances are short enough. Indeed, such applications exist in the area known as "datacom" (for data communication) that distinguishes it from "telecom" (for telecommunication). Datacom works well at 0.850 microns, even though this wavelength band would be completely unworkable for long-distance telecom applications because of the large dispersion and absorption that would accumulate over large distances.

Fortunately, the material dispersion of glass fiber changes with wavelength, and in one of the happy coincidences of nature, the combined material and waveguide dispersion happens to vanish around a wavelength of 1.3 microns. This wavelength is centered inside the second transparency window, which is a more attractive window than 0.850 microns because it has less attenuation. This coincidence was not lost on fiber engineers: the first transatlantic fiber-optic cable installed in 1988 was based at this central wavelength working at a (conservative) bandwidth of 280 megabits per second with repeater stations every 70 kilometers.

It would seem that this should be the end of the story for long-distance fiber communications. By working at a wavelength of 1.3 microns, where dispersion vanishes, it should be possible to transmit high data rate pulses without the problems of broadening. But this is an easy trap to fall into. Remember that high data rates require wide bandwidths. And wide bandwidths would force some wavelength channels to fall outside the center wavelength of 1.3 microns where dispersion vanishes. Therefore, even though the central wavelength of a channel may not experience dispersion, the wavelengths on either side of the frequency spectrum will. This is known as second-order dispersion, which again leads to broadening of the pulse. The ultimate bandwidth of the 1.3-micron band is thus still limited to data rates less than 1 terabit per second over 70 kilometers.

One last strike against the 1.3-micron band is that the fiber loss at 1.3 microns is still not as low as at 1.55 microns. Since repeater stations carry with them considerable cost, low fiber loss has compelling financial benefits. The fiber engineers were able to find clever ways of designing special fibers that could shift the zero dispersion wavelength from 1.3 microns to 1.55 microns. Furthermore, by using even *cleverer* engineering, they were able to design fibers that even had small second-order dispersion at 1.55 microns, which would allow fibers to carry the highest possible data rates the longest possible distances. The second transatlantic fiber optic cable (installed in 1991) works at this central wavelength at a bandwidth (again conservative) of 560 megabits per second. Because of the lower loss, the distance between repeater stations was pushed out to 150 kilometers.

This would seem to be all that is needed to access the 30-terabit-per-second data rates that can be supported within the 1.55-micron window. But the fiber is not the only component in the transmission system. Fiber systems are serial systems, which connect laser transmitters to fibers that pass through multiple optoelectronic repeaters and more fibers, finally connecting to receivers—all in a line. The whole system only operates as fast as its slowest component. The exponentially increasing data rates on fiber systems have never pushed the limits on the actual data-carrying capacity of the fiber. The bottleneck technology has always been the optoelectronic components—the lasers and modulators and their associated drive electronics. Let's look at the physics behind why these electrical components are the principal obstacles to the multi-terabit-per-second Internet. Are these bottlenecks inescapable? Or can they be overcome to fill the full 30-terabit-per-second bandwidth of the fiber in a 1.55-micron telecommunication band?

ELECTRONIC BANDWIDTH BOTTLENECKS

Electrons may be good at control, but they have their speed limits. The first-generation optoelectronic machines of light rely on electronics either to generate light, to modulate it, or to detect it. The speeds at which electronic devices operate are subject to their own laws of physics, just as basic physics principles limited the bandwidth of the fibers. But in electronic devices, the physics principles are different, and more severe. For instance, the mass of the electron gives it inertia that must be overcome by forces to accelerate it to high velocity. Even at their highest velocity, the electrons do not approach the speed of light. This means that it takes time for an electron to travel distances inside electronic devices. While the size of the devices is getting ever smaller (and with the decrease in distance comes an increase in speed of operation—Moore's Law again), their ultimate speeds remain much lower than the potential bandwidth of the optical fibers. So, the bandwidth bottleneck shifts from the physics of fiber to the physics of the optoelectronic machines.

There are two characteristic times associated with electrons that move and are stored in solid-state electronic devices. The first of these is the time it takes an electron to travel across the device. This time is called the transit time. The second is the time it takes for enough electrons to accumulate to operate the device. This time is called the RC time (which refers to the device resistance R and capacitance C). Depending on the size and shape of the device, one time or the other will be longer. And in all cases, the slower process limits the rate because the system is only as fast as its slowest component. For instance, if the RC time is larger, then the maximum data rate that the device can drive is the inverse of the RC time—and similarly for the transit time. It is therefore usual to try to reduce both times together.

The best way to reduce both the RC time and the transit time is to reduce the size of the device. Because the transit time is equal to the distance divided by the electron velocity, decreasing the distance and increasing the velocity should produce smaller transit times. Decreasing size is a practical approach that has been the principal means of sustaining Moore's Law for silicon electronics. There is the added benefit that as the size gets smaller, the electric fields that drive the electrons get larger (for a fixed working voltage). It might be expected that larger forces on the electrons would make them go faster, but this is where the intricacies of semiconductor physics clamp down on the ultimate speed of electronic devices.

Electrons in semiconducting materials such as silicon are not free to move around, but are held in chemical bonds that keep the solid material together. A small number of electrons (on the order of parts per million) can be introduced into the material attached to impurity atoms like phosphorous that are called dopants. These added electrons move through the crystal, but not freely because they sense all the other electrons that are held in the chemical bonds. Under the applied force of an electric field, the electrons accelerate up to a maximum velocity. Unlike a truly free electron, further increase in the electric field produces no additional velocity. The maximum velocity in silicon is about 10 million centimeters per second, which is 0.03 percent of the speed of light. Other optoelectronic semiconductors, such as gallium arsenide and indium phosphide, share this common speed limit, despite their considerably different chemical constituents.

To get an idea of how this speed limit for electrons affects the speeds at which electronics operate, consider a device that has a length of one tenth of a micron, or 1,000 Ångstrom. An electron traveling at the maximum speed will traverse this distance in 1 picosecond. A 1-picosecond transit time corresponds to a data rate of about 100 gigahertz—a rate that barely touches the bandwidth of 30 terabits per second of the transparency window around 1.55 microns in silica fibers. Higher speeds require shorter distances for the electrons to travel. However, there are practical limitations that prevent this—partly due to physics and partly due to engineering.

The current way to fabricate solid-state devices is to use light in a process known as optical lithography. Ultraviolet light is passed through a silica plate called a photomask that has been patterned with chromium with the identical pattern as the eventual electronic devices, but at a bigger size. The image of this photomask is reduced in size by a lens system, which projects the pattern onto a semiconductor coated with a light-sensitive polymer film called photoresist. Wherever the transparent part of the mask illuminates the photoresist it undergoes light-induced polymerization. After exposure, the silicon wafer with the exposed photoresist is developed and the unexposed resist is dissolved away, leaving a miniaturized pattern of resist that perfectly matches the pattern on the photomask. The wafer is then sent through additional processing steps, including more photolithographic steps that define transistors and the metal wires connecting them.

Because this process of photolithography is an optical process, it is subject to the laws of optical diffraction. Just as light diffracts off the iris of the eye to define a minimum spot size on the retina, the light diffracting off the optical mask defines a minimum resolvable line size equal to half the wavelength of the light. To make lines that are much smaller will require new technology that goes beyond the capabilities of optical lithography. Alternative approaches are currently being pursued that have succeeded in making exceedingly small devices, much smaller than one tenth of a micron. One approach uses a finely focused electron beam that moves point by point to directly write small features, but this lacks the principal advantage of optical lithography—the parallel advantage of imaging. Tenth-micron feature size therefore represents a practical limit to solid-state device size and limits electronic (and hence optoelectronic) devices to data rates under 100 gigabits per second.

But electronic devices are only one part of optoelectronic systems. The other important component of a fiber-optic communication system is the laser. Light from a laser needs to be turned on and off—called intensity modulation—to represent optical bits of "1's" and "0's." Light from a laser diode can be modulated by directly controlling the electrical current delivered to the device. The current does not need to be turned all the way off to make the light go to zero—all that is necessary is to reduce the current slightly below the threshold for lasing. The amplitude of the electric current modulation can therefore be very small, allowing high-speed light modulation using high-speed drive electronics. But there is still the question of whether the laser can respond fast enough to the changing electrical currents.

The characteristic time associated with a laser turning on and off depends on the intensity of light coming out of the laser. If the laser emits higher powers, it turns off faster. This may seem counterintuitive. Usually, larger amplitudes take longer to decrease to zero than smaller amplitudes. But in lasers there is the added mechanism of stimulated emission that was discussed in chapter 2. Stimulated emission is the process where one photon stimulates an excited atom to emit a second identical photon. If more photons are present in the laser medium, then more of the excited states are induced to emit; in other words, the de-excitation of excited states through stimulated emission happens faster when more photons are around. When the calculations are done, and the typical parameters of a semiconductor laser are put into the equations, the maximum modulation rate of a semiconductor laser turns out to be only about 40 gigahertz. Direct laser modulation does not quite get up to the rates of the high-speed electronics.

Direct modulation of lasers, though simple, is not the only means to modulate the intensity of laser light. It is also possible to modulate the light by sending it through an optoelectronic shutter called an optical modulator. Simple modulators are made from special materials whose optical properties change as electric fields are applied. These are called electro-optic modulators. No electrons move through these devices, so they are limited in speed only by the RC time. For conventional devices, the data rate approaches 10 gigabits per second, but no further. More sophisticated modulators called traveling-wave modulators get up to frequencies of 40 gigahertz, but higher frequencies are still difficult to achieve.

All these different optoelectronic devices—electronic drive circuits, diode lasers, and electro-optic modulators—have a bandwidth bottleneck that cuts off between 10 gigahertz to 100 gigahertz. The physical principles operating in each of the devices are very different, yet they all converge on this limiting range of maximum operation frequencies. This convergence is a fundamental consequence of electromagnetic interactions. The wavelength of a 100-gigahertz electromagnetic source is 3 millimeters. It is not easy to generate wavelengths that are smaller than this using electronic means.

This frequency of 100 gigahertz is roughly the dividing line between optics, which relies on the emission and absorption of photons by quantum states of atom and molecules, and radio-frequency electromagnetics, which relies on the transmission of waves from antennas. Therefore, all the electronic technologies pull up short at the 100-gigahertz boundary.

TIME PARALLELISM

So how do you put 30 terabits per second into a fiber if your light sources and optoelectronic control devices operate only as fast as 100 gigabits per second? More practically, how do you get even 40 gigabits per second onto a single fiber if you want to use a tried-and-true laser transmitter that only runs at the much more conservative (but equally more reliable) rate of 100 megabits per second? The answer is through a process known as time-division multiplexing (TDM).

Time-division multiplexing is a form of optical parallelism that uses time as an additional parallel dimension. TDM interleaves the data pulses of several different signals, each of which operates at a lower data rate. For instance, if there are forty separate signal channels, each at a base data rate, these can be combined into a signal that operates at forty times the original data rate. By the use of extensive time-division multiplexing, multiple low-rate signals of 100 megabits per second can be multiplexed up forty times into the 40-gigabit-per-second range.

Time-division multiplexing has been the approach of choice to get telecommunications systems operating up to 2.5 gigabits per second, and recently up to 10 gigabits per second. TDM is also the basis of the synchronous optical network (SONET) protocol that dominated fiber-optic network architectures through the 1990s. This architecture has been thoroughly tested and implemented in virtually all the long-haul optical networks. Because of its robustness, there is considerable impetus to see how high TDM can go. For instance, systems have been built that operate solely through TDM at 40 gigabits per second. However, conventional optoelectronics fail for 1 terabit per second and higher because the optoelectronic modulators cannot operate at those speeds. On the other hand, we can ask whether we could ever fill the complete 30-terabit-per-second bandwidth of optical fiber through TDM. Such a feat would require data pulses of only 30 femtosecond duration. Can such short pulses actually be produced reliably if electronics can never approach this time scale?

ULTRA-FAST LASERS

As we saw, direct modulation of laser diodes or electro-optic modulation of light gives data rates only up to 100 gigabits per second, which corresponds to 10 picosecond pulses. To generate laser pulses of 1-picosecond duration or even shorter requires completely different physics. The challenge is to have a laser emit a 1-picosecond pulse in response to an excitation that lasts significantly longer than that. For instance, an exciting pulse may be the electric current supplied to a laser diode by fast electronic circuits. This electrical pulse might be 10 picoseconds or longer, but we want the laser to respond by emitting a pulse that is shorter than that by a factor of 10, or even more. In this case, the output of the laser is clearly not linearly proportional to the stimulus, indicating that we require some form of non-linear response of the laser to the electrical stimulus. Fortunately, lasers happen to be strongly non-linear in how they behave and in how they respond to externally imposed perturbations. These intrinsic laser non-linearities provide precisely the means to generate ultra-short laser pulses in response to slow excitation.

The population of excited states in a laser grows linearly with an increase in the exciting power only up to the point that the laser crosses the lasing threshold. Once the laser starts lasing, even a large increase in the amount of energy pumped into the laser produces virtually no increase in the population inversion—its value becomes clamped at a level that can go no higher. This is because of stimulated emission, which provides a feedback effect called gain clamping that is one of several forms of strikingly non-linear behavior in lasers. A key to making fast lasers is to use such laser non-linearities to take a slow process, like the electrical modulation of the drive current of a laser diode, and turn it into a much faster process by accelerating the rate of stimulated emission.

To explain how this happens, we first need to define a laser "mode." When lasers produce light, the properties of the light coming from the laser are defined in terms of laser modes. Each is a resonance of the laser cavity composed of two mirrors at each end of the laser medium. A particularly easy resonance to understand is the distance a single photon travels in a single trip around the laser cavity. This round trip takes a time equal to twice the total length of the cavity divided by the speed of light. A mode, or a resonance, occurs when the photon properties are the same after one round trip as before the round trip. It occurs only when the length of the laser cavity is exactly equal to an integer number of wavelengths of the light.

To form very short picosecond pulses in a laser, all the modes need to cooperate in a collective manner. For instance, if the phases of all the different modes lock in step with one another, then at one point in time and space all the waves add together constructively to give a strong intensity, while away from the center of the pulse, the waves add destructively.

To lock the phases of all those modes together to produce a short pulse in a semiconductor diode laser, it suffices to excite the laser with a periodic sequence of electrical current pulses. The repetition rate of the current can be relatively long, such as 20 picoseconds, which is compatible with laser drive electronics. A key requirement to achieve short pulses is that the periodic modulation of the pumping energy must exactly match the round-trip time of the photons in the cavity. Photons that are passing through the gain medium when the gain is a maximum are amplified, while photons that are passing through the medium when the gain is a minimum are attenuated. This forms an initial weak pulse of photons in the laser cavity that is synchronized with the pump repetition.

Once this initially weak and relatively long pulse forms, the growth of this pulse in amplitude and the decrease of the pulse duration are automatically supplied by the intrinsic non-linearities of the laser medium. The different photon modes pool their energy and synchronize their phases through a feedback cycle. Higher intensity and shorter pulses produce more non-linearity. In turn, the larger non-linearity produces higher intensity and short pulses—and the cycle starts again. By having all the photon modes bunch together, they attain the highest intensity by achieving the shortest possible pulse duration. This self-organization of the photons produces a single packet of photons that bounces back and forth inside the laser cavity. In this situation, all the modes are said to be locked in synchronization with each other, hence this type of laser operation is called mode-locking. The output of a mode-locked laser is a steady stream of extremely short but very intense laser pulses.

The duration of an individual pulse depends on the specific details of the type of laser, but typical pulse durations from this type of mode-locking are in the range of 1 picosecond, even though the electrical current only needs to drive the laser with slow repetition rates of about 20 picoseconds. Actively mode-locking the laser by modulating the gain of the laser at a frequency equal to the round-trip frequency of the circulating photon packet therefore succeeds in producing ultra-short laser pulses that are sufficient for attaining 1-terabit-per-second data rates through time-division multiplexing. But we would like to go farther. The full fiber bandwidth is 30 terabits per second, requiring laser pulses of only 30 femtosecond duration to fill that bandwidth. Such pulses are achieved by relying even more heavily on laser non-linearities in a process known as passive mode-locking.

Passive mode-locking is distinguished from active mode-locking (just described) by dispensing with the requirement of periodic external pumping. This is achieved by using the optical non-linearities of a laser system to start and sustain *self*-oscillation. Self-oscillation is actually a very common, natural phenomenon.

When a violinist draws a bow across a violin string with a steady pressure and velocity, the string naturally oscillates. The bow provides steady energy to the string, sustaining the oscillation, but the oscillation occurs naturally and on its own. Nothing about the bowing of the string imposes the oscillation or the oscillation frequency on the string. The length of the string and its tension uniquely defines its resonant frequency. How, then, does the steady supply of energy to the string produce a time-varying oscillation? The answer is through the non-linearity of the force of the bow on the string. The resin used on the bow string causes the bow to stick and slip across the violin string. As the string vibrates, it gives a feedback force on the bow which causes a steady rate of stick and slip that automatically matches the natural resonance frequency of the string. With a steady force and velocity, this causes a uniform self-sustained oscillation. But without the bow string non-linearity, the violin would never play.

Passive mode-locking is a similar type of self-oscillation that occurs in lasers under appropriate conditions. The locking of all the laser modes together into a single circulating laser pulse is a form of self-oscillation. Optical non-linearities in the laser medium provide the non-linear mechanism that is needed to initiate and sustain this passive mode-locking. The initiation process is similar to the case for active mode-locking, but now there is no external control or stabilization of any kind. All that is needed in the laser cavity is some energy loss mechanism that gets smaller as the intensity gets higher. Intensities get higher when photons bunch together. Therefore, because non-linearities give proportionally stronger effects for stronger laser pulses, there is a tendency for natural fluctuations of higher intensity to experience less loss on average per round trip. This positive feedback amplifies high-intensity fluctuations and suppresses low-intensity fluctuations in a beam of photons.

The high fluctuations grow into a single circulating packet of photons that contains all the energy output of the laser. Because shorter pulses have higher intensities and lower losses, this mechanism produces laser pulses that are as short and intense as can be physically sustained by the laser medium. In the best cases, laser pulses may be only several femtoseconds long. Such pulses are so short that they contain only a few optical cycles of the electric field.

Apart from the ability to produce ultra-short laser pulses, the greatest advantage of passive mode-locking is that no external feedback is needed to sustain the oscillation. This makes passively mode-locked lasers very easy to operate, and very robust. An increasing number of solid-state lasers have been found that are able to support mode-locking. With the ready availability of ultra-fast laser sources that generate laser pulses down to 30 femtoseconds, massive TDM can in principle be used to multiplex up to the 30-terabit-per-second rate that fills the fiber bandwidth. But do we really want to do that?

COLOR PARALLELISM

Let us consider again our example of the actively mode-locked semiconductor diode laser with the 1-mm cavity length. This laser emits a 1-picosecond pulse every 20 picoseconds. It requires 50 gigahertz electronics to drive it, which is an available technology (though it pushes the limits). By using TDM, twenty of these lasers could be used to generate data pulses that could be multiplexed up to 1 terabit per second without the need for inordinately fast optoelectronics; but then we are faced with the problem of demultiplexing. How do we break the multiplexed signal back down again into its individual channels, using only 50 gigahertz or slower optoelectronics? One answer, which we explore in the next chapter, is to use optical non-linearities to perform the demultiplexing. This approach, though still in its infancy, performs all operations in the optical domain without ever needing to resort to slow electronics. On the other hand, venture capitalists and stockholders of the large telecommunications companies are not willing to wait for terabit-per-second systems. They want them now! Alternative, and shorter-term, solutions to filling the fiber bandwidth need to be developed. (A list of many of the most active optical companies is given in Appendix B.)

The best alternative is called wavelength-division multiplexing (WDM). Wavelength-division multiplexing is a form of optical parallelism that uses wavelength (or color) as an additional dimension for sending signals in parallel. This approach starts with multiple signals that have already been multiplexed up to a base data rate of 2.5 gigabits per second using TDM. These signals are then encoded at different wavelengths. For instance, four different signals can be sent down the same fiber at the same time, but at four different wavelengths. To do this, all you need is four lasers with different wavelengths, each operating below the 40-gigahertz electronics limit. These signals are combined passively, just as in the case of time-division multiplexing, before being coupled into a single transmission fiber. The demultiplexing is as simple as using filters, as on a radio dial, to tune to each respective wavelength. When tuned to a specific channel, only that channel will be detected, because the other simultaneous signals will not make it through the filter.

Wavelength-division multiplexing puts only minor requirements on the electronics because standard optoelectronic speeds are sufficient to generate each separate signal. Furthermore, the fabrication of filters that only let through one channel and block all the others is primarily an engineering challenge. Therefore, this multiplexing approach does not face the technological challenges of massive time-division demultiplexing; nor does it suffer from the problem of pulse distortion from dispersion that very short pulses experience in the time-division approach.

Going beyond wavelength-division multiplexing is something called dense wavelength-division multiplexing (DWDM), which means that many different wavelengths and channels are used—all down the same fiber at the same time. For instance, 128 different wavelength channels, each with a base data rate of 2.5 gigabits per second, could be separated by 100 giga-hertz across the fiber transparency window around 1.55-micron wave-lengths. This would use up 12.8 terahertz of bandwidth, while achieving a multiplexed data rate of 320 gigabits per second, which is one third of a ter-abit per second. These rates have already been achieved in laboratories, and soon should find their way into commercial systems.

But this does not provide the full data rate that can be supported by fiber. To push these numbers farther, consider individual channels with data rates of 40 gigabits per second on each. If these are transmitted at fre-quencies that are separated by 100 gigahertz, then 300 different wave-length channels would span the full 30-terahertz bandwidth of the fiber, with a multiplexed data rate of 12 terabits per second. Smaller channel sep-aration could improve this multiplexed data rate even further, approaching the full bandwidth of the fiber.

Clearly, dense wavelength-division multiplexing fully benefits from the parallel advantage of light. When the channel intensities are chosen appro-priately, the optical beams do not affect each other, which is just what we want from photons as information carriers. A thousand channels can travel along with each other, all at the same time, just like radio stations across the frequency spectrum of the radio bands.

Wavelength-division multiplexing is expanding rapidly into the long-haul market because of its clear advantages. It uses electro-optic modula-tors and TDM to construct the base channels, which are then encoded at the different wavelengths. In this way, it uses the best features of fast opto-electronics with TDM, then fills fiber bandwidth using WDM. Going to dense WDM is more challenging because of the difficulty of designing net-work architectures that keep track of all the different signals at all the dif-ferent wavelengths. These architectures are advancing and becoming more sophisticated in their ability to switch and route multiple signals at multiple wavelengths.

But in all this discussion of filling fiber bandwidth, a central problem of network bandwidth has been overlooked. This has to do with the band-width bottlenecks of the whole system, remembering that the speed of the network is only as fast as the slowest component. Even if we succeed in us-ing much of the available bandwidth for data transmission through fibers, what happens when the data is attenuated in the fiber to the point that it needs to be regenerated to continue on its way down the next fiber? This is where the all-optical Internet comes in.

THE ALL-OPTICAL INTERNET

Despite all the advances that have improved the purity of silica fibers, and after all the "muxing" and "demuxing" schemes, a laser pulse still cannot go from Philadelphia to New York without losing most of its energy. This means that all that optical information traveling down the fiber at terabit-per-second data speeds needs to come to a crashing halt every 100 kilometers or so to get regenerated by electronics—slow gigabit-per-second electronics—the old bottleneck. There must be a better way.

The dream of the all-optical Internet is simple and sweet. Think of optical signals in the form of data packets on the global network. In the all-optical network, these packets would never leave the optical domain. At a network node, packets would be added and dropped just like cars getting on and off highway ramps that connect seamlessly to other highways. If you have traveled in your car long distance in this country, you know that you can drive from Boston to Washington without ever having to get out of your car (if you have enough gas). The all-optical network would be like this. The data packets would never leave the all-optical highway. No need to regenerate. No need to convert to slow electrons.

This is far from the reality of the optoelectronic networks that we live with at the beginning of the twenty-first century. Signals need to be converted from optics to electronics and back to optics every 100 kilometers. This would be like being on a bus that has to stop at a gas station every 60 miles. Traveling from Boston to Washington would be interminable under these conditions. And it gets even worse. Think of every intersection of every road as a place where you would need to stop, get off the bus, tell a traffic controller where you want to go, and then get on a new bus going in the right direction. How many intersections are there between Boston and Washington? How long would this trip take? This is how the optoelectronic network handles information today. Rather than an open highway system, it is more like a traffic jam. There is no getting around this tedious O/E/O conversion when relying on optoelectronic regenerators and switches. But the all-optical Internet will change all this. All the data packets will stay in the optical domain from start to finish. How can this be accomplished?

Several requirements need to be satisfied by an all-optical Internet. First, no electronic regeneration would be allowed. When the data signal weakens through propagation down the fiber, the signal is boosted "on the fly" by passing through optical regenerators that amplify the signal without the need for electronics. Second, data packets on the major trunk lines will be added from and delivered to connecting networks without the data packets ever leaving the optical domain. This operation requires routers and switches that are all-optical and do not resort to optoelectronics. Third, the data rates of the packets must be irrelevant to the operation of these routers and switches as well as to the optical regenerators. Doubling the TDM data rates or the DWDM channel density should have no effect on the performance of the all-optical components supporting the network. In a colorful adjective adopted by some network service companies, such network devices are said to be "agnostic." The systems do not care what form the data is in or what rate it has; they just amplify it and route it to where it needs to go. These are the major requirements for the dream of the all-optical network.

FIBER LASER AMPLIFIERS

The first step toward the all-optical Internet has already begun with the replacement of some of the old O/E/O repeaters by optical amplifiers. As we saw, the O/E/O repeaters convert photons into electrons, electronic circuits amplify the data, and electronic laser drivers convert the signal back into photons. This old approach to amplification works well for lower data rates, but it presents a bottleneck for the terabit-per-second Internet. In contrast, all-optical amplification is much simpler, and it is free from the bandwidth bottlenecks of optoelectronic conversion. On the face of it, optical amplification is extremely simple. A laser, after all, is simply an optical amplifier. If a laser receives a small signal of photons, these stimulate the emission of additional photons that add to the signal. By traversing the laser medium only once, dramatic amplification of the signal is possible without ever needing to invoke electronics.

The obvious advantages of optical amplification for fiber-optic telecommunications were recognized early by fiber researchers, but the advantages had to be translated into practice. For many years, researchers sought the best laser gain medium. Some of the early favorites were semiconductor laser amplifiers. Because semiconductor lasers were already used to transmit data and to regenerate signals in optoelectronic repeaters, it made sense to use them to amplify the weakened signals by simply passing the signals through the semiconductor amplifiers without converting to electronics. This approach was tried, but it faced many practical difficulties, the principal one being that laser amplifiers lased on their own rather than passively waiting to amplify existing data.

The problem was the mismatch in the optical properties between the fiber carrying the data pulses and the semiconductor. The mismatch made it difficult to integrate these two material systems together. A better solution would be to have a length of fiber act as a laser gain medium. This would allow the amplifier and transmission fiber to be joined seamlessly. The task, therefore, would be to find a glass fiber that could act as a laser.

Glass lasers had been known for some time. Invented in 1961 by Elias Snitzer, working at the American Optical Corporation, it used glass that was doped with atoms of the rare earth called neodymium. Rare earth atoms called Lanthenides (because the row starts at the element lanthanum) occupy a special place in the periodic table of the elements. They are in the row that is physically separated from the rest of the chart. This physical separation of the rare earth elements from the rest of the periodic table mirrors the physical role they play when they are inserted into materials, especially insulating materials.

The periodic table is a striking visual representation of quantum mechanics. First, it represents nuclear physics in general as the nuclei of the atoms acquire one additional proton, stepping through the table, starting at the top row with hydrogen. Second, it reflects the quantum mechanical properties of each electron added to match each proton in order to keep the atom electrically neutral. These electrons go into quantum states called electron shells. There are only four types of shells, and each holds only a specific number of electrons. They are the s-shells (2 electrons), p-shells (6 electrons), d-shells (10 electrons), and f-shells (14 electrons). The arrangement of the periodic table is a simple reflection of the sequential filling of these different types of shells. As the table steps across the Lanthenides, the electrons fill the first f-shell.

The f-shell is special in atomic physics because the electrons are packed tightly into it. Normally, when an atom is placed in a material, its electrons form chemical bonds with the surrounding atoms. This is true for oxygen and hydrogen in glass. In fact, it is this strong bonding of oxygen and hydrogen in the silicon dioxide which causes the trouble with hydroxide impurity absorption in the silica fibers that limits data transmission only to specific transparency windows. But with the rare earth atoms, the electrons in the f-shell are isolated from the chemical bonds of the surrounding atoms. These f-shell electrons therefore are free to maintain their regular atomic energy levels, mostly independent of the material in which they are incorporated. This practical isolation of the f-shell electrons of the rare earth elements is a boon for laser physics because a rare earth element like neodymium always emits nearly the same optical frequencies independent of the matrix in which it sits. In addition, because there are so many different ways electrons can fill up the fourteen f-shell states, there are many atomic transitions associated with a single rare earth atom. Each transition involves photons of different colors, giving considerable flexibility in the choice of photon wavelengths.

The success of getting neodymium-doped glass to perform as a laser raised hopes that rare earth elements inside silica fibers likewise could act as amplifiers. Neodymium was not appropriate for this application because there were no atomic transitions (electrons dropping from excited states to ground states and emitting photons in the process) to produce photons with wavelengths around the important values of 1.3 or 1.55 microns. However, another rare earth element called erbium had transitions very close to 1.55 microns. In 1987, researchers at the University of Southampton in England produced the first fiber amplifier that used erbium atoms in silica. This was just what was needed for all-optical amplification in fibers. Because the fiber amplifiers have virtually the same optical properties as ordinary fiber, this removed the problems with spontaneous lasing that had plagued semiconductor amplifiers. Furthermore, the fiber amplifiers are fundamentally compatible with the transmission fibers themselves. The transmission fibers are spliced seamlessly onto the amplifiers in a perfect match. The technology of erbium-doped fiber amplifiers matured so quickly that the twelfth transatlantic cable, installed in 1995, uses them in place of the old optoelectronic regenerators. Fiber amplifiers are spaced every 40 kilometers to boost the signal. Terrestrial long-haul systems now also incorporate the erbium-doped amplifiers as standard components.

Erbium in silica glass has another physical property that is particularly important for fiber-optic telecommunications: it has bandwidth! An isolated atom of erbium has specific atomic transitions that are very narrow, i.e., that have very little bandwidth. But even though the transition energy does not change much when the atoms are incorporated in another material, an important change in the optical transition does take place. The sharp atomic transition turns into a broadened emission bandwidth because the rare earth atom, despite the relative isolation of its f-shell electrons, does interact by a small amount with the surrounding atoms. For erbium atoms in silica glass, the atomic bandwidth spreads out to around 3-terahertz centered at 1.55 microns, which is in the middle of the best transparency window of the silica fiber.

This 3-terahertz bandwidth has a direct impact on the data rate that can be amplified by the erbium amplifier. In the best case, when channels are separated by only their bandwidth, the 3-terahertz bandwidth of the fiber amplifiers could ultimately support a data rate of 3 terabits per second. While this is still below the full 30-terabit-per-second potential of fiber optics, it is clearly sufficient to support the data rates that should get us through the next decade. More important, the erbium fiber amplifiers are all-optical. The optical data signals never leave the optical domain, thereby removing the optoelectronic bottleneck—at least in terms of reamplification. The amplifiers are also agnostic to the data format, which is a particularly important feature of the all-optical Internet. Because the amplifiers are passive, they simply amplify whatever signals are passing through them. If Internet engineers change the wavelengths of the channels (within the 3-terahertz bandwidth), or if the fiber line is upgraded from channels running at 10 gigabits per second to 40 gigabits per second, the optical signals are simply amplified. Here, in a single technology, we satisfy two of the three requirements for the all-optical Internet: no optoelectronic conversion, and data format agnosticism, at least as far as data amplification is concerned.

But you can't expect to solve all problems in a single stroke. There is still the problem of dispersion that broadens the pulses as they propagate down the fibers. Even with the best engineering, the data pulses still spread out over time and start to overlap with one another if the data rates are too high.

And optoelectronic regeneration performs more than simple amplification. It practices the 3R regeneration discussed earlier: reshaping, retiming, and reamplifying. By replacing the optoelectronic regenerators with the erbium-doped fiber amplifiers, only the last of these is performed. The data pulses still spread, and the timing slowly drifts with distance. These two effects limit the data rate that can be supported even with these all-optical systems.

The twelfth transatlantic telephone cable (the first commercial system to use fiber amplifiers) runs at a data rate of only 5 gigabits per second. Current terrestrial optical systems are running at 10 gigabits per second and still use optoelectronic 3R regeneration. The use of fiber amplifiers reduces system cost because the numerous fiber amplifier stages, distributed at 40-kilometer intervals, are significantly less expensive than the regeneration stations. Although fiber amplification has pushed the distance between the optoelectronic 3R stations from 140 kilometers out beyond 400 kilometers, and thus far fewer of the optoelectronic stations are needed in a long-haul system, the optoelectronic timing and reshaping remain serious bottlenecks that prevent the use of the full fiber bandwidth. Solutions to this problem must draw from non-linear optical effects discussed in the next chapter. But first, let's pause to consider how much information we really "need" to run our lives. We may wonder if we each personally need a gigabit per second. Surprisingly, we do—mostly because of our hungry eyes.

HOW MUCH INFORMATION DO WE NEED?

If we consider that we talk and think at a rate of about 25 bits per second, then in eight non-stop hours we process 1 million bits of information: a data rate of about 1 megabit per day. This is certainly an underestimate of the information that we are bombarded with daily, considering that it is now possible to connect your computer to an ethernet cable that delivers 1 billion bits in a single second (gigabit ethernet). Why do we need a billion bits in a second if we have trouble assimilating a million bits in a day?

First consider music. Digital music is stored as binary data that represents the amplitude of sound as a function of time. Music is sampled at a rate of 44.1 kHz, which requires a sample to be taken every 11.3 microseconds. This sampling rate produces a music bandwidth of 20 kHz, which is the limit of the human ear. The sampled sound amplitude varies over several orders of magnitude and is digitized into discrete values that take on any of 65,536 values from minimum to maximum, corresponding to 16 bits ($2^{16} = 65,536$) of digitized amplitude per sample. Sixteen bits of information every 11.3 microseconds equals a data rate of about 1.41 megabits per second, which is a long way away from 1 gigabit per second.

But even this much audio data rate would almost never be transmitted in practice over the Internet. This data rate is a linear one-to-one digitization of the acoustic amplitude. However, music has considerable redundancy, and we know that redundancy can be exploited to reduce the number of bits needed to transmit meaning. For instance, redundancy might arise through extended times of quiet that do not need full 16 bits of amplitude, or low-frequency bass that does not need to be sampled at 11.3-microsecond intervals. By taking advantage of this redundancy, the data stream can be reduced using efficient compression codes. Also, in the digital world there is little noise (bit error rates are typically smaller than 1 bit error per billion bits sent), so redundancy is not needed for accurate information transmission.

The popular audio data file format known as MP3 is a good example of how much can be achieved with good data compression. The acronym MP3 stands for MPEG Level III, where MPEG stands for Motion Pictures Expert Group. The MPEG standard was developed by the entertainment industry for efficiently recording multimedia formats onto optical compact discs (CD) and CD-ROM (read-only memory). Level III of the MPEG standard uses compression algorithms to take advantage of the redundancy in music to significantly reduce the amount of data needed to store music in digital formats. For instance, Level III uses sophisticated psycho-acoustic models (models that explain how we construct sound inside our minds based on what we receive from our ears) to sample the music in multiple subfrequency bands and with adaptive segment lengths. Music can be compressed from 1.41 megabits per second down to as low as 64 kilobits per second for stereo and 32 kilobits per second for mono. These are compression factors of 20 and 40, respectively, although digital music designers claim that at least 256 kilobits per second is required to make the music indistinguishable from the directly sampled music.

Next, consider video. A standard digitized image from a digital video camera typically consists of 320 by 240 pixels, or a total of about 77,000 pixels. The intensity incident on each pixel is digitized into 8 bits for the three colors red, green, and blue (RGB). The frame rate for video is 30 frames per second. This produces a combined data rate of about 55 megabits per second, with no interleaving of one frame to the next. When including interleaving, high-quality digital video transmission requires up to 165 megabit-per-second data rates. While this data rate may approach within a factor of 6 of the gigabit per second that we are trying to fill, the MPEG optical CD standard reduces this, using redundancy in images. For instance, redundancy might be expanses of solid color in which only the edges need to be defined, or many features in a scene may not change from one frame to the next. In video, compression by a factor of 50 is common. Compression therefore reduces the estimated data rate to only a few megabits per second.

Watching movies on the Web is not a highly sophisticated use of the Web resource, but it is one that many consumers would like to have. If we could get about 6 megabits per second into our homes, then we could watch any movie ever made, any time we wanted. This service is called Movie-on-Demand.

FLASH-FORWARD

Let's look at the demographics of Movie-on-Demand for a small town with a population of about 40,000 people. On any given night, maybe 4,000 households would be receiving a movie. The data rate that is needed to support this demand is 400 gigabits per second, which is nearly half of a terabit per second. Over a two-hour period, this constitutes a total data of nearly 3,000 terabits, or 3 petabits. This data would either need to be stored locally by the service provider, or else ported in from some regional storage location to reduce the need for many local storage facilities. If it is ported from a regional storage location, then the trunk line from the storage facility to the town would need to handle a terabit per second. This high data rate would then be broken down into lower data rates that eventually lead into the individual homes on the gigabit ethernet fibers running at 1 gigabit per second, but needing only 6 megabits per second for a movie. What do we do with the remaining 994 megabits per second of data rate?

Consider a typical family of four. Mother and Father are working parents with a son and a daughter. After dinner in the evening, Mother is in her den working on-line. She is downloading every encyclopedia article on hurricanes. At the same time she has the movie *All About Eve* (compressed) playing on the high-definition television (HDTV) screen. She is using a net data rate of 25 megabits per second. Father is in the workroom, building a wood cabinet for the new Internet appliance he bought. He is watching a woodshop program that had aired several days previously, but which he has ordered from the Internet service provider at the standard 6 megabits per second. Meanwhile, the daughter is teleconferencing with several friends. They are working on a project for art class. Each of them has a video camera and electronic sketchpads, which everyone can see all at the same time. She is also running music videos on a separate monitor, though she doesn't have much time to watch since the teleconference has become highly animated. Her net usage is 50 megabits per second. Finally, the Son is running a flight simulator to get certified for a pilot's license. The technical training is through distance learning from a state university with a good aeronautics program. His performance on the flight simulator, which is transmitted as moderately compressed HDTV, is being monitored in real time by a computer at the university. His net usage is by far the highest at 400 megabits per second because of the high-resolution graphics he needs for the virtual reality simulation (nearly all of that bandwidth needed to feed the eyes).

In total, our (perhaps not so typical) family is using a little under 500 megabits per second of data in their home. This usage is not an unreasonable scenario, because what we have learned about the Internet is that bandwidth always gets used. It is like buying a new computer and deciding on the size of the hard drive. Almost everyone has underbought disc space at least once. In that case, the hard drive fills far faster than the buyer could originally have imagined. Bandwidth on the Internet is the same way. All past estimates of future net usage have always underestimated the actual usage. Both users and providers continually find ways of burning through bandwidth. There is a famous "law" that states that "work expands to fill the time allotted." On the Internet, the equivalent principle is that all services expand to fill the bandwidth provided.

In our example of the family, an important service was left out that could easily burn through the full gigabits per second provided by the fiber to the home. This service is that of intelligent agents. An intelligent agent is a software program that works on behalf of its user. Its job is to actively scan the Web for items of interest to the user. It does this by matching the attributes of information found on the Web with previous preferences and behavior of the user. The agent uses artificial neural networks to perform the matches. The agent runs non-stop twenty-four hours a day, surfing the Web, going from link to link and assessing the interest level of what it finds. It compares and contrasts similar Web pages and sifts through the chaff to find the kernels of insight. The agent, being software, can receive and assess Web pages as fast as the Web can provide them. The computer within which the agent resides is itself a machine with a multi-gigahertz processor, fully matched with the speed of the gigabit ethernet. The personal agent can therefore burn through a full gigabit per second, non-stop, twenty-four hours a day.

That burn rate will drive the need for more bandwidth. The biggest consumer of the bandwidth will be a multiplicity of intelligent agents, each configured for different tasks. This is perhaps the most significant need right now on the Internet—the intelligent management of information. The Internet has become so immense, carrying virtually all the information anyone may want to access, that information has actually become almost inaccessible. It is a problem of dilution. With so much information, what is relevant is lost, like the proverbial needle in a haystack. The smarter search engines that are available on-line today are at the level of amoebas compared to the intelligent personal agents that will work for us tomorrow. When these personal agents mature, the nature of the Web will change. The true revolution of "information on-demand" will not start until then. When it does, the agent's demand for bandwidth will provide the real economic incentive to drive fiber to the home and into the box.

The "box" itself will by that time be radically altered. Today, we watch televisions, listen to CD players, or surf the Web on personal computers. These separate units will all be replaced by Internet appliances—as they already have been to some degree. Listening to music, watching movies, and surfing the Web will all be part of the Internet. The distinction between computers and television will disappear, merging into boxes that take bandwidth from the net and turn it into entertainment and information. The optical network will connect seamlessly to the Internet appliance box, porting optical information inside. What will be inside that box?

COPPER RULES

It is hard to compete with copper inside the box when the goal is to send as much information as possible from one point to another while at the same time taking up as little space as possible. Copper has the lowest resistance to electrical current of any of the practical metals. This means that you can send electrical information far and fast—which is why copper electrical lines are the conduits of information on circuit boards inside computers today. Even on the silicon chips attached to the circuit boards, copper has recently replaced aluminum as the material comprising the fine tenth-micron traces that carry current from one transistor to another. Copper rules virtually uncontested inside all computers.

What, then, is the future role of optics inside the box? In existing computer architectures, optics cannot compete. Copper already transmits signals at the speed of light—and nothing, not even optics, goes faster than that. It is not that the electrons in the copper wires are traveling at the speed of light. Signals are not sent by sending electrons physically from one side of the wire to the other. Instead, it is the force on the electrons that transmits the information. The force is from electric fields, and these fields travel at the speed of light.

To understand this, think of water in a pipe. If you suddenly push on the water at one end of the pipe, the water at the other end of the pipe is ejected. You do not need the actual water molecules that you push on to get to the other end. The pressure that you apply on one end travels to the other end and ejects the water there. How fast does this pressure "information" travel? In this example, it travels at the speed of sound in water (1480 m/s). For electrical signals on copper wires, the relevant speed is the speed of electromagnetic waves—and they travel at the speed of light. Therefore, the claim that photons are faster than electrons for transmitting information just does not hold water, and replacing wires with fibers will not gain much.

Another reason why optics cannot compete with copper in current architectures is the wavelength problem. As noted in chapter 2, the mass of the electron makes its quantum mechanical wavelength very small. The typical "size" of an electron wavelength can be a billionth of a meter compared to the millionth of a meter for a wavelength of light. Light wavelengths are therefore a thousand times larger than typical electron wavelengths. This wavelength mismatch enters directly into the issue of electronics versus optics. The wires carrying the electrons can be very small. In current technology, these wires are about one tenth of a micron, which is ten times smaller than the wavelength of light.

Finally, there is the recurring problem that light is never good as an agent of control. For the same reason that we seek the use of optics to allow light beams to pass through or along each other without affecting one another, optics is typically not in a position to control information. It supports the flow of information, but does not decide what information to send. That decision is always left up to the strongly interacting electrons in electronic devices.

LIGHT INSIDE THE BOX

Has optics nothing to offer for computers? On the contrary, there *is* light at the end of the tunnel, because copper does not win on all fronts. For instance, the reason for smaller electronic device sizes is to increase speed. But increased speed of electronic transmission starts to make the copper wires act like antennas—antennas that transmit and receive. At high speeds, all those individual copper wires that were supposed to direct information point to point start to broadcast their signals everywhere. This effect is called electromagnetic interference, and it gets worse as the electronic speeds and densities get higher.

When electronics approach 100 gigahertz (Moore's Law currently predicts this will occur around the year 2012), this interference will be so severe that isolated communications channels will be impossible on the chip. All data transmission will be broadcast as electromagnetic interference. Although it may be possible to design new chip architectures that dispense with point-to-point data transmission and use exclusively wide-area broadcasting, such a revolutionary change is not likely to occur. A more evolutionary approach is to remove the effects of electromagnetic interference, so that higher speeds can still be achieved without the need to sacrifice point-to-point data transmission.

Optical data buses inside the box are the clearest way to solve the broadcasting problem. If optical waveguides are used, the optical beams remain confined to the path of the waveguide routed from point to point. When the communication is between boards inside the computer, the relatively large size of the optical waveguides (on the order of microns) presents no serious problem because board-to-board distances of many centimeters are much larger than the size of the data bus. But if the waveguide is to be placed on a single semiconductor chip, the micron sizes needed for light confinement are much larger than the copper connections, and the optical waveguides would take up an unacceptably large fraction of the chip surface that is better used to pack in more transistors. Therefore, the size of an optical waveguide relative to the size of a copper data bus represents a fundamental limit to the use of optics inside conventional electronic computers. Optics can make inroads into the box only so far as the distances involved are much larger than a wavelength of light. This fundamentally restricts optics to "long-distance" data transmission over high-speed data buses and trunk lines that broadly distribute information on the computer boards.

On the other hand, point-to-point transmission will not be the only use for optics inside the box. The first application for optics in conventional computers is as a means to distribute the central clock pulses to synchronize the operation of all the individual chips. This application will actually be achieved through the use of free-space optics, without even requiring confinement inside waveguides, because the information received by all the chips is the same—the clock pulses. When the information is the same everywhere, broadcasting is the best way to send the information around. It may seem like a contradiction to use optics for broadcasting when the original problem of electromagnetic interference from electronic buses was specifically broadcasting. But in this application, optics is more reliable. Furthermore, in free-space optical interconnections there can still be considerable use of point-to-point transmission. After all, tightly directed laser beams are an excellent means of transmitting information.

Board-to-board free-space transmission will follow the clock distribution application in a natural evolution as purely electronic computers become hybrids of optics and electronics, using each for their best advantage. It may take some time for optical waveguides to migrate onto single boards, primarily because of the need for new technologies and architectures. Yet the evolution in this direction is inevitable. Even more challenging, and farther out in time, is the migration of optical waveguides onto single chips, because this will become economically feasible only when electronics approach the 100-gigahertz speed range and electromagnetic interference problems of electrical interconnects would otherwise shut down the chip. But the need for speed will eventually push even this limit.

So, hybrid optoelectronic computers certainly lie in our future. They are a natural extension of the optical Internet. Fibers will bring optics into the box, where information will stay in the optical domain in optical buses that distribute the information around the boards and to the individual chips. Only then, when the information needs to be used, will it finally be converted into the electronic domain for processing. In the distant future, long after gigabit ethernet has given way to terabit ethernet, the composite data rate entering the box at lightning optical speeds will be multiplexed down to speeds sufficient for optoelectronic conversion and for real-time electronic processing.

However, light remains dumb in these hybrid optoelectronic computers of the future where optics works solely as the messenger of electronics. Although assigned to a time much later in this new century, these machines of light remain solidly in the first generation described in chapter 2. But light can drive intelligence too, if we engineer it. What is needed is the ability of light to perform control—in particular, the control of light by light. When this is accomplished, the intelligence of light will sweep away the hybrid machines that bind light in service to electronics. These second-generation machines of light will appear first as intelligence in the all-optical Internet. But just as optics inexorably evolved and invaded the heretofore inviolate realm of electronic computing, so too will optical control enter into our homes as intelligent agents working on our behalf. The next chapter explores how this will happen.

7 The All-Optical Generation

The Control of Light by Light

... A KNOWLEDGE OF MATERIAL PROPERTIES WILL LEAD TO THE DESIGN OF MANY NONLINEAR [OPTICAL] DEVICES THAT WILL PERFORM FUNCTIONS IN THE VISIBLE SPECTRUM THAT CIRCUIT ELEMENTS PERFORM AT LOWER FREQUENCIES.

Nicolaas Bloembergen, 1964

The machines of light of the second generation move into a new realm, where light becomes the active agent of control. Everything we think we understand about the architecture of intelligence changes. The discrete transistors and logic gates of electronics disappear; in their place appear exotic optical devices of unfamiliar shapes and surprising behavior. The replacement is not one-to-one, and even functions have changed. Nothing precisely resembling the function of a transistor or a logic gate can be found. Instead, new components, like coupled fibers and arrays of mirrors or finely scribed gratings, become the elementary units that make up the new machines.

The purpose of the machines is different as well. No longer are manipulations of bits by logic units and math co-processors the principal function of these machines of light. Instead, demultiplexing composite signals into their component channels and routing information to the right locations is the main goal. The intelligence required to thread information through optimal paths across the Web challenges the processing power of conventional computers.

Indeed, with the vast quantity of information on the Internet, intelligent management is critical, otherwise a tangled mess results. Information must be routed and protected, with fast recovery when a channel goes down. Information must also be filtered, to extract the gems of wisdom from the

Web out of the tons of detritus generated daily. All these operations require intelligence. What form will it take? Since the information is already in the optical domain, it makes sense to keep it there. Let light be both master and servant of information on the Net—both controller and messenger.

Because the Net is distributed, that is, it is spread over wide areas rather than localized like the processor of a computer, optical intelligence will naturally also be distributed with local dense clusters connected by a few long communication links—analogous to a neural network. The Net therefore becomes intelligent, global in extent, with hundreds of millions of nodes, calculating and routing and reconfiguring; all optically implementing the intelligence of light.

LIGHT IN CHARGE

For all the desire to have light *take* charge, light *has* no charge. This is what prevents photons from interacting with each other in a vacuum. Photons also have no mass with which to exclude other photons from occupying the same space. As we have seen, these are the properties that make photons excellent messengers, but poor controllers. To execute control, photons need to interact. They need to get in each other's way. While this is impossible in free space, photons inside matter can enlist electrons as intermediaries. Light can interact with light through the interceding polarizable medium, as long as that medium is non-linear. So, what does it mean for a medium to be "non-linear"?

Physicists like to simplify things by thinking in terms of "ideal" entities, so they define an "ideal" linear spring as one that stretches in linear proportion to the force applied. This means that if you double the force on the spring, it stretches twice as much—simple. When we discuss dispersion and atomic polarization, the amount that the atom's electron shell stretches in an electric field is linearly proportional to the electric force acting on the electron. This is the regime of linear optics. However, any real spring, like a rubber band, gets stiffer if you pull too hard so that it no longer stretches in linear proportion to the applied force. The polarization of electrons by the electric field of a light wave in matter is no different. As the electric field pulls harder, the polarization of the atoms no longer changes linearly with the electric force. This is called non-linear polarization.

Consider a non-linear medium as a high-intensity light beam travels through it. The electric field of the light pulls on the electrons, inducing non-linear polarization. A second light beam traveling through this medium senses the non-linear polarization and propagates at a different velocity. The law against photon interaction is lifted inside matter by letting two photons interact with each other through the mediation of non-linearly polarized electrons. An important process for all-optical control is known as the optical Kerr effect, in which the refractive index of the non-linear material is a simple function of light intensity. Thus, one light beam under certain conditions can alter the velocity of a second light beam, delaying it or advancing it.

This change in propagation time can be extremely useful in optical interferometers (that use sensitive phase differences between two light beams to produce constructive or destructive interference) to control the light intensity at the output of the device. Optical interferometers are exquisitely sensitive to minute changes in the time it takes a pulse to traverse the device. When an interferometer contains a non-linear material, the output intensity depends on the travel time of one beam influenced by another, constituting optical control of light by light.

Clearly, non-linear optics makes it possible for light to control light. But the catch is that it usually takes large electric fields to make the medium vary sufficiently to affect another light beam. Strong electric fields in a light beam produce high intensity and therefore require high energy. Obtaining useful changes in the optical properties of a non-linear crystal can typically require concentrating a kilowatt of energy from a laser into a single square centimeter. This energy density is sufficient to melt the plastic chassis of your personal computer. Can you imagine trying to build an optical computer using laser intensities at this level? Fortunately, there are practical solutions that get around this problem of meltdown.

One way to circumvent the need for high energies is to compress the energy of the laser light into a pulse of very short duration. In the last chapter, we saw that a non-linear laser medium generates pulses with durations of only picoseconds, or even several femtoseconds. In these ultra-short light pulses, the energy stays the same, but the *intensity*, the energy per time, gets extremely large because the duration gets extremely small. For instance, a laser pulse with a duration of 1 picosecond (able to support a terabit-per-second data rate), with an energy of only a microjoule (a very small amount of energy), would have the peak power of a megawatt. Therefore, small energies in sufficiently short pulses can produce strong non-linearities and hence the prospect of control.

A second way to establish strong non-linear interaction between light beams without using much energy is to force the light beams to interact with each other over long distances. The influence of one light beam over the propagation of a second light beam can accumulate as they travel side by side over many kilometers (as in an optical fiber), accumulating small effects into large ones. This makes non-linear optics in fibers particularly attractive, because long interaction distances are relatively easy to come by.

The ability to focus weak beams to achieve high intensities again favors non-linear optics in fibers because light, in order to be launched into the optical fiber, must always be focused down to the size of the cores of the fibers, which are only several microns in diameter. Fibers therefore have the dual advantages of long interaction distances and high intensities, making them prime candidates for the implementation of optical intelligence.

It may seem a contradiction that optical fibers are excellent media in which to have light controlling light through optical non-linearities. The previous chapter extolled the virtues of fiber *linearity,* which allows multiple signals, as in TDM and WDM, to travel down the same fiber without affecting each other. This apparent paradox is resolved by considering the dividing line between linear optics and non-linear optics. The essence of the non-linearities is that they depend on intensity as well as on the frequency and coherence of the light. If intensities are small, then non-linearities do not hamper the signal propagation. Furthermore, if the separate signals share no coherence, that is, if the phase relationship between them is random, they likewise can travel together with no adverse effects. Therefore, although all materials are non-linear in a general sense, they are all approximately linear at low intensities. On the other hand, if high intensities are used, and if individual signals share coherence, then indeed one propagating signal will affect another. This type of interaction forms the basis of the control of light by light inside fibers.

It is even possible for a single signal pulse to interact with itself through the optical non-linearities of the fiber. Such self-interaction in fibers turns out to be an excellent way automatically to defeat the degrading effects of dispersion in fibers by creating a special type of laser pulse that maintains a perfect shape without broadening as it travels. That type of pulse, surprisingly, is like a canal wave.

CANAL WAVES IN THE FIBER

A weak pulse of light in any material broadens (the duration gets longer) as it propagates. Even in an optical fiber, when a light pulse has a central wavelength at the zero dispersion point, the pulse still broadens because of the finite bandwidth of the pulse. Wavelengths that are a little shorter or longer than the zero dispersion wavelength travel at slightly different velocities. This is a natural consequence of the inertia of electrons, which causes different frequencies to travel with different velocities (linear dispersion). Furthermore, dispersive behavior is not restricted to light waves in matter; it happens with any wave propagating in almost any physical medium (except for light in vacuum).

This universality was probably not known to J. Scott Russell as he rode his horse along a narrow barge channel in Scotland in 1838. However, as an astute observer and an amateur scientist, he recognized an unexpected and novel phenomenon when he saw a large canal boat stop suddenly in the channel, producing a single large wave that had a smooth and rounded swell that moved forward along the channel. Russell kept pace with the wave on horseback, noting that it kept its shape perfectly as it traveled. Intrigued by this behavior, he pursued the wave for more than a kilometer before he was prevented from going further. In all that distance, this solitary wave never deviated in its form, without change in shape or height. Russell was so impressed by this event that he published his observations in the *Reports of the Meetings of the British Association for the Advancement of Science* in 1844. The importance of the discovery was clear—he had found a wave phenomenon in which a wave experienced no dispersion and hence no broadening as it propagated. Nearly half a century passed before a mathematical theory was able to explain the existence of such a solitary wave in shallow water.

The non-linear wave equations that appropriately described the phenomenon required the velocity of the wave to depend on how large the wave is. Water turns out to be a strongly non-linear medium. In open water higher waves travel faster than lower waves. This causes the center of a wave to travel faster than the surrounding tails of the pulse, broadening the wave as it travels. We saw earlier that dispersion also broadens waves. In a canal, for instance, the confinement of the water wave to the channel produces a type of dispersion that allows shorter wavelengths to travel faster than longer wavelengths. Therefore, in a water wave containing a bandwidth of frequencies, the higher frequencies travel faster and arrive earlier than the lower frequencies. This produces something known as a "chirp," so-called because in the case of a sound wave a chirped pulse sounds like the chirp of a bird.

The remarkable feature of a medium that has both dispersion and non-linearity is that these two broadening mechanisms can cancel out. In other words, the non-linearity can balance the natural dispersion of the medium. If the balance is perfect, then the non-linearity exactly cancels all the effects of dispersion, and the pulse travels with no broadening—hence Russell's solitary wave.

Solitary waves are therefore somewhat common, with the important property that they propagate without broadening. There is also a subset of solitary waves with the added benefit that they can pass through each other without affecting each other's pulse shape. These collision-impervious solitary waves are called solitons.

In 1973, only three years after the first demonstration of low-attenuation glass fibers, Akira Hasegawa of Bell Laboratories realized that optical fibers produce the same type of dispersion for light (at wavelengths longer than 1.3 microns) as canals do for water, and that glass fibers have the right type of non-linearity to balance this dispersion. He therefore predicted that optical solitons should be possible in these fibers. Seven years later, Linn F. Mollenauer, also at Bell Laboratories, demonstrated that such optical solitons could indeed be formed in single-mode silica fiber and were free to propagate without broadening.

The potential value of optical solitons to data communication through fibers arises for several reasons. First, there is no strictly prohibitive distance-dependent data rate for soliton propagation as there is for conventional light pulses. Second, the solitons' ability to pass through each other without disturbance makes them good candidates for wavelength-division multiplexing. Finally, even when their central wavelength is well away from the zero dispersion wavelength of the optical fiber, they form and propagate without broadening. This is particularly important for broadband telecommunications where all wavelengths need to be used, not just those that are at the zero dispersion point of the fiber.

On any given fiber, there is only one wavelength for which a conventional light pulse experiences no dispersion. In common single-mode fiber, this wavelength is near 1.3 microns, although we saw that clever engineering can shift the zero dispersion wavelength to be near 1.55 microns (the wavelength of minimum attenuation in silica fiber). But to prevent broadening, conventional pulses would need to have wavelengths in a relatively narrow bandwidth around this zero dispersion wavelength, wasting much of the optical bandwidth of the fiber. Solitons, on the other hand, can form and propagate across broad bandwidths.

Solitons sound too good to be true—and there is a catch. To continue propagating without broadening, a soliton must maintain its amplitude. After all, it is the amplitude of the wave which drives the non-linear balance that keeps conventional dispersion in check. But fibers can transmit light only about 100 kilometers before most of the energy is gone. A soliton that experiences such attenuation will not maintain its pulse width, and the intensity of the pulse will eventually drop below the minimum needed to sustain the soliton. Optical solitons in fibers therefore have this Achilles heel: they can propagate forever without broadening as long as they can keep their energy constant. In ordinary fibers with even the lowest attenuation, data transmission using solitons is not feasible.

This is where the erbium-doped fiber amplifiers discussed earlier play an essential role, because they provide the kind of energy recharge that a soliton needs to keep its shape. Furthermore, the fiber amplifiers can be placed much closer together than 100 kilometers, providing a form of distributed amplification for the soliton. The long-haul terrestrial and transoceanic transmission systems that currently use erbium-doped fiber amplifiers are thus good candidates for soliton transmission.

In addition, other amplification methods can be used to supply the appropriate distributed amplification needed to sustain solitons, such as a process known as Raman gain. This uses one laser beam as a pump wave that propagates down the fiber supplying energy to the signal beams. The advantage of the Raman approach is that it can support wider bandwidths than the limited 3-terahertz bandwidth of the erbium-doped fibers. Raman gain may therefore be a better candidate for broadband soliton transmission.

Transmission over 1 million kilometers has been achieved in laboratory demonstrations using solitons and TDM to support a data rate over 1 terabit per second. If past trends continue, such "hero" experiments may become routine and move into the marketplace in three to five years. The soliton transmission systems would provide a bandwidth of a terabit per second that is immune to pulse broadening over wide ranges of wavelengths, thus enabling the use of WDM. Solitons also solve two of the three 3R regeneration processes, taking care of regeneration (by the distributed amplifiers) and making reshaping unnecessary.

Solitons are an example of the potential usefulness of non-linear optics in the second generation of optical devices, although light is still a passive messenger and not an example of the control of light by light. In some sense, a soliton may be viewed as a light pulse that controls itself by maintaining a constant pulse width. Nonetheless, the full potential of non-linear optics still rests with interactions among separate light beams, allowing light directly to control the flow of information traveling on other light beams. Such all-optical machines of light are the holy grail of the all-optical network.

THE HOLY GRAIL

Keep information in the optical domain! That is the imperative. But how to do so when so much needs to be done to keep networks working? Network switches and routers are not so much relay devices as they are computers. The sophistication of network switches has grown rapidly, drawing from the rapid advances in silicon computers. Maintaining the Internet requires considerable computational power and intelligence. Communication lines need to be practically fault-free. Users of the telephone, for instance, expect perfect performance. How many times have the lights gone off in your home, but your telephone still worked? How many times has your personal computer crashed, but your telephone line stays live? We put up with faults in our electric power and computers, our air conditioners and refrigerators. But we expect the phone always to be there. Accomplishing this feat of reliability takes Herculean computational effort on the part of the phone companies.

The key phrase for the net service companies is "performance monitoring." The protocols of the network, such as the synchronous optical network (SONET), require electrical monitoring of system performance. Typically, there are more electrical wires in a fiber cable than there are optical fibers. The fibers are used for the high optical data rates, but the wires are used constantly to send electronic information back and forth among the switching stations to tell how the net is performing. Though these monitoring signals can be relatively slow and low-bandwidth, the existing networks rely heavily on this electronic surveillance.

Surveillance by itself is useless unless action can be taken based on the information. This is where intelligence comes in. To provide customers with fault-free communication, immediate action is needed if a line goes down. And lines do go down. All it takes is one errant backhoe operator to kill a trunk line carrying terabits per second to a major metropolitan area. All the information going down that line ceases immediately. Is the information lost? In many cases, no. The network has such redundancy, such multiplicity of nodes and links—one manifestation of the Architecture of Light— that information can be cloned or retrieved or rerouted in an instant. If you were carrying on a phone conversation over that trunk line, you would never know the line went down. Restoration is so fast that it lies beyond your ability to perceive because we talk and listen at only about 25 bits per second, and certainly not at gigabits per second or terabits per second.

But what happens to a high-speed bank transaction when that trunk line goes down? Is the restoration fast enough to protect *it*? As the bit rates increase, the answer is increasingly becoming no, because electronic intelligence is approaching the limit of its ability to protect the information. Furthermore, the multiplicity of wavelength channels puts a severe load on the electronic circuits.

And finally, all this performance monitoring and switching and routing faces the old conversion bottleneck of converting light into the electronic domain and back again. Soon, this approach will no longer be sufficient. When the Internet goes all-optical, the intelligence to monitor and maintain the Net will need to be all-optical as well, with optical control and optical logic. Just as erbium fiber amplifiers replaced O/E/O repeaters in the fiber links, all-optical logic will replace silicon in network intelligence. What form will all-optical logic take? What will the machines of light of this second generation look like?

The definitive technological solution for all-optical intelligence has not been chosen yet, much as in the early days of semiconductor logic. The first transistor in 1947 was made out of germanium, and germanium remained a favorite material of electronics engineers up to the 1960s. But there is no Germanium Valley in the south San Francisco Bay area. There was a shakeout of technology in the early 1960s among many competing possibilities, and silicon technology won. Now Silicon Valley is firmly entrenched, and almost nothing can displace it. Even semiconductors that are supposedly "better" than silicon have no chance because the technological investment in silicon is too great. The technology is set in stone.

Not so for the all-optical Internet. For the moment, any technology can still win, and the possibilities are almost limitless. This is what is driving the recent spate of light wave technology start-ups and the numerous acquisitions of these companies by optical networking companies. With the rise of e-commerce on the World Wide Web, trillions of dollars are at stake—and no one knows which optical technology will dominate the future structure of the Internet.

Although the winning technology of the machines of the second generation has not been selected, the functions that this all-optical intelligence must perform are clear. We saw in the last chapter that all-optical networks require three principal capabilities in order to eliminate every optoelectronic conversion from source to destination (the Internet appliance box in your home or office). These attributes are, first, no optoelectronic regeneration; second, all-optical switching and routing of the data packets; and third, agnosticism in the face of data rate and format.

The removal of optoelectronic regeneration has partially begun through the use of fiber amplifiers and will continue with the use of solitons. However, retiming remains a problem even for solitons. Optical fibers stretch and shrink with changing temperatures through the day. They vibrate when trucks drive by. These mechanical effects cause the arrival time of the optical pulses to drift. In addition, there are fundamental sources of timing jitter in the solitons themselves. Because solitons are non-linear, they are susceptible to a type of timing noise called Gordon-Haus noise (after the two theorists who first predicted the effect) that linear pulses do not experience. This jitter can be extremely fast, involving pulse-to-pulse variations that accumulate over long distances. All-optical regeneration will need to face and remove these problems.

The second challenge for all-optical control of information on the Internet is through all-optical routing and switching. The saving grace of this requirement is that much of the routing and switching can be performed at speeds much lower than the data rate of the communication channel. Although the data rates can be gigabits per second or terabits per second, routing recovery and restoration (when a line goes down, or a more optimal route is identified) can occur at rates as low as a MHz (microsecond) or even a kHz (millisecond) because of the reasonably long times between successive packets of information on the fiber. These times are easily handled by mechanical switches such as miniature mirrors etched into silicon, or tiny bubbles in liquid optical waveguides based on ink-jet printer technology.

However, other requirements of routing are much more difficult to attain. Take demultiplexing. When a wavelength-multiplexed TDM data packet arrives at a switching node, perhaps only 1 bit out of 1,000 and only 1 wavelength out of 100 needs to be taken off the optical information highway, while its place is taken by a new bit at a new wavelength for transmission downstream. This process is known as Add/Drop multiplexing. Though optoelectronics can do this up to about 40 gigabits per second, when the systems go toward terabit-per-second data rates, this function must become all-optical. Removing a bit from a packet and replacing it with a new bit is fundamentally a control process that affects the information content of the optical pulses. Only non-linear optical approaches can provide the degree of control needed at these speeds.

Finally, the all-optical approaches should be agnostic to data rates and format so that older infrastructure can be used to carry new lightwave standards and services when they come along, rather than needing costly new hardware. Mirrors are examples of agnostic components. Light bounces off mirrors in the same way whether it carries a data rate of 1 bit per second or 1 trillion. It also ignores what color the light is. But mechanical mirrors are only solutions for slow routing processes and cannot be used for fast functions like Add/Drop multiplexers. The challenge is to develop agnostic non-linear optical processes that are independent of data rate or color. Possibilities abound for materials that can be brought into the service of all-optical intelligence to govern the flow of information on the Internet.

Looking far into the future, when the battles to attain all-optical networks are a distant memory, it is possible that information will control information, all in the optical domain, without speed limits. That is, the functions dictated by a control beam may depend on the information contained in that beam. Thus, there can be direct dynamic interaction among streams of optical information. But before this can happen, we need to develop architectures that allow one beam to control another. For instance, one such architecture uses non-linear interferometers whose light output depends on input control beams.

TREADING PATHS LIGHTLY

Interferometers are the most sensitive optical instruments that can be built. The intensity of their light output can change 100 percent just by making tiny changes in the refractive index of a material placed inside them, producing a form of amplification or gain. In any kind of control system, large gain is always important.

There are numerous possible configurations for interferometers, all with their own special names, such as Michelson, Mach-Zender, Sagnac, and others, named after the individuals (most of them from the nineteenth century) who devised them. Even within these classes of interferometers, there are many ways to implement them. The light beams can be in free space, or confined inside planar waveguides, or inside fibers, or in combinations of these. Each specific configuration and implementation has its own attributes and advantages for controlling light intensities. Each of these can also incorporate non-linear materials. Such design flexibility opens up a number of ways to allow light to control light.

Interferometers are strongly sensitive to wavelength, which makes them natural devices to use in WDM applications. If several wavelengths enter an interferometer, only a selected number will appear at the output. The selection process that decides which wavelengths emerge from a non-linear interferometer can depend on the light intensities—a twist on the control of light by light that allows light to control wavelength.

Before discussing the advantages of non-linear interferometers for all-optical control, we first take a close look at linear interferometers, in particular, the Mach-Zender interferometer shown in the adjacent figure. It consists simply of two conventional mirrors, and two half-silvered flat plates of glass called beamsplitters. In addition, it contains an optical component called a phaseshifter (shown in the figure by the box with the symbol Φ in it) that varies the phase of a light beam passing through it. (Remember that the phase of a wave is expressed as an angle, with a wave crest at $0°$, the trough at $180°$, and the next crest at $360°$.) The interferometer has one input port, and two output ports. Light detectors are placed at both output ports.

Inside the interferometer, the input light beam shines on the first half-silvered beamsplitter, which splits the beam into two beams, one that continues to propagate in the same direction as the incident beam, and a second that propagates at a right angle to the incident beam. If the silvering is done correctly, each beam carries exactly half of the original intensity of the incident beam. This plate is called a 50/50 beamsplitter. The process of splitting the beam into two is a form of cloning because the two resultant beams have coherent properties that are identical to the original beam. This maintenance of coherence is crucial for the operation of the interferometer. After the beamsplitter, the two beams follow two distinguishable paths known as Path 1 for the upper beam and Path 2 for the lower beam. The Path 1 beam passes through the phaseshifter, then each beam is reflected by a mirror that directs it onto the second beamsplitter.

The behavior at the second beamsplitter is the same as at the first, but now there are two incident beams rather than only one. Each beam is half transmitted and reflected. The reflected beam of one is now combined with the transmitted beam of the other, and vice versa. The light leaving each output port therefore consists of an equal superposition of the two beams from the different paths inside the interferometer. The intensity at the detectors is different in the two ports, and each detected intensity depends on the phase Φ that was imposed by the phaseshifter on the beam in Path 1.

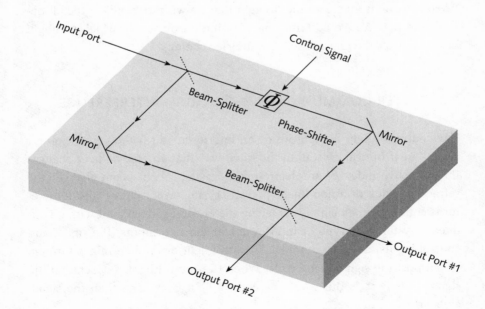

CONTROLLED MACH-ZENDER INTERFEROMETER

This type of interferometer can control the amount of light leaving one port or the other by virtually 100 percent by changing the phase in the phaseshifter. The phaseshifter is therefore a key element for the control of light, and there are several ways to construct it.

One type of phaseshifter uses a special material called an electro-optic crystal that has the property that its refractive index (related to the material polarization that controls light speeds inside the material) is a function of applied electric field. By changing the refractive index of the electro-optic crystal, the wave following Path 1 in the interferometer acquires a slightly different phase. If the optical phase of the beam is as large as 180°, then this crystal has the full range for controlling the output of the interferometer by 100 percent. Many electro-optic materials are available that can impart this phase, using only several millimeters of material and using electric fields that are easily accessible. We saw in the last chapter that in the best cases these materials can be used to modulate the phase of light up to the 40-gigahertz range. Therefore, electro-optic crystals inside interferometers are sufficient to provide high-speed modulation of data for telecommunications, at least into the range of gigabit-per-second data rates.

However, such an electro-optic interferometer uses the same electro-optic conversion from electronics to light that we wish to avoid for the all-optical Internet. We would rather have an interferometer in which one light beam controls the phase inside the interferometer.

BETTER COMMUNICATION THROUGH INTERFERENCE

The control of light by light inside an interferometer is the perfect job for a non-linear optical crystal. In the same way that an electric field changes the refractive index of an electro-optic crystal, a light beam changes the refractive index of a non-linear optical crystal. A non-linear interferometer is constructed by simply replacing the electro-optic crystal with a non-linear crystal. This type of interferometer has two inputs (the signal and control inputs) and two outputs. A control light beam determines through which port the signal beam exits. When the control light is absent, all the signal exits Port 1. But when the control light is present, then the signal exits Port 2.

In this non-linear interferometer, the physics of non-linear optical phenomena provides its strongest advantage in the switching speed. Earlier in this chapter, I described how a non-linear medium allowed one light beam to alter the propagation of another light beam. Non-linear optics is an instantaneous process (within limits that are of no importance to optical communication), with no time delay between the application of one beam or another. The control of light by light has no intrinsic speed limit other than the propagation time of the light beams. As long as a signal pulse and a control pulse are present together in the non-linear optical crystal, the signal pulse will be switched to the second output port. Light pulses as short as 30 femtoseconds (generated in mode-locked lasers) could therefore switch between the two ports bit by bit at speeds equaling the full bandwidth of optical fiber.

To control synchronization and alignment between signal bits and control bits, it is possible to put the control beam into the front-end beamsplitter of the Mach-Zender interferometer. The control pulses split along the same two paths taken by the signal pulses, and one of them interacts with the signal pulse as they co-propagate inside the non-linear optical crystal. In this configuration, the control and signal beams share a long interaction length through the crystal, maximizing the non-linear interaction between them. At the output beamsplitter, the control beam exits along with the signal beam.

This configuration has the added advantage that it can work when the control beam has a different wavelength than the signal beam. As they pass through the non-linear crystal, the linear properties of the crystal impart a different path to the control beam than the signal beam. This ability of an interferometer to differentiate among beams of different colors makes it a valuable asset for WDM applications.

An exciting prospect for non-linear interferometers is the ability for *information* to control *information,* as contrasted with the relatively simple procedure of flipping a switch. When the control beam is composed of data bits just as the signal beam is, then the information content from the two beams directly interacts. For instance, if two pulses are coincident in both the signal and control beams, then Port 2 emits a pulse and Port 1 does not. But if a pulse is present in the signal but not in the control, Port 1 emits a pulse and Port 2 does not. Finally, if no pulse is present in the signal beam, then neither port emits a pulse. If you look closely at this sequence of possibilities, you will notice that Port 2 of the non-linear interferometer has the function of a logical AND between the two beams, while Port 1 is a logical NAND (a logic gate that is the negative of the AND). Though this is only rudimentary logic, it is the first step to higher functions in which information controls information all-optically.

The non-linear interferometer will be the fundamental element in all-optical control just as the transistor was the basis for electronic control. The optical signals in this device can be data that is switched or routed; or the optical signals can be control programs. The control beam, for instance, can come from the output of another non-linear interferometer that was switched by other control beams. Logic operations can be performed in this way, and the basic logic gates of a "universal computer" can be constructed. This is the first step toward all-optical intelligence.

To be compatible with the optical fibers that will constitute the medium of the all-optical Internet, non-linear interferometers are made out of fibers similar to those used for data transmission. Thus, there are no problems coupling light from the telecom and datacom fibers into these switches and out again. Fibers also have the distinct advantage, described earlier in this chapter, of having long interaction lengths over which the non-linear effects can accumulate. It is possible to construct fiber non-linear interferometers using the relatively weak optical non-linearities of the glass itself as the optical control medium. Conversely, sections of erbium-doped fibers or semiconductor optical amplifiers can be added to the fiber paths in the interferometer. Using these techniques, switching speeds up to 100 gigabits per second have been demonstrated in the laboratory. These rates are just the beginning. Higher rates supported by instantaneous interactions will allow the optical logic to smoke along at the speed of the data rate, in the best case up to 30 terabits per second.

In one form or another, non-linear interferometers will appear in the marketplace and in field installations within a few years. These will be the first links holding together a growing intelligent fabric that will perform all the switching, routing, and multiplexing needs of the all-optical Internet. Indeed, when these non-linear interferometers are combined into logic gates, the optical Internet itself starts to look like a computer—one that spans continents and the world. Such an idea forces us to rethink what constitutes a "computer," and what functions we want computers to perform for us.

RETHINKING COMPUTERS

What is a computer? We have become so comfortable with our personal computers that we start to lose sight of how a computer is defined. What does a computer do? In the early days, they were primarily glorified (and fast) calculators. The name "computer" was even borrowed from an existing profession that consisted of people whose job it was to compute numbers. In the early half of the twentieth century, when someone would say, "I will have these numbers checked by our computer," he was actually referring to a human being. The first electronic computers replaced the human computers and appropriated their name. But how often do you use your PC to compute numbers? The functions of the computer these days seem mostly non-numerical, such as word processing or surfing the Internet. Yet for all these applications, the information is stored as binary numbers. The computers are still computing numbers; only now they just represent words, sounds, and images.

But personal computers are hardly the most common computers in the world today. Most computers are never even seen. They are part of coffeemakers and anti-lock brakes and thermostats. The industry that uses the largest number of computer chips is the automotive industry. In these days of electronic ignition and power everything (windows, steering, brakes, etc.), computer chips are controlling almost every aspect of the car's performance.

Similarly, when you use digital telecommunication, your voice and data are fragmented into packets that are dispersed over numerous trunk lines and switching nodes. In data transfer from Chicago to Atlanta, say, parts of your conversation may be switched through Dallas, while other parts are switched through Baltimore. Which parts are sent where all depends on the most effective path in terms of cost and load. Furthermore, your bits are interleaved with the bits of many other subscribers. Such complex switching functions can only be performed by high-end and high-speed computers that are constantly figuring out how to break apart the signal, send it through the best nodes, and put it all together again at the destination with complete accuracy. Therefore, we are already relying on considerable "intelligence" simply to port information around on the Internet.

Are these switches really computers? Maybe they perform complex operations, but are they *universal* computers in the sense of a Turing machine? A Turing machine was the conceptual computing machine devised in 1937 by Alan Turing, (1912–1954) the brilliant British mathematician who helped break the secret *Enigma* code of the Germans in World War II, and who was one of the founding fathers of modern computer science. Turing was interested in finding out what tasks could be considered computable versus those that were incomputable. For a theoretician, the definition of computability does not include the time needed to solve the problem. If a problem can be solved in principal, even if it takes longer than the age of the universe to compute, it is still deemed to be computable. On the other hand, there are some problems that are incomputable. Turing's original motivation for constructing his idealized computing machine was specifically to see if it could decide which problems were computable and which ones were not.

This computability problem, or *Entscheidungsproblem,* was one of the twenty-three famous open problems outlined by David Hilbert (1862–1943) of Göttingen University in 1900. To mark the new century, Hilbert composed a list of the greatest outstanding problems in mathematics. He presented these at the Second International Congress of Mathematics in Paris. He anticipated that these problems would be solved before the new century was over, and that their solution would place mathematics on equal footing with formal logic. Hilbert's second question asked whether it was possible to prove the consistency of a mathematical system from within the system. Largely in response to Hilbert's challenge, and also as a review of the recent developments in symbolic algebra, the English mathematician and philosopher Alfred North Whitehead collaborated with Bertrand Russell on a three-volume tome published between 1910 and 1913 called the *Principia Mathematica,* whose name mirrored Isaac Newton's Seventeenth-century *Principia.* The goal of the new *Principia* was to firmly derive mathematics by using only propositions of logic. The *Principia* was uniquely visual in its use of symbolic algebra to define logical propositions.

The *Principia* was a tour de force, even though it was unable to establish mathematics unambiguously as a consistent branch of logic. Then, in 1931, a young Austrian immigrant to the United States by the name of Kurt Gödel (1906–1978) working at the Institute for Advanced Study at Princeton, shattered Hilbert's hope to prove the completeness of mathematics, by proving the reverse instead—that certain well-defined statements could be neither proved nor disproved when using the finite set of axioms of a logical system. Gödel's discovery of undecidable propositions is considered to be one of the greatest events in modern mathematics. It turned the belief in absolute mathematical truth on its ear. It also derailed two thousand years of progress toward the goal of proving that all of pure mathematics could be derived from a finite number of fundamental logical principles. Leibniz had been one of the chief advocates of this program, and it was in the pursuit of this ideal that he dreamed up his universal characteristic of visual symbols that would serve as tools of discovery. After Gödel's proof, all hope of achieving Leibniz's dream vanished. Turing, spurred on by Gödel's discovery, went further by considering whether a mechanical process, that is, an algorithm composed of discrete steps, existed that could be used to identify propositions that *were* provable. By envisioning just such a mechanical process, Turing was able to show that it was impossible to devise any such algorithm.

Fortunately, Turing's abstract project on the decidability problem had far more practical consequences. For though his "machine" was meant only to be a set of abstract functions, his conceptual model contained many of the components that later became standard in modern computers. For instance, a processing unit that makes decisions by comparing input data to the internal state of the unit; the notion of a program of logical steps; and the idea of a memory to store intermediate results of the computation, were all there in the original concept of the Turing machine.

Turing was also able to prove that *any* problem that was computable could be computed by a Turing machine. This means that Turing machines are *universal computers.* No computable problem is outside their scope. Furthermore, Turing concluded that all universal computers were equivalent. This conjecture, known as the Church-Turing hypothesis, opens the door on an infinite number of ways to construct universal computers, and launched a search for the best ways to do so.

From these first axiomatic beginnings of computer science, progress was rapid, and several practical universal machines were in operation by the middle of the 1940s (primarily associated with the Allies' war effort against the Axis). Binary data storage was recognized as the cleanest and most error-free means of manipulating data in a real machine that has real noise. The relevant system for binary propositions was Boolean logic, which introduced logic gates into computer science. The foundations of universal computers became even more solid when it was understood that any universal machine could be constructed by combining only two logic gates, the AND and the XOR (exclusive OR), into more complicated logic gates.

As we saw in chapter 3, it was because of the fundamental importance of the XOR gate to universal computing that it came as such a shock in the early days of research into neural networks when Marvin Minsky demonstrated in his 1969 monograph that simple two-layer perceptrons could not implement the XOR. This blow delayed work in neural networks for over a decade before multilayer networks regained momentum. With the introduction of hidden layers, neural networks also became members of the class of universal computers: anything that is computable should be computable using a neural network. By analogy, the all-optical fiber network, with its power to switch and route and reconfigure, and its massive connectivity, may itself be viewed as a universal computer.

INTELLIGENT OPTICAL FABRIC

An intelligent optical Internet requires an even more important resource than mere speed; it also requires connectivity. There are currently 100 million hosts on the Internet. Each of these hosts has 1 million logic circuits. That means that there are, even today, about 100 trillion logic gates connected loosely through the Internet. This is a number that exceeds the number of neurons in the human brain by at least a factor of 10,000. Can such an interconnected network have the brainpower of a small town? At the moment, direct connectivity to those logic gates is hampered by slow optoelectronic interfaces.

Nonetheless, distributed computing is already going on in those millions of hosts. In the mid-1990s, researchers conceived the idea of using the vast idle computer power represented by all the personal computers connected to the Internet to perform the Herculean task of sifting through radio data in the search for extraterrestrial intelligence. The computing power needed to analyze the reams of data was non-existent in single computers, or even for distributed computers on a local area network. However, the task could be doled out to the millions of computers on the Internet, most of which are idle at any given moment. By creating a computer application analogous to a screen saver, the researchers were able to give each PC owner the ability to crunch the numbers on parts of the immense data set. Periodically, the individual computers would send their results automatically over the Web back to a central computer, where the individual results were compiled and assessed. At the peak of the project, 500,000 personal computers were enlisted. The best part of this scheme was that, once the software was installed on the machines, the owners could use their machines normally with no further responsibility.

Although no extraterrestrial intelligence has been discovered as of this writing, the project represents a bold new approach to massively parallel distributed processing. Furthermore, it demonstrates the potential power of tapping into all those nodes on the Internet. The bottleneck that keeps the nodes from being truly interconnected is the same optoelectronic bottleneck that separates the optical Internet from the electronic processors. But as we saw in the last chapter, the distance above which optics rules and below which electronics rules is constantly shrinking. When the optical fibers of the all-optical Internet go directly inside the box and couple with the optical data buses inside the hybrid optoelectronic computers, then the last significant barrier between the network and the computers will be gone. When that happens, the network will become a fast, fully interconnected neural network, with the potential for intelligence—true intelligence. That is, if intelligence is computable at all.

In a nutshell, that is the biggest question. Is intelligence computable? If so, then any universal computer, including the optical network, could, in theory, be programmed to exhibit it. Remember, though, that computability says nothing at all about the time and cost of such a computation. Though intelligence might actually be computable, it might take longer than the age of the universe to compute something as complex as intelligence.

The possible computability of intelligence was one of the areas in which Alan Turing had a direct interest. He even devised an ingenious test to ascertain when a machine could be said to be intelligent. The test consists of an Examiner, who poses questions via a keyboard to both a human subject and to a potentially intelligent machine. The Examiner can ask any question of either of the two. Both subjects have the goal of convincing the Examiner that they are human. To achieve this end, the human and the machine can answer the questions truthfully, or can lie if that best achieves their goal. If, at the end of a sufficiently long testing period, the Examiner cannot distinguish which of the test subjects is the computer and which is the human, then the computer is deemed "intelligent."

Turing's test is a wonderfully pragmatic approach to the problem of intelligence, and was very much in keeping with the dominance of behavioral psychology during the fifties. The question is completely operational rather than philosophical or even mechanical. If the machine behaves in a manner that is indistinguishable from an intelligent human, then who is to say that the machine is not intelligent? On the other hand, the Turing Test is a set of rules rather than a set of questions, and the cleverness of the Examiner to a large degree decides the outcome of the test.

The intelligent optical fabric that will drape the world, with its multiplicity of nodes and interconnectivity that exceeds the physical constraints of a human body, may indeed be intelligent in the operational sense of the Turing Test. If its behavior becomes indistinguishable from that of a human, then perhaps it will deserve the name of "intelligent being" that we guard so jealously for ourselves. Aside from issues such as whether an intelligent machine would have a soul, it will become our constant ethereal companion as we live our lives in continuous connection to the optical network. In the distant future, we may even plug ourselves into the network through neuro-optical interfaces and become the intelligent nodes to replace the artificial ones. What, then, might we accomplish?

But the crucial feature that has been missing in this optical intelligence of the fiber network is the Parallel Advantage of Light and Image. The optical machines of the optical network are still the same binary digital ones that sit on our desktops. Serial data in these machines represents the world in bits of ones and zeros. Though these machines are universal, are they sufficient to develop the rapid intelligence we would want out of our machines of light? Does a binary representation have enough depth or nuance to implement optical intelligence in the time scale of human thought?

The work of Whitehead and Russell—though fundamentally ill-founded because they were specifically trying to develop a consistent system that Gödel later proved could not exist—did develop visual tools that partially bridge the gap. These tools are closer to Leibniz's universal language than any other efforts have approached. One of the goals of the new *Principia* was to present "the perfectly precise expression, in its symbols, of mathematical propositions." In the tradition of Leibniz, Whitehead and Russell were keenly interested in providing an accurate and unambiguous visual symbolism shared by both mathematics and logic. They stated that "it is a subsidiary object of this work to show that, with the aid of symbolism, deductive reasoning can be extended to regions of thought not usually supposed amenable to mathematical treatment."

Their symbolism and notations were, in fact, extensive and exhaustive. A small dictionary of terms is required to read even the simplest propositions. For instance, the following propositions are written in the Whitehead-Russell notation.

The law of excluded middle:

"p is true, or not-p is true."
$\vdash \cdot p \vee \sim p$

The law of contradiction:

"It is not true that p and not-p are both true."
$\vdash \cdot \sim (p \cdot \sim p)$

The law of double negation:

"p is the negation of the negation of p."
$\vdash \cdot p \equiv \sim (\sim p)$

A statement of relation:

"'a exists' is equivalent to 'x exists and x is a'"
$\exists ! a \cdot = \cdot (\exists x) \cdot x \epsilon a$

and so forth. When looking at the these strings of strange symbols, it is easy to envision them etched on glass beads strung together in a hotly contested match of the Glass Bead Game.

The new *Principia* was therefore a partial success. Two centuries after Leibniz formed his ideal of a symbolic language of human thought and knowledge, a thorough and complete effort to establish such a language was complete. Beginning with simple definitions and laws, the *Principia* moves upward into ever more complex constructions and derivations of logical propositions and relations—all in an unambiguous visual notation, requiring no words or "language."

The probability that such a symbolic language could ever be adopted for human communication is small. The symbols are numerous and highly arbitrary. Learning such a language is only possible for the few mathematicians and logicians interested in such things. But the real value of the notation is that the language could become that "instrument of discovery" of Leibniz's dreams. It would be a visual calculus, a type of Glass Bead Game played by master mathematicians to explore the beauty of the universe.

This symbolic language foreshadows the possibility that we can construct machines of light which use visual symbols as a language of intelligence. Such visual machines will go far beyond the digital fiber networks in efficiency and multiplicity of interconnection. These will be the computers with hologram hard drives and adaptive optical neurons.

8 The Telling Image

Holographic Computers and the Architecture of Light

IT IS QUITE POSSIBLE TO TRANSLATE, BY MEANS OF A HOLOGRAM, A
CHINESE IDEOGRAM INTO ITS CORRESPONDING ENGLISH SENTENCE, AND
VICE VERSA.

Dennis Gabor, 1971

We can move beyond the serial intelligence of fiber to machines in which images become the units of information. In these visual machines, images control images. Such machines are not necessarily digital in nature, nor do they need to be classified as "universal" computers in the sense of a Turing machine. Instead, they have specialized talent; in particular, the talent of processing and analyzing visual information.

These machines represent the evolutionary end point of visual and optical communication. Where human visual capability and speed end, artificial visual machines begin and go beyond human experience. These are the last of the classical machines of light that play the Glass Bead Game in their luminous heads.

In such a computer, when images control images inside non-linear optical crystals, a great opportunity for cross-connection arises. When 100 million pixels connect independently with 100 million others, the number of interconnections exceeds that in the human brain. In such a computer, images are both data and control program. One image "tells" the computer what to do with another image. This computer would be highly reconfigurable because functions would be defined by the images sent into the computer. The architecture would remain wide open, like the brain of a newborn child, with potential to be molded into any number of possible configurations.

The parallelism we would gain by moving from one dimension (bits per time) to two dimensions (images per time) is tremendous. Wavelength-division multiplexing currently pushes physics to the limit just to get 1,000 different wavelengths propagating down a fiber together. But an image the size of only 1 square centimeter contains approximately 100 million pixels (where a pixel size is defined by the size of the wavelength of light) and improves parallelism almost a million-fold. The immense advantage of the parallelism of the image is clear. The challenge is to develop the architecture that can tap it.

KEEPING THE PHASE

The technology that is best suited to exploit this massive interconnection potential is optical holography. Holography is the art of creating images without lenses. The idea was conceived in 1947 by the Hungarian-born electrical engineer Dennis Gabor (1900–1979) (later to receive a Nobel Prize in 1971) as a way of getting additional information out of electron waves in electron microscopes. Though he was able to demonstrate the principles using ordinary light sources, optical holography only became practical after the invention of the laser. Holograms today most often are seen as flashy 3-D images on credit cards, or on the cover of *National Geographic,* or in novelty shops. Though many of these demonstrations are merely cute or eye-catching, other holographic applications serve purposes of security, such as anticounterfeiting holograms on credit cards and personal checks, which represent the largest market for holographic products. But these applications are hardly high-tech and have little or nothing to do with optical intelligence.

The true value of holography lies in the physical structure of the hologram that is created when two beams of mutually coherent light interfere inside a holographic medium, that is, a medium that can record the interference pattern between two or more light beams. That two beams (at least) are required to generate the hologram reflects the fact that holograms allow separate streams of information to interact. This physical mixing of information through light is the basis of all higher-order optical functions in intelligent optical computers. How do holograms do this? The secret is in the phase. (Remember that the phase of a wave refers to where the crests and troughs lie.) The holograms naturally and automatically mix optical information by directly recording, not just the intensity, but also the phase of individual images.

Holograms are created in a manner very similar to the interferometry we discussed in the last chapter. To use an interferometer to do holography takes only a slight misalignment of the two beams at the interferometer output so that they cross at a small angle. In the region where the beams overlap, there are alternating bright and dark strips called interference fringes that produce a two-dimensional pattern that can be viewed by eye on a white screen, or on photographic film. The interference fringes on the film are caused by successive conditions of constructive and destructive interference as the beams come in and out of phase, varying periodically across the area of overlap. If the film is exposed for the correct amount of time, the regions that see high intensity are strongly exposed, while the regions of low intensity are barely exposed at all. When the film is developed, the interference pattern appears as zebra stripes on the film. The pattern is a record of the changing phases of the two beams, and can be made to recreate not only how bright the light was, but also where it came from.

That is remarkable. Photographic film only responds to intensity—not to the phase of a light wave. When you take a regular photograph of an object or scene, the reflected intensity from the object is mapped directly to silver particle density on the film. None of the phase information of the object is seen in the negative. But in a hologram, by bringing in a second reference beam that is coherent to the first, the phase information is turned into a periodic intensity variation through the process of interference.

If both laser beams are simple blank beams, the stripes on the film are perfectly periodic and constitute a rudimentary hologram. Clearly, we would like to do more than that. We would like to have one of the light beams come from a real-world object—a flower, a toy car, a person, anything light can illuminate—and we would like to make a hologram of it. When we bounce a laser beam off the object, the reflected beam has a complicated form which contains all the phase information of the object that tells where the light comes from. We call this information-bearing beam the object beam. The other beam we keep blank, with no information on it. This we call the reference beam. When the object beam crosses the reference beam, the interference pattern is a complex pattern of swirls and blotches in which nothing of the object is recognizable. This complex interference pattern encodes the phase information (and therefore the 3-D information) of the object. The Holography recording process is shown in the figure.

The next step is to retrieve the phase information and recreate the object wave that has all the properties of the original wave. This is accomplished when the recorded hologram is illuminated by the same reference light beam that was used to write the hologram in the first place, as illustrated. This illumination beam carries no information—it is a blank wave. But when it propagates through the hologram, it scatters into many directions— the same directions that the original object wave had. This scattered wave travels off *just as if* it had come from the object. In this way, the full potential of holography is realized as a form of 3-D optical memory: the ability

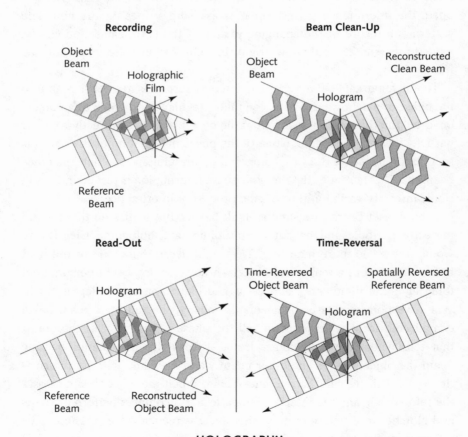

HOLOGRAPHY

to re-form a complicated wave that propagates with all the properties as if it were coming from the original object. If the reconstructed wave is a perfect replica of the original wave, then looking at the reconstruction should be indistinguishable from looking at the original object. That is why reconstructed holograms have parallax (when you move your head from side to side, closer items move faster than farther items), and why you can look "behind" objects in the foreground. The original 3-D scene had these properties; so does the reconstructed scene.

It is important to make a distinction between the hologram and the image that is created by scattering light off the hologram. The term *hologram* is reserved for the exposed and developed film (or any medium that can record a hologram). If you look closely at the "hologram," all you see are dark blotches and crazy stripes on the film. You do not see anything resembling an image because you are only looking at the object's phase. On the other hand, when you shine the reference beam on the hologram, you see the reconstructed image, which looks just like the original object.

The ability to record and read holographic data from an appropriate medium is more important than just a parlor trick. The value of holographic storage to computing comes from the quantity of information that can be stored. We will see that holographic memory benefits from the massive parallelism of the image, and has the potential to store terabits of data inside the volume of optical crystals that can hold much denser holographic information than mere film.

A CRYSTALLINE *MONA LISA*

Leonardo would have approved of the subject for the first extensive demonstration of holographic optical memory. In 1994, a research group at Stanford University under the direction of Lambertus (Bert) Hesselink, a professor in aeronautic engineering, stored a full-color digital version of the *Mona Lisa* inside a holographic memory crystal, distributing the information as holograms throughout the volume of the crystal. The image was written into the crystal and, subsequently, the read out virtually error-free. The two images of the *Mona Lisa*—before storage and after the read out— are indistinguishable to the eye. In both the "before" and "after" shots, she continues to smile her ambiguous smile and to peer demurely, if also somewhat self-possessed, out of her digital canvas.

Bert Hesselink is one of the energetic leaders in the field of holographic optics. He has long been pursuing realistic holographic data storage systems. Many previous demonstrations of holographic data storage had focused on one aspect or another of this technologically challenging goal. However, there are many requirements for successful performance of a holographic storage system, and all of them need to be satisfied in a single system. These requirements include high storage capacity, high signal-to-noise ratio, and high-speed access. Hesselink's *Mona Lisa* project succeeded in bringing these all together into a single system.

The argument in favor of holographic data storage in crystals is fairly easy to make when it is based on theoretical grounds. For instance, on the back of an envelope I can write down the simple equations that show how holographic data storage can store 1 terabit in a crystal that is only 1 centimeter on a side, with data transfer rates of 1 gigabit per second, and random access times less than 100 microseconds. These specifications are simple consequences of the size of the wavelength of light, of the parallelism inherent in the optical image format, and of the spatial storage of the data in the crystal volume.

One pixel from an image can be stored in an area equal to the square of the wavelength of light. Assuming that light has a wavelength around 1 micron, an image of 1 square centimeter contains approximately 100 million pixels. If the pixels are digital, i.e., black or white, then each pixel represents a single bit. Such a data image is called a page. Many pages can be stored, one next to the other, inside a crystal in a format called a stack. Pages can be placed as close together as a single wavelength inside the crystal. Therefore, in a cubic centimeter of crystal, there can be a stack of 10,000 pages—equaling a total capacity of 1 terabit of binary data. Furthermore, if the readout of the information is performed a page at a time, even if that readout is as slow as ten pages per second, it still corresponds to a data rate of 1 gigabit per second.

These performance characteristics far outstrip the capabilities of any hard drive, certainly any that were available at the time of Hesselink's experiments in 1994. Given such potential, it is easy to see why there has been so much interest in developing holographic data storage. For this reason, the Advanced Research Projects Agency of the U.S. Department of Defense funded the work at Stanford University, as well as several other groups, to develop holographic storage systems.

The Stanford group chose digital data storage rather than analog image storage because digital data is much less susceptible to noise, which has always been a severe handicap to holographic storage. The use of coherent laser light to create holograms almost always produces flaws in the images which are caused by interference of the image beam with stray light that comes from the optical elements making up the optical instrument. Holographic images therefore have intensity variations that constitute a significant source of noise. Digital data, on the other hand, can be nearly impervious to such variations because of the high contrast between a 1 and a 0. Furthermore, the researchers were able to create a data format that was largely free from the intensity variations of the holographic system. This approach significantly decreased their bit error rate, which is one of the principal merits of a digital information system.

The *Mona Lisa* was therefore digitized into differential pairs of pixels using a digital format that encodes the locations and colors of the individual pixels of the image. They used fairly low-resolution digitization, which required only 163 kilobytes of data to describe the image. The data were stored inside a crystal of lithium niobate. This is a special type of transparent non-linear optical crystal that translates the intensity interference pattern into a refractive index grating that forms the physical hologram inside the crystal. The change in the index lasts for an extended period of time; just what is needed to write a hologram and retrieve it. The data were stored by shifting the angle of the reference beam for each page within a single stack, and by spatially shifting the reference beam between four different stacks. The data were read out by repeating the same angles and positions of the reference beam and recording the diffracted reconstructed beams with a digital video camera. During the data readout, standard error correction protocols were used to ensure faithful reproduction of Leonardo's masterpiece.

The result of this data storage and retrieval process was a color image of the *Mona Lisa* in which only a single bit, out of approximately 1 million, was in error. The data were also read out at a rate of about 6 million pixels per second. The performance of this system was impressive, and competitive at the time with other technology for storing compressed video signals or for storing uncompressed images. The work was a milestone in the science and technology of holographic data storage and established a new baseline for the state-of-the-art.

Unfortunately, though impressive, the performance of this state-of-the-art system fell far short of the full potential of holographic storage. The total information stored was only about 1 million bits—not the 1,000-fold higher terabit level that is desired. The data transfer rate of the system was only about 1 megabit per second—not the 1,000-fold higher gigabit-per-second speed that everyone wants. The storage density was about 10 million bits per cubic centimeter—not the 100,000-fold higher capacity that is sought.

In defense of the experiment, it is important to point out that the original silicon memory chips did not perform even that well. In the early days of silicon integrated circuits, 163 kilobytes was an almost inconceivably large number. Any technology has a learning curve, and sometimes that learning curve just keeps rising as the technology constantly improves—Moore's Law, for instance. Silicon chips started modestly, but have continued to get faster, with greater transistor densities, for over thirty years. Given that much time, holographic optical memory would certainly improve as much.

On the other hand, even though not every computer on every desktop will one day have holographic optical memory, at some time in the future such memory will find its way into the marketplace. I can predict this with some confidence because of the moving frontier between optics and electronics described in chapters 6 and 7. So much information is already in the optical domain that there will be a benefit to keeping it there.

Also, when personal computers on desktops become the hybrid optoelectronic machines of the second generation of the machines of light, they will be using light inside the box. The all-optical Internet by that time will be a far-flung global computer. Even when silicon or magnetic storage achieves the terabit/gigabit-per-second storage/bandwidth goal, it will never be compatible with optical information, especially optical information in image format. There will always be that bottleneck of optoelectronic conversion from the optical domain to the electronic domain and back—a bottleneck even now being eliminated in all-optical networks. Therefore, information transmission and storage in the network will be best achieved all optically—in the end. But holography has much more to offer than 3-D storage of vast amounts of data. Holograms and holographic reconstructions are also useful for finding or enhancing features in an image.

FURTHER ADVENTURES IN HOLOGRAPHY

There is a logic to holograms, and with practice it is possible to gain an intuitive feel for how holograms behave under different circumstances. The reconstruction from holographic memory starts when we shine a reference beam onto the hologram. The hologram *completes the picture* by recreating the missing object beam. This is the general behavior of holograms; they *complete the picture*. Whatever beams were present during the hologram recording are recreated when the hologram is illuminated by just one of the original beams.

Knowing this, we can supply the *object* beam to the hologram, but not the *reference* beam, and let the hologram complete the picture. In this case, the clean reference beam is missing, so the hologram creates one. The process of taking a complex beam and creating a clean beam has important uses in real optical systems. It performs what is known as beam cleanup (shown in the figure on page 176). When a laser beam bounces off less than ideal surfaces, it produces optically scrambled beams that are hard to manipulate optically and detect cleanly. By passing such a dirty beam through the hologram, the information is "cleaned up" by turning it into a uniform beam that is easy to send through lenses and into photodetectors.

Let's look at another example. Take the blank reference beam and run it backwards through the hologram (as in the figure). What will the hologram produce? Think about making a video of a simple propagating wave. If you run the video backwards, by reversing the direction of the videotape and hence reversing the apparent direction of time, the wave propagates backward. Therefore, a plane wave (or blank beam) that travels backward (by reflecting exactly back along its original path) is equivalent to a time-reversed wave.

If we imagine making a video of the beam cleanup process shown in the figure, where the complex object beam is incident on the hologram and a transmitted blank reference beam is created, we can run this video backwards. We find the reference beam running backwards into the hologram, and the hologram recreating the complex object wave—but now running backwards. Therefore, if we shine a reference beam backward on the hologram, we get an object beam that behaves as if it were time-reversed, and it propagates back until it converges on the exact surface of the original object. This makes it possible to create a time-reversal mirror.

A time-reversal mirror reverses wavefronts. If a complex wave hits a time-reversal mirror, it bounces off in exactly the same direction from which it came. A useful property of time-reversal mirrors is their ability to act as perfect retroflectors. No matter what direction the incident beam comes from, the reflected beam exactly retraces its path. No ordinary mirror can do this. Although certain arrangements of mirrors can send parts of a beam back on itself, such as corner cubes that are the basis of retroflectors on cars or highway signs, these cannot exactly match the incoming wavefronts. Time-reversal mirrors can.

A second, related property of the time-reversal mirror is its ability to send light rays back through distorting media. As an example of this, consider smearing petroleum jelly on window glass and then trying to look through it. You can't. The jelly mixes up the rays and hopelessly distorts the image. But the time-reversal mirror makes it possible to see through such a distorting screen. The trick is to have a two-way imaging system. The object of interest lies behind the smeared screen, and in front of a time-reversal mirror. The light is transmitted through the screen, through the object, and then off the time-reversal mirror. The mirror makes the beam propagate back, retracing all the different paths through the distorting screen. When the beam emerges from the screen again, all distortion is removed—it runs exactly backwards to compensate all the distortion it acquired going forward. What remains on the beams is the information of the object.

Yet another useful application of holograms borrows from the behavior of neural networks. In the previous cases of beam cleanup and time reversal, the reference beam carried no information. It was just a blank beam (a plane wave). However, both the object and the reference beams can carry different information (different images). In this case again, the hologram completes the picture. First, the hologram is recorded when the film is exposed simultaneously to the two different object beams, as in the Associative Memory Figure. Let us say the objects are a sphere and the edge of a box. Although both beams are now object beams, *each acts as the reference for the other*. During readout, one object beam or the other, but not both, are sent through the hologram. The hologram then reproduces the missing beam. If we send in the sphere beam, it reconstructs the box beam. And if we send in the box beam, it reconstructs the sphere beam.

This function is very much like human associative memory. The hologram "associates" the box with the sphere. When the hologram sees "box,"

Recording

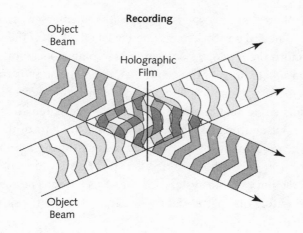

Object
Beam

Holographic
Film

Object
Beam

Associative Recall

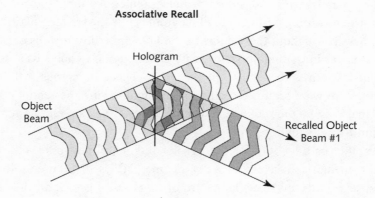

Hologram

Object
Beam

Recalled Object
Beam #1

Object
Beam

Recalled Object
Beam #2

Hologram

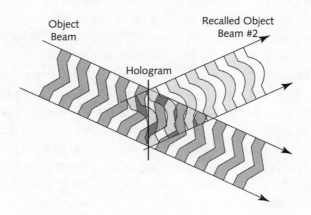

ASSOCIATIVE MEMORY

it remembers "sphere," and vice versa. Associative memory was one function of a Hopfield neural network mentioned in chapter 3. It is therefore interesting to explore the analogy between holographic association and the
structure of neural networks. In the neural net, the association is contained
in the weights of the synaptic connections among the neurons. These
weights are adjusted so that when one pattern is presented to the input
neurons, the output neurons fire in such a way that they form the associated pattern. The adjustment of the weights is done during a training period, after which the weights are fixed. The distribution of weights
constitutes the memory of the system for the association. The memory is
read out by presenting one pattern at the input, and the network regener-
ates the target pattern at the output.

Notice how the language describing the associative neural network
closely parallels the description of holographic recording and reconstruction. The recording period of the hologram is like the training period of the
network. Throughout the volume of the hologram, tiny regions of periodic
patterns of alternating optical density called gratings connect the features
of one pattern with features of the other. These numerous little optical
gratings are what scatter (or diffract) the light during the readout process
and that may be viewed as the synaptic connections among the input and
output neurons (light beams).

Another parallel between holography and neural networks is the nature
of the memory. In a neural network, memory is distributed. No single
synapse records any specific feature of a pattern. Instead, all the features
are distributed over all the synapses. This is why distributed memories remain robust in the face of damage or partial erasure. The memory might
degrade a little, but all the features remain. The hologram works the same
way. All features of an image are distributed throughout the volume of the
hologram. Conversely, every small volume of the hologram contains information about the whole image. This makes it possible to take a hologram
recorded in film, cut out a small section, and when the reference beam illuminates this small section, the full image is reconstructed. What gets lost in
this procedure are not any specific features but the overall clarity of the reconstruction. The reconstructed image has a lower spatial resolution than
the original full-hologram reconstruction. The smaller the hologram fragment, the less spatial resolution and clarity the reconstruction has; but
lower resolution is a small price to pay for the robustness of the memory.

For many visual recognition processes, a coarse reconstruction is all that is needed for positive identification.

However, an important feature that is missing in the analogy between holography and neural networks is a non-linear response function in the case of the hologram. The non-linear response of a neuron is important for thresholding to allow one answer, and only one answer, to emerge from the network rather than all answers at the same time. In our specific associative holography example, the hologram responds linearly to the input. While the reconstructed image is the associated image to the exact input, imperfect inputs produce imperfect outputs using this straightforward holography. This is not how neural networks work. For a flexible neural network, even an imperfect input should produce a relatively good reconstruction without cross-talk from other stored images. But more of this later.

Let's look at one last useful application of holograms that makes it possible to extract specific features from a scene. The writing process for feature extraction looks just like that for holographic memory, with a few adjustments. For instance, when an object beam containing a text of letters is sent through a lens, the lens breaks apart the object wave into a combination of spatial frequencies (periodic patterns in an image). By recording the spatial frequencies of the object beam rather than the image directly, it is possible to get a match between the spatial frequencies of one object with another test object.

When we want to extract a specific feature or pattern from the text, we put that feature onto the readout beam. Consider when the input is a page of English text, and the target is the letter E. The task is to find every location on the input text that contains the letter E. The letter E has a unique spectrum of spatial frequencies that differentiates it from all the other letters of the alphabet. Each spatial frequency spectrum is a unique fingerprint for that letter. The input, which consists of all the possible letters, is a linear sum of the spectra of each of the letters. In the readout process, the spectrum of the E in the target matches that part of the hologram associated with the E's in the text, but is mismatched to all the other parts of the hologram associated with the other non-target letters.

An important feature of this example is the ability of holograms to record phase. The interference fringes in the hologram have just the right orientation (associated with the phase and location of the E's) to send the reconstruction beam back to the exact position of the E's in the text. To read out the information, a beamsplitter is placed in the path of the scattered reference beam to direct the light to a video camera. Every place where the letter E occurs in the page lights up with a bright spot on the video screen. The bright spots are called correlation peaks. These occur wherever the target letter is correlated with a letter in the text. The apparatus described in this example is therefore called an image correlator.

This particular holographic process extracts features from a scene and is called content-addressable memory. That is, when we scan a text for the letter E, we are searching for specific content in memory. Traditional computers do this also, but if the content cannot be ordered in a way that allows a binary search to be performed, then the search has to go sequentially through every element in memory. Thus, in a search for the letter E in a text of ASCII characters, if there are N characters, the computer will step through all N sequentially until the end of the list is reached. The time for this sequential search is linear in N. If N is a large enough number, like the exponential growth of information on the Internet, the search might take an unacceptably long time, even with today's high-speed computers.

On the other hand, searching for content in an image is a parallel search process. All the E's are present at the same time, and all share the same spatial frequency fingerprint. The search and identification of the locations takes only as long as it takes light to pass through the optical components. Of course, reality intrudes on this rosy scenario. No useful application is without its bottlenecks. In the case of image-content search, the bottleneck is in the interface device that presents the information to the holographic medium, and that detects the bright spots of light where the content is identified. These interface devices, for the moment, are optoelectronic devices like spatial light modulators and charge-coupled-device cameras connected to electronic computers. The speed of the content-addressable search is limited by the speed of the electronic devices. This situation will change when computers begin to live more completely in the optical domain. The information in optical computers will already be parallel data structures (images) that are stored and accessed without needing electronic conversion.

Even with the optoelectronic interfaces, content searching of images has important applications. Far more challenging tasks than finding the letter E in text are encountered routinely. For instance, matching fingerprints is much more difficult than finding letters. Not only are all fingerprints different (representing an "alphabet" of 3 billion prints in the United States alone), but every instance of the same fingerprint from the same person will be different depending on who does the fingerprinting, or how the fingerprint is left behind by the individual. Needless to say, writing a computer code to match fingerprints is a difficult task. An optical "fingerprint computer" is a natural candidate to perform this task faster and better than any conventional computer. Other worthwhile applications of content search in images abound. Identifying camouflaged enemy tanks in a cluttered battle scene, tracing retinal marks in a retinal security scan, finding faces in a crowd, locating Waldo in comic books—these are all tasks that require feature detection in an image. Where electronic computer programs struggle to do this task, optical computers do it naturally.

In spite of the value of these optical machines, and the strong analogy between such holographic image associators and neural networks, they are still missing the key element of a non-linear threshold (the intelligent decision maker) that is essential to the operation of all neural networks. The next section describes how a non-linear response is added to holography to complete the analogy with optical neurons.

HOLOGRAPHIC NEURAL NETWORKS

The key element missing in the hologram readout of the associative memory application was the decisiveness of the output of the optical neural network. If a degraded or incomplete object beam is presented to a hologram, the recalled object will also be degraded or incomplete. If the degradation is severe enough, the reconstructed object is unrecognizable. But there are many instances where human associative recall works in the presence of noisy or incomplete data. Almost every sensory input we receive is in this category. Something as simple as having a conversation in a crowded and noisy room uses our natural neural networks to perform this task with little conscious effort. Likewise, visually, we rarely see a complete picture. Even when reading highway signs or billboards, there are many distractions and imperfections that mar our vision. Highway glare and haze or weak eye glasses all conspire to scramble the visual message. Yet, we often do well in these situations because our natural neural networks perform associative recall and classification on partial or noisy sensory data.

One of the most difficult tasks to program into a computer is to recognize human faces. This is probably for the same reason that drawing a human face is one of the most challenging skills an artist can master. As humans, we are extraordinarily sensitive to the slightest nuances in facial symmetry and expression. This is because our visual neural networks have been honed since birth to use facial cues when interacting and communicating with others. Our inborn ability to get milk from our mother and to survive conflicts with our siblings depends on this fine skill of recognition. In chapter 4, I mentioned the "grandmother" cell that was supposedly a neuron buried deep in the brain which responded when a baby saw its grandmother. Though this fictitious cell is a half-joke, it has some truth to it; not that there would be such a highly specialized cell for facial recognition, but that the visual neural networks are highly trained and fine-tuned to perform high-level recognition tasks. Not only do we recognize faces that we see clearly; we also recognize faces that are half obscured, or are partly in shadow, or are seen from odd angles, even partly from behind. We are extraordinarily good at working with faulty or partial views, yet arriving at clear recognition.

Not so for electronic computers. To a computer, all faces look alike. We all have two eyes, a nose with two nostrils, two ears, and a mouth. Differences in hair color or skin tone, or the presence of facial hair, provide some of the most striking cues to identity difference. But in the absence of hair or strong pigment, facial features are very similar among all humans. Furthermore, unless a photograph is a mug shot, photos or electronic images are taken under lighting conditions and angles that vary dramatically. Trying to get a computer to recognize a face under all this variability is considered to be one of the hardest tests for artificially intelligent visual recognition systems.

Associative holographic memory is one step toward generating a visual recognition system that is able to handle the nuances of face recognition. For the next step, it is necessary to add to the image correlator an element that makes decisions. Decision making, as we learned in chapter 3, requires non-linearity. When combined with feedback, this makes it possible for neural networks to eliminate wrong possibilities and provide clear identification. When this is done, not only does a perfect input elicit a perfect response, but any partial input will work as well, as long as enough information is present to allow the identification to be unambiguous.

It took only a year or two after John Hopfield published his seminal paper on neural networks in 1982 before optical scientists recognized the parallels between the massive interconnection properties of holograms and the interconnections of neural synapses in neural networks. Furthermore, the extensive parallelism of optical interconnects could be implemented with optoelectronic devices that could provide the necessary non-linear neuron responses. Dmitri Psaltis, a physicist at CalTech in Pasadena, and his group were among the first to implement the Hopfield model, using light-emitting diodes and photodiode detector arrays, in 1984. They quickly extended their work to combine holographically defined synaptic weights with non-linear thresholding.

The holographic neural network of Psaltis's group performed image associative recall and classification using the linear correlation properties of holograms, and non-linear decision-making elements in a feedback loop. This holographic neural network worked on the basis of the image correlation process described as content-addressable memory with a slight alteration that used two holograms instead of one. The purpose of the experiment was to take a partial or noisy image of a face and recall the complete face from the holographic memory.

The experimental arrangement consisted of an iterative feedback loop that incorporated gain to balance the losses incurred when passing around the loop. An argon laser (that emits a bright green beam of laser light) provided the gain. The partial image to be recognized illuminated a liquid crystal light valve (LCLV). The liquid crystal light valve technology is closely related to the flat-panel displays on Sony Watchman portable TVs and computer monitors. This device acts as an optically addressed mirror to the argon beam: its reflectivity is high everywhere that the intensity of the input data is high, and is low where the input data is dark. On the first trip around the loop, this optically written mirror did nothing more than impart the input information onto the reflected argon laser beam.

The image carried by the reflected laser beam was transformed by a lens into its spatial frequency spectrum, and hit the first hologram, which stored several different faces. The operation of the first hologram was identical to the operation of image correlation. The target image diffracted from the hologram and was transformed by a lens to produce a bright spot at the correlation plane. The stored image that most closely resembled the input image had the brightest spot. Up to this point, only *linear* correlation had been performed.

The *non*-linear thresholding process occurred in the second half of the loop where the bright spots at the correlation plane were transformed by a second lens onto the second hologram that was nominally the same as the first hologram. The diffracted information from the second hologram was transformed one last time by a lens into a superposition of all the stored images, but weighted by the intensity of the correlation spots of the first correlation process. The stored image that best matched the input image was brightest in the output of the second hologram. This is where the non-linear part of the process began.

The superposed recalled images, with the best matched image as the brightest, were combined with the original input image, and these collective images fell on the liquid crystal light valve. When the intensities of the correlated images were combined with the original image intensity, the brightest correlated image reinforced the intensity of the original input image. Therefore, on the second time around the loop, the original incomplete image had been augmented by features of the whole image stored in the holograms. There was still some contamination, or cross-talk, from the other incorrectly recalled images; but these contributions were small, and got smaller on each consecutive round trip. Finally, after only a few iterations, the image reflected from the liquid crystal light valve was the complete recalled image.

Psaltis's holographic optical neural network created a considerable stir at the end of the eighties. It succeeded in demonstrating how concepts of neural networks could be combined with visual image recognition using the full advantage of optical parallelism. As a proof of principle, it was a tour de force that changed how people thought of optics and holography. On the other hand, the non-linear thresholding device was slow and represented a bottleneck for the operation of the neural network. Furthermore, the fixed holographic memory required a separate and slow hologram recording process.

For these reasons, the overall performance of the system was not up to the level of electronic systems that did the same things at that time. The advantages of parallel optical processing in neural networks were outweighed by engineering problems. The continuing challenge of such machines is to build them out of robust components that are reliable and inexpensive.

We are still waiting for this technology to gain an economic foothold with incentives for constant improvement. But in some ways, the door has already opened. For instance, in the machines of the second generation, holographic optical memory is only one of the two primary functions of an optical computer. The second, equally important function of any computer is processing. It is possible to have holograms that act as image-processing units, avoiding optoelectronic devices like the liquid crystal light valve. Crystals called dynamic holographic materials make this possible.

MOVING HOLOGRAMS

To tap the full potential of holography for optical control and processing, it is necessary to go beyond the static hologram. All the previous examples of holographic reconstruction used a material (like Kodak film) that had been exposed and developed into a permanent hologram. The static hologram is a good example of optical memory, but we would also like to use holography as a way to process light and images in real time. By this, I mean that the recording and readout should be occurring at the same time—*and all the time*. If the image information on the beams is changing, then the hologram should change to match it.

Continuous real-time holography, called dynamic holography, is performed using non-linear optical crystals. The only difference from the previous examples of holographic memory/readout is that the recording beams and the readout beams are present all at the same time. A dynamic hologram is generated by a transient change in the crystal's optical properties in response to the periodic stripes of high and low intensity generated by the interfering beams. If the interference patterns move, the material responds accordingly with moving optical gratings. One important difference between static holography and dynamic holography is that the dynamic hologram adapts in real time to variations in the optical beams. This makes it possible to compensate for changes that might arise due to mechanical vibrations or thermal changes in the optical system. This adaptive ability is also a key aspect of holographic neural networks that adapt and learn—but more of this later.

The important improvement we gain by using a non-linear optical crystal to record holograms is the ability to compensate for a turbulent environment that vibrates and drifts ceaselessly. Because light is so sensitive to minor changes in path length (remember the interferometer), most interferometric devices need to be carefully isolated from their environments, at considerable cost in optical hardware and engineering. Dynamic holography provides a solution by replacing static beamsplitters with dynamic holographic gratings. The path lengths are kept fixed by the dynamic hologram as it adjusts and adapts to the changes caused by thermal expansion or vibration, making the interferometer insensitive to mechanical vibrations or shocks.

The dynamic response of these holograms also benefits time-reversal mirrors. The previous example of time reversal used a static hologram, but the reversal is perfect only if the reflected reference beam is perfect. In real applications, laser beams are constantly being buffeted by a noisy environment. Furthermore, the time-reversed object beam might be the right beam for the object at the time when the hologram was recorded, but the object might have changed during the time of the recording and development of the hologram, making the static hologram obsolete. But if the hologram is constantly being written and updated as the object moves and sways in the breeze, the time-reversal mirror will always send back a perfect time-reversed beam.

This has a particular advantage when looking through turbulent media. Any turbulent fluid can prevent imaging. For instance, telescopes have difficulty seeing through our atmosphere, either to image astronomical objects, or to transmit laser communications to orbiting communications satellites. Turbulence causes stars to twinkle at night, and makes the sky blue and sunsets red. Atmospheric turbulence is why the Hubble telescope flies above the atmosphere to get the most dramatic images ever of our universe.

Adaptive time-reversal mirrors fix these problems. As such, time-reversal mirrors are part of the field of adaptive optics, which covers a broad range of optical systems designed to conform to changing environments. Many of these systems have sensors and actuators connected by feedback electronics to move optical components, such as mirrors or lenses, that compensate for time-varying changes in image quality. In sophisticated telescope systems, a large mirror can be segmented to enable the actuators to move each segment separately. Such mirrors are called "rubber mirrors" because of their flexibility. Using adaptive optics and rubber mirrors, land-based telescopes will someday be able to acquire images almost as good as the Hubble, at considerably less cost.

In contrast, the time-reversal mirror belongs to a different class of adaptive optics that requires no active feedback or complicated software to drive it. The time-reversal mirrors are "self-adaptive." Appropriate changes in the hologram occur automatically as the signal interferes with the reference beam and impresses this interference onto the hologram. Specialized time-reversal mirrors already have been commercialized as components in self-aligning laser cavities, and dynamic holographic gratings play key roles in adaptive interferometers.

THE DREAMING MACHINE

Around 1984, when Psaltis's group at CalTech was pursuing optoelectronic approaches to optical neural networks, an intensely imaginative assistant professor by the name of Dana Anderson had newly arrived at the University of Colorado. He was struck by the similarity between competitive learning in neural networks and the competition among laser modes that takes place inside a laser resonator. As discussed, lasers have many modes that all oscillate inside a laser cavity. Getting these modes to cooperate produces ultra-fast pulses with picosecond and femtosecond pulse durations. But laser media can also have competition among modes, rather than cooperation, as they compete for net gain. The competition causes one mode to win out and suppress the oscillations of the other modes. Anderson realized that this behavior of laser mode competition is analogous to competition among neurons. Furthermore, because an optical resonator can support images, a mode can be an image. In this way, images can interact and compete directly.

By drawing on the massively parallel interconnection properties of holograms, just as Psaltis was doing at that same time, Anderson made the analogy between competing laser modes and neurons more explicit. He constructed a ring resonator that used a holographic storage medium for the neural interconnections, and a photorefractive crystal called barium titanate as a dynamic hologram to provide the gain for which the resonator modes would compete. The resulting resonator was not a laser; but it shared many of the same dynamics, including mode competition.

Each of the many resonator modes interacted with the pump beam to write individual dynamic gratings inside the gain crystal. The individual gratings redirected energy from the pump beam into their specific mode, amplifying it for the next pass around the feedback loop. As one mode became more intense, through a random intensity fluctuation, its dynamic grating grew stronger, deflecting more of the pump beam into that mode, and robbing energy from the other modes. The process iterated until only a single mode received all the pump beam energy. This type of competition is called winner-take-all because only a single mode survives.

In the absence of any input, this resonator had the peculiar habit of "dreaming." Even though one mode would win at a time, its supremacy was constantly being challenged by the other suppressed modes. Slight drifts in the temperature of the resonator, or intensity fluctuations caused by dust particles in the laser beams, would constantly be trying to unseat the winning mode. Sometimes, these perturbations would be sufficient, or fast enough, that the dynamic hologram of the winning mode was unable to track them, and the grating of a usurper would suddenly get the lion's share of the pump beam energy and become the new king of the modes.

The output of such a resonator behaves like a person dreaming. If there are many different holograms stored in the holographic memory, the output of the resonator randomly recalls one, then another—like dreaming, drifting undirected through the day's experiences.

However, when a partial image was injected actively into the resonator, the mode that best matched the input quickly gained superiority over the other modes. If the injected information was ambiguous, matching more than one mode, then the system randomly switched among those modes, but not among the others that did not match. The recall therefore reflected the ambiguity of the input, while still eliminating the bad matches.

This work was important for three reasons. First, it equated the natural resonances of optical cavities with the natural responses of neural networks. Second, it moved optical neural networks into the all-optical regime, requiring no optoelectronic interfaces. The dynamic holograms in the photorefractive crystal provided the decision-making non-linear threshold for the winning mode. The third new twist introduced by the experiment was the emergence of natural behavior. It was not only that the system could dream, but also that new modes (images) that were never stored in the holographic memory could emerge. The system therefore exhibited a degree of creativity. It thought up answers that had not been preprogrammed into the holographic memory. The creative behavior of this optical apparatus, which is merely a collection of a few inanimate optics, raises an interesting question about whether human creativity and intuition is somehow connected to our ability to dream.

More sophisticated demonstrations that expanded the capabilities of these dynamic holographic neural networks followed Anderson's initial work. The winner-take-all strategy of the first experiment was expanded into a paradigm of local mode competition that used dynamic holographic crystals inside stand-alone modules. Successive applications began to use these modules as discrete components in a form of optical circuit board, just as transistors and capacitors are combined inside special purpose integrated circuit modules. Miniaturization of the modules also took place, and free-space propagation was in some cases replaced with fiber optics, making the systems more compact and economical.

Other applications expanded as well. Using the concepts of mode competition and modular design, devices were constructed that could perform as optical spectrum analyzers that could break apart the spectrum of a symphony; as speckle demultiplexers for multiple data signals transmitted down multimode fibers; as sequence generators that could step through an ordered set of modes or images; and as optical delay lines that were used in neural networks for voice recognition.

The growing number of imaginative demonstrations using these concepts and modules has sustained an excitement about the capabilities of adaptive holograms. These applications operate fundamentally with images, including speckle fields, that are fully parallel data structures that tap directly into the Parallel Advantage of Light and Image. The improving modularity of the devices is also forming the basis of a new Architecture of Light. Architecture requires forms with distinct functions that are assembled in a system with complex structure and behavior. The modules are beginning to provide those distinct functions, and the assembly of the modules into systems is the beginning of overarching and unifying principles of design.

EVEN PLENTY OF ROOM CAN EVENTUALLY BE FILLED

With such bright potential from these image machines, combined with the imminent arrival of the all-optical Internet, we seem poised in the entryway to the second generation of the machines of light. But many of the proof-of-principle demonstrations that I have described are already ancient history. Anderson's and Psaltis's optical neural networks first operated over fifteen years ago. At the time, it looked as if the inauguration of such networks into specialized market niches was imminent. The benefits of optics over electronic computers were clear. But as is well known, Moore's Law has pushed the performance of silicon-based computers far beyond where they were in the mid-1980s. The technology of silicon has tremendous momentum—enough to keep the technology doubling every eighteen months. It is therefore a moving target that optical computing has had difficulty overtaking. That is about to change.

The speed of personal computers has already begun to taper off as of the writing of this book. Although processor speeds continue to increase along the path ordained by Moore, and gigahertz machines have been introduced into the market, there is a growing bottleneck inside the computer architecture that is strangling the benefits of fast clock speeds. Getting information from cache memory to the processing unit is the bottleneck that has already forced the speed of software bench tests to veer off the exponential slope of Moore's Law. The processor, though capable of great speed, has to idle while it waits for the information it needs to do its next operation. This will become an increasing problem if Moore's Law keeps going. Some solutions are already being explored by the silicon computer architects, such as multi-threading, which is a tactic to anticipate what information the processor will need, not for the next operation, but down the road, and getting that information into fast memory where the processor can quickly access it. But even this strategy is only a stopgap. There is a much more fundamental bottleneck.

If you project Moore's Law for transistor size into the future, and count how many electrons are needed to switch a single device, you find that by the year 2020, a transistor should operate on only a single electron. I do not believe we will have large-scale silicon processors operating with single electron transistors by that time. Whole new technologies would need to mature and match the exponential trends of silicon to make that happen. Even though thousands of scientists and engineers are trying hard to make this happen, there are problems facing the electronics industry that are every bit as difficult as the technological problems facing optical computing. Therefore, silicon's momentum must slow, and the slack will be taken up by optics. The machines of light of the second generation will face, for the first time in thirty years, a level playing field. And just as light-in-the-box marries the best features of light and electronics inside digital computers, I predict that electrons-in-the-light-beam will combine the strong electron interactions with the parallelism of the image.

A tantalizing scenario is emerging that pushes both optics and nanoelectronics to their very limits—in quantum devices. The single-electron transistor will by necessity be governed by quantum effects. Why not use that to advantage? In the new quantum generation, photons and electrons will collaborate as equals when they leave the classical world and enter into the strange and powerful world of quantum communication and computation. This is the new frontier where optics and electronics merge into the machines of light of the third generation—the Quantum Optical Generation.

9 The Age of Entanglement

Quantum Teleportation and Cryptography

" . . . BECAUSE NATURE ISN'T CLASSICAL, DAMMIT . . ."
Richard Feynman, 1981

Quantum mechanics is a venerable field of study. The year 2000 marked the one hundredth anniversary of the original quantum hypothesis proposed by Max Planck in November 1900. Few current fields in physics or engineering are as old as quantum mechanics. It predates relativity, both special and general. It predates nuclear and particle physics. Quantum mechanics even predates universal acceptance of the molecular hypothesis, that is, that all matter is made up of individual molecules in thermal motion. It may be hard to believe, but this happened only after Einstein's paper on Brownian motion was published in his miracle year 1905.

Quantum mechanics was a topic of study long before the beginnings of modern solid-state physics, and indeed quantum theory formed the basis of the modern theory of solids. All of modern electronics, with its semiconductor chips and computers, is a younger field of study than quantum mechanics. At the time of Planck's announcement, no one knew that the Milky Way was a galaxy of stars. Nor did anyone realize that the so-called nebulae were other galaxies in a vast universe of galaxies. The discovery of the expanding universe by Edwin Hubble (1889–1953) happened decades after Planck's announcement in Berlin, and evidence for the Big Bang came only several decades after that. All in all, most of the fields of physics that hold our attention today are upstarts in comparison to quantum mechanics.

If quantum mechanics is so old and mature, why is it the focus of so much attention? When we read late-breaking science news in popular magazines, quantum devices are in the headlines, including the recent fervor about quantum communication and computation. For such an old field of study, one for which *all* theoretical aspects have long ago been verified experimentally, why does it hold onto popular imagination so strongly?

The answer is not that quantum mechanics is unintuitive. Ask any college freshmen taking introductory physics whether they think physics is intuitive, and they will fill your ears with exasperation and frustration at the seemingly unintuitive subject. Even seasoned physicists are often stumped and surprised by ordinary physics. Systems as well understood as electromagnetics or old-fashioned mechanics can be unintuitive. Spinning tops or collections of magnets can raise hour-long debates among highly educated and savvy physicists.

In the Physics Department at Purdue University, I can usually be found between 9:30 and 10:00 a.m. attending Professor Ramdas's Coffee Club in the Solid State Library down the hall from my office. This is a loose group of nuclear, high-energy, and solid-state physicists. We have both theorists and experimentalists among our members. One of the coffee club members, Marty Becker, is an emeritus who travels around Indiana giving physics shows to schoolchildren. He is always coming to coffee with bars and rods, balls and magnets, pails of water, or whatever, all parts of demonstrations he is developing for his show. Without fail, his demonstrations— all of them fundamental in nature and certainly classical—raise energetic arguments among the attendees. It is not unusual for there to be as many conflicting explanations of the phenomena as there are people in the room. Classical physics is largely unintuitive to us all. Quantum mechanics, in this sense, is just as unintuitive. Therefore, it isn't that quantum behavior is unintuitive. It is that it is so utterly implausible.

The physical behavior of extremely lightweight particles, like electrons and protons, defies Aristotelian logic. The logical problems of quantum mechanics are not even that deep. They run into trouble right at the beginning of Philosophy 101 with an apparently obvious tautology: an electron is *either* a particle, *or* it is not a particle. This sentence is clearly true. But in quantum mechanics, I can also make the following true statement: an electron *is* a particle, *and* it is *not* a particle. This sentence is a contradiction in classical logic (violating the proposition $\{\vdash \cdot \sim (p \cdot \sim p)\}$ in the notation of Russell and Whitehead), but it lies at the core of quantum behavior.

For indeed, an electron is a particle, and it is not a particle. It is a wave, and it is not a wave. It is found precisely where you observe it to be, yet it is nowhere before you observe it. You can know its momentum to infinite accuracy, yet only at the price of not knowing where it is. You can equally well pin it down precisely inside an atom, yet its momentum can take almost any value at all . . . . Every statement seems to be either a contradiction or a restriction. This is quantum mechanics! It is not the fact that quantum mechanics is unintuitive that gives it its allure, but that it lives in states that cannot logically exist.

But they do exist. It is an unassailable fact that every prediction of quantum theory has been experimentally verified, to date. There are no stones unturned. Every system, from solids to liquids to gases to plasmas to high-energy particles, bears out every aspect of quantum theory. Quantum mechanics is one of the most thoroughly tested theories in physics, and it has passed every test flawlessly. Therefore, its logical implausibility, though a nuisance to philosophers, causes no trouble for the practicing physicist. We take the laws of quantum theory, derive their consequences, and look for those consequences in the laboratory.

So we can say without fear of contradiction that quantum measurements performed on particles on our side of the universe instantaneously affect the outcome of experiments performed on particles on the other side of the universe. Unbelievable! We further assert that a quantum computer can simultaneously compute the answer to a million questions all at the same time, by performing only a single computation. Audacious! Let's see how it is done.

INTERFERING PHOTONS

It is always best to start with those things with which we are most familiar. Before describing the quantum behavior of light, I shall begin with the interference of coherent light, which has been discussed in several applications in the preceding chapters. We will see that much of what we understand about classical light (light made up of electromagnetic waves) can be used with only slight modification when we begin to talk about the quantum of light—the photon. For instance, we saw that interference of light inside non-linear interferometers will allow light to control light in the all-optical Internet. And interference inside holographic crystals is the origin of imaging computers that use the full parallelism of visual images. Interference in these examples occurs because waves satisfy the *principle of linear superposition,* which says that any wave can be described as a sum of individual waves. For light, the electric fields of individual waves add together to produce a resultant wave that experiences constructive or destructive interference. The interference of light waves is our point of departure as we begin our discussion of quantum optical machines.

Long before Dennis Gabor thought of holography, the ingenious Thomas Young devised a simple and elegant experiment that demonstrated the wave nature of light. Young (1773–1829) was an English physician and physicist who, in his spare time, helped decipher the Rosetta stone and demonstrate once and for all that Egyptian hieroglyphics were phonographic in nature, shattering the romantic notion that the magic symbols could be an instance of Leibniz's universal "character." As a physician, his principal interest was in the physics of visual perception. He was the first to measure the change in curvature of the eye as it focused at different distances, and he discovered the cause of astigmatism. The three-color theory of color perception—that only the colors of red, green, and blue are needed to perceive all the colors of the rainbow, which is the basis for every color computer screen today—was also one of Young's significant accomplishments.

It was through his interest in the perception of light that he came to study the effects of light passing through tiny holes in opaque screens. When he passed light through two such holes and allowed the light transmitted from each to overlap on a distant screen, he observed bands of light alternating with bands of darkness. This was an astounding discovery that defied perceived commonsense at the time: that light added to light could produce darkness. Yet it is precisely this interference effect that I employed to describe holography in the last chapter. Young was able to explain the effect as a consequence of the wave nature of light. He went on to explain the colors of soap films based on this theory, as well as to explain polarization of light waves. Despite his genius, he was disparaged by the professional English physicists of his time, principally because Isaac Newton had proposed that light was composed of particles. In England, to disagree with Newton was sacrilege and heretical. On the other hand, the Continental physicists were not so loathe to debunk Newton, and Young's work gained wider acceptance after work by the French physicist Augustin-Jean Fresnel (1788–1827) confirmed his hypothesis.

An idealized experimental arrangement of Young's double pinhole experiment has a single pinhole that emits light of a pure color and illuminates two pinholes situated a small distance apart in an opaque screen. The light emitted from each pinhole illuminates a distant viewing screen, and the field of illumination of each hole overlaps with the other. On the observing screen, bands of light alternate with bands of darkness, demonstrating the coherent interference of the light coming from both pinholes. A bright band on the screen is obtained when the difference in the distances from the two holes allows the waves to add constructively. Conversely, a dark band on the screen is obtained when the difference in the distances from the two holes allows the wave amplitudes from each pinhole to subtract to produce destructive interference. If either pinhole is blocked by an opaque obstruction, the interference pattern disappears and is replaced by an even illumination from the unobstructed pinhole.

Up to this point, the discussion has been purely classical. But now we do a simple experiment to take us out of the classical regime and into the quantum realm. We reduce the intensity of the source so that it becomes extremely weak—much weaker even than moonlight. At this stage, we need to relate the intensity of light to the flux of photons. A light beam is a stream of individual photons, like drops of rain falling in a summer shower. In the pinhole experiment, we can reduce the intensity of the source so low that there can only be a single photon in flight at a time between the source and the observation screen. We replace the screen with a photo-sensitive plate that records the arrival of photons, allowing the photon hits to accumulate over time on the plate. This plate is analogous to the photodetector used in your digital camera.

When we turn on the experiment, the photo plate responds at the positions hit by a photon. After only several photons have been detected, the photo plate may look like a set of random spots. No discernible pattern of bright and dark bands can be seen. As we continue the experiment, the spots start to clump, and there are the beginnings of a pattern, but it is still rough. After continuing for a longer time, the photo plate has bands of bright and dark and begins to look like the expected bright and dark fringes that we see in the classical experiment.

This new version of the experiment is fully in the quantum domain. The light travels as photons and arrives at the photo-plate as photons. The photo plate responds at specific positions that are hit by single photons. There is no room in this description for classical electromagnetic waves, nor even for the interference of electric fields. The absence of classical interference is made clear by the conditions of the experiment, which allow only a single photon to be in flight between the source and the screen at a time. Since only one photon is present, its electric field neither adds constructively to, nor subtracts destructively from, the electric field of any other photon. Yet the interference pattern slowly develops on the photo plate, just as in the classical interference experiment. Where does this interference pattern come from if the photons cannot interfere with each other?

The quantum answer is that the photon interferes with itself: an answer that warrants considerable discussion. Though the photon has an electric field associated with it, we cannot view the quantum experiment as an interference of the electric field of the photon with its own electric field. Instead, something else must be interfering to generate the interference pattern that we see accumulating on the photo plate. To understand what is interfering, we need first to understand something of quantum wave mechanics.

WAVE MECHANICS

Wave mechanics for quantum systems was developed in 1927 by Erwin Schrödinger (1887–1961) (at age forty). Schrödinger was able to show that the behavior of quantum particles could be understood as special functions, called wavefunctions, that obeyed a straightforward wave equation that came to bear his name. The result of this theory was an understanding that, in the quantum world, particles behave like packets of waves. This is the famous wave-particle duality that has so perplexed quantum philosophers—how best to understand objects that are both particles and waves at the same time.

The meaning of the wavefunction of an elementary particle, like an electron, was not initially obvious. That interpretation was supplied by Max Born (1882–1970), a German theoretical physicist at the University of Göttingen. He suggested that the squared amplitude of a quantum wavefunction at a place and an instant in time is proportional to the probability for finding an electron at that place and time. This interpretation was radical—equally as radical as the original quantum hypothesis. Whereas the wavefunction of an electron could be accurately and uniquely specified, the electron's location could only be predicted with a probability governed by the amplitude of the wavefunction.

If you take a hundred atoms, all in exactly the same quantum state (that is, the electrons of each atom are all described by the same wavefunction), and measure the positions of the electrons in each of them, you will get a hundred different answers. But if you continue preparing more atoms in identical states and measure those, you will slowly build up a distribution of electron positions that tend to cluster close to the nucleus of the atom. With enough measurements on enough atoms, you will eventually have a smooth distribution of electron positions that exactly match the squared amplitude of the electron wavefunction for that quantum state. The important feature of this description is the difference between where the electron is *before* the measurement, and where the electron was found *during* a single measurement.

The wavefunction for an electron is a well-defined smooth function of position. At any radius away from the atom nucleus, there is some value for the wavefunction. We therefore say that an electron *occupies* this wavefunction, meaning that the electron is simultaneously everywhere where the wavefunction has some non-zero value. In this sense, an electron surrounds the nucleus all the time. But in the act of measurement, let us say a measurement of the position of an electron using a microscopic probe of some kind, a single electron must be found at only a single location.

Photon wavefunctions behave in the same way. When Young's apparatus contains only a single photon, that photon is governed by a single wavefunction. The wavefunction fills all the space inside the apparatus, just as the electron wavefunction filled all space around the nucleus of the atom. Part of the wavefunction passes through one pinhole, and part of the same wavefunction passes through the other. When these parts of the wavefunction overlap on the screen, the amplitudes of the wavefunction add and subtract in just the way that the electric fields of classical light waves would. When the path length differences make the crests and troughs of the wavefunctions line up, constructive interference occurs, and the squared amplitude of the quantum wavefunction is a maximum. Using Born's interpretation, this means that there is a high probability to detect the photon at this location. On the other hand, in regions of destructive interference, the squared amplitude of the photon wavefunction vanishes, as does any chance to observe the photon at that position.

You will note that the quantum theory gives the same answer as the classical theory. It looks like a sleight of hand to say that a photon is governed by an interfering probability wave, while at the same time classical interference of the light fields produces exactly the same intensity pattern. This starts to look like a metaphysical question. If the quantum theory predicts an outcome that is identical to classical theory, do we really care? And more important, can the quantum theory predict any behavior that is impossible classically? The answer is yes—in volumes! The entire field of quantum information rests on specific differences between classical and quantum behavior. To illustrate the unnatural quantum behavior of photons, I turn to a process known as "quantum seeing in the dark."

"QUANTUM SEEING IN THE DARK"

In your mind's eye, envision a diabolical terrorist who places Young's apparatus in a crowded theater. Inside the apparatus there may be (or may not be) a bomb that will detonate any time it is hit by a photon. If the bomb is there, it is placed behind one of the pinholes. As a member of the Quantum Bomb Squad, you are called in to determine whether the apparatus contains the bomb or not. Your goal is to detect the presence of the bomb without detonating it. However, all you can use to detect the bomb is a source of photons. How would you use photons to detect a photo-sensitive bomb without detonating it? If you shine photons (let's say by opening the apparatus) on the bomb to see if it is there, then it will go off and you lose your job (if not your life). But if you were a good quantum student in school and have full faith in the Born interpretation of the quantum wavefunction, you devise a way of using quantum interference to detect the bomb without detonating it, at least with odds you are willing to live with. This is what you do.

Take the apparatus, turn on the photo plate, and then hold your breath as you send in a single photon from the source. The single photon can pass either through the open hole, or through the hole with the bomb behind it. It will do either with a 50 percent probability. If it passes through the hole with the bomb, then it detonates, destroying valuable property, and you lose your job on the Quantum Bomb Squad. On the other hand, if it passes through the open hole, it will register a flash on the photo plate. This is where your understanding of quantum mechanics is crucial.

If the photon hits a location on the photo plate that would be inaccessible when *both* pinholes were clear, that is, a position of destructive interference caused by the wavefunction interference from the two pinholes, then the bomb must be present and you should evacuate the theater. In this result, *you* have detected the bomb with a photon, yet the *bomb* detected no photon because it passed through the other pinhole. How does the photon detect the bomb without detonating it, or even touching it? The answer is that the photon wavefunction extends throughout the apparatus. If the bomb is blocking the pinhole, it also blocks the photon wavefunction and prevents interference at the photo plate. Therefore, blocking the wavefunction is not the same as blocking the photon itself. The wavefunction just determines where the photon is *likely* to go.

Unfortunately, the odds are not great that the photon will hit exactly at a location of complete destructive interference. It is more likely that the result will be ambiguous (by hitting in a location that would be accessible whether the pinhole is blocked or not). Then you will need to send in another photon, with another 50 percent chance of detonation. And if that result is ambiguous, you need to send in yet another photon, until you are most surely going to need to find a new job. Fortunately for you, there are higher-probability ways of detecting bombs in the dark.

One way is to replace Young's apparatus with a simple interferometer composed of a half-silvered beamsplitter, two mirrors, and a photodetector. This configuration uses the beamsplitter to split the possible photon paths. When photons hit the beamsplitter, they either continue traveling to the right, or are deflected upwards. After reflecting off the mirrors, the photons again encounter the beamsplitter, where, in each case, they continue undeflected or are reflected. The result is that two paths combine at the beamsplitter to travel to the detector, while two other paths combine to travel back along the direction of the incident beam.

The paths of the light beams can be adjusted so that the beams combining to travel to the detector experience perfect destructive interference. In this situation, the detector never detects light, and all the light returns back along the direction of the incident beam. Quantum mechanically, when only a single photon is present in the interferometer at a time, we would say that the quantum wavefunction of the photon interferes destructively along the path to the detector, and constructively along the path opposite to the incident beam. It is clear that the unobstructed path of both beams results in the detector making no detections.

Now place the light-sensitive bomb in the upper path. Because this path is no longer available to the photon wavefunction, the destructive interference of the wavefunction along the detector path is removed. So, when a single photon is sent into the interferometer, three possible things can happen. One, the photon is reflected by the beamsplitter and detonates the bomb. Two, the photon is transmitted by the beamsplitter, reflects off the right mirror, and is transmitted again by the beamsplitter to travel back down the incident path without being detected by the detector. Three, the photon is transmitted by the beamsplitter, reflects off the right mirror, and is reflected off the beamsplitter to be detected by the detector.

In this third case, the photon is detected *and* the bomb does *not* go off, so that you have succeeded at "quantum seeing in the dark." The odds, now, are much better than for Young's experiment. If the bomb is present, it will detonate a maximum of 50 percent of the time. The other 50 percent, you will either detect a photon (signifying the presence of the bomb), or else you will not detect a photon (giving an ambiguous answer and requiring you to perform the experiment again). When you perform the experiment again, you again have a 50 percent chance of detonating the bomb, and a 25 percent chance of detecting it without it detonating, but again a 25 percent chance of not detecting it, and so forth. You keep sending in photons until you have either detonated the bomb, or detected it. Your chances of success in the end are one in three. These are much better odds than for Young's apparatus, where only exact detection of the photon at a forbidden location would signify the presence of the bomb.

It is possible to increase your odds even above one chance in three. You do this by decreasing the reflectivity of the beamsplitter. In practice, this is easy to do simply by depositing less and less silver on the surface of the glass plate. When the reflectivity gets very low, let us say at the level of 1 percent, then most of the time the photon just travels back along the direction it came and you have an ambiguous result. On the other hand, when the photon does not return, there is an equal probability of detonation as of detection. This means that, though you may send in many photons, your odds for eventually seeing the bomb without detonating it are nearly 50 percent.

These are about the best odds you are going to get, but it is impressive in itself. To be able to "see" something without ever having the photon "touch" it is only possible in a quantum world. This serves to illustrate how one must reason when dealing with quantum systems. Next, we need to understand a physical property of photons called photon polarization, because quantum information can be stored in the two orthogonal polarizations of light.

PHOTON POLARIZATION

One of Thomas Young's innumerable contributions to physics was the idea of polarization. He correctly understood that the electric field of light has an orientation perpendicular to the direction of propagation. When the electric field points in a constant direction, say in the vertical direction, or along a 45° diagonal, we say that the light has linear polarization.

In a plane, there are always two mutually orthogonal (right-angle) directions, like the x and y axes pointing in the horizontal and vertical directions. Any linearly polarized wave can be expressed as the sum of two polarizations that point along these two mutually orthogonal axes. What you call "vertical" or "horizontal" is actually your choice. For instance, you could call a line making a +45° angle the "vertical" axis relative to a line making a -45° angle that you would call "horizontal." The choice of a direction changes only how you describe the wave's polarization—it cannot change the actual physical state of the wave. This is an important feature of all physics. It is a form of relativity. Your choice of a coordinate frame, even the frame's orientation, cannot alter the physics. We are free to choose and define any axis as "vertical," and the orthogonal axis as "horizontal." Any choice is arbitrary, yet equally valid as a way of describing the electric field or the wave.

When we stop thinking of light as classical electromagnetic waves and think instead of photons, the notion of polarization remains, but the interpretation changes. A photon has a polarization just like a classical light wave, but the polarization now is associated with the photon wavefunction. If a photon is originally polarized at an angle relative to the horizontal, we say that the wavefunction is a linear combination of *two* wavefunctions describing two *different* photons, one that has a polarization along the vertical and another that has a polarization along the horizontal.

Nature has provided us with an ideal method for separating a flux of photons into the ones polarized along the vertical from the others polarized along the horizontal. This is accomplished using a crystal of calcite that has the chemical name of calcium carbonate. It is the most common constituent of limestone and marble. In its pure crystalline form, it is transparent and colorless, and is noted for its property of double refraction; anything you look at through the crystal has a double image. This is because natural light has equal amounts of orthogonal polarizations, and the calcite crystal directs light of the two polarizations along two different directions that leave the crystal in two different locations, called the H and V "ports" (for horizontally and vertically polarized photons).

The calcite crystal is known as a polarization analyzer. It takes any input beam and breaks it down into its vertical and horizontal components. As an optical device, we say that it has one input port and two exit ports. Detectors are placed at both of the exit ports. If the crystal is very pure, none of the light energy is absorbed, and all of the light is detected. For a classical light wave with a polarization angled at 45° relative to the horizontal axis, half of the intensity is detected in the V port, and half is detected in the H port, because the electric field of the photon has equal parts of V and H.

Now let's consider the quantum behavior of the calcite when we send in a single photon polarized at 45°. In the quantum case, the entire photon emerges whole from either one port or the other, but never both ports, and never as a fraction of a photon. A photon with a polarization of 45° is a superposition of two different photons, one with a vertical polarization and one with a horizontal polarization. The photon has a 50 percent probability of exiting the V port, and a 50 percent probability of exiting the H port. If it exits from the H port, it has 100 percent H polarization. Similarly, if it exits from the V port, it has 100 percent V polarization.

When we consider the action of the calcite crystal on a single photon, we may ask an apparently simple question: Does the crystal simply observe the polarization of the photon, or does it modify it by rotating its polarization? Let us assume, for the moment, that the second option is true, that the crystal modifies the photon. Many materials rotate the polarization of a light beam. For instance, a solution of corn syrup rotates the polarization of a light beam as it propagates through the liquid by a process known as optical activity. Corn syrup is optically active because the sugar molecules, called dextrose, in the syrup have only a right-handedness. Light polarizes the dextrose molecules, and the re-radiated light field is rotated slightly to the right. This effect accumulates over distance into a macroscopic rotation of the polarization of the light beam.

With this in mind, we can try to explain the effect of the calcite crystal as polarization rotation. For a 45° polarized photon passing through a calcite crystal, the crystal either rotates the polarization right by 45°, or left by 45°. But this is not deterministic as it was in the case of the corn syrup.

For the syrup, the rotation was always to the right. In the case of the calcite, the photon polarization for a series of identical photons is rotated right for half of them (on average) and left for the other half. On any given instance, it is impossible to predict which will occur. Since the result is indeterminate, it is impossible to assign a specific physical rotation mechanism to the process. Therefore, we have no choice but to accept that calcite is *not* rotating the polarization, but rather is making a quantum observation, that is, determining whether the photon has V or H polarization.

This example illustrates *the fundamental indeterminacy of quantum mechanics.* It is impossible to predict exactly which polarization will exit the crystal for a single incident photon. This type of indeterminacy was what Einstein was unwilling to accept. He viewed such an experiment as evidence that quantum mechanics was incomplete. In this regard, it is important to make the distinction between "incomplete" and "incorrect." Einstein never considered quantum mechanics to be incorrect. He was fully aware that quantum theory accurately predicted the outcomes of quantum experiments. In fact, he was the theoretician who, using quantum theory, correctly predicted many of those outcomes. Einstein's argument against quantum mechanics was rather that, in those areas where it could say nothing, as in the prediction of the result of a single observation of a single quantum particle, some deeper and more complete theory *could* predict the outcome. It is in this sense that Einstein considered quantum mechanics to be incomplete.

THE EPR PARADOX

It is fitting that the most imaginative and sustained attack on the completeness of quantum theory was devised by Einstein (along with Boris Podolsky and Nathan Rosen) in the EPR paradox of 1935. The paradox was introduced briefly in chapter 2, but let's consider it here in more detail because it is the best way to understand quantum entanglement and quantum teleportation. To illustrate the paradox, I use a formulation along the lines proposed by the American physicist and quantum philosopher David Bohm (1917–1992) that is simpler to think through. This formulation begins with the self-annihilation of an atomlike entity called positronium into two photons.

Positronium is an electron bound to its antimatter pair, a positron, in a quantum state similar to that of a hydrogen atom. Unlike hydrogen (which is stable for times at least as long as the age of the universe), the electron and positron annihilate each other in a flash of energy that produces two gamma rays. The atom lives for only about a tenth of a microsecond, on average, before annihilation. When the positronium is initially at rest, and is in its ground state, the atom has no linear momentum and no angular momentum. By the law of conservation of momentum, the final state must also have no net linear or angular momentum. We therefore immediately conclude that the two photons must travel in opposite directions, carrying equal amounts of energy and momentum, and the sum of their individual angular momentums must be zero.

Now consider a thought experiment in which many individual positronium atoms sequentially self-annihilate, and the linear polarization of the two decay product photons are observed by two observers, who are located opposite each other and very far away from the source. (It has become a well-established tradition, in discussions of this sort, to give the name "Alice" to observer A and "Bob" to observer B.) We insist that the difference between the observation times must be much shorter than the time it takes for photons to travel from the source to either observer. This ensures that no information about one measurement *causally* (that is, traveling at the speed of light) affects the outcome of the other measurement.

In Bohm's thought experiment Alice and Bob each have a crystal of calcite with single-photon detectors placed at both the H and V output ports of their respective crystals. Each chooses any angle they please from observation to observation. Neither Alice nor Bob knows what the other is doing. Each chooses a large number of angles, recording in their notebooks whether the H detector or the V detector flashed for each case.

What each observer sees locally, as the experiment is progressing and as they randomly choose their measurement angle, is that whenever their H detector flashes, the V detector does not flash, and vice versa. Each photon leaves the crystal from either one port or the other, but never both and never none. The observers also note that there is equal probability for the photon to appear in the H port as the V port. In other words, their local data is extremely uninteresting; they just see a long random string of photon hits in either one detector or the other, with a 50/50 probability for each detection regardless of what angles they choose for their crystals. No other structure is visible in their data.

When the experiment is over, Alice and Bob pack up their equipment and travel back to the source to compare their seemingly random data of "H's" and "V's." To their surprise, they find that whenever they had accidentally chosen the same angles for their crystals, they got exactly the same results. If Bob saw his V detector flash, then Alice saw her V detector flash. There were never any exceptions. One way to interpret this result is that when a polarization measurement is made on one photon, the twin photon *instantly* acquires the identical polarization. The effect is instantaneous, which means that no matter how far apart the two photons are when the first measurement is made—whether they are at opposite sides of an experimental optical bench in a laboratory or at opposite sides of the universe—as soon as the first measurement is made, the second photon instantaneously has the identical polarization. This "influence," being instantaneous, must occur at speeds exceeding the speed of light. Such an "influence," or effect, is called "non-local" to contrast it with conventional forces that only exert their influence at speeds limited by the speed of light.

To banish non-locality, as well as randomness, from the interpretation of quantum theory required the existence of some unknown element that determined ahead-of-time what polarization a photon would assume during a measurement. This unknown element is called a hidden variable.

Hidden variable theories sprang up in abundance in the early days of quantum mechanics in attempts to solve the randomness and non-locality problems. One idea was that each quantum particle carried along with it some hidden variable that determined whether it would pass through the V port or the H port. Such a hidden variable would solve the non-locality problem because the photon polarizations are predetermined. Each photon would already know how their twin would pass through a polarizer and therefore would require no influence traveling faster than the speed of light to tell them. It was in the context of hidden variables that Bohm proposed his alternative EPR paradox, based on measuring polarizations. We can ask whether any of these hidden variable theories might actually be able to complete the quantum picture of reality.

This was the question asked by John Bell, a physicist working at CERN in the early 1960s. He proved, using arguments about probabilities, that all hidden variable theories (if they permitted only local interactions among particles) must be false. The proof was surprisingly simple, and produced what has come to be called the Bell inequality. Any local hidden variable theory must satisfy the inequality. Quantum systems, on the other hand, violate the inequality. Devising a physical experiment that unambiguously demonstrates a violation of Bell's inequality was a challenging prospect. The definitive demonstration came in 1981–82, when Alain Aspect and his research group at the Institut d'Optique Théorique et Appliquée, Université Paris-Sud in Paris performed a series of experiments of increasing sophistication that violated Bell's inequality with extremely high confidence. The most important aspect of these experiments, and the aspect that made them so difficult, was the need for the detection events of the two photons to be separated far enough so that no signal moving at the speed of light could travel from one side of the experiment to the other during the time of the measurements. This condition was absolutely necessary to guarantee that no local interaction (defined as an interaction limited by the speed of light) could explain the correlation between the two measurements.

The experiments by Aspect used an atomic beam of calcium atoms in excited states that radiated two photons as they fell back to their ground state. The two photons carried away polarizations in the same way as the two photons from positronium. The use of calcium instead of positronium significantly simplified the experiments because the atomic beam produced copious numbers of visible photons that are relatively easy to analyze for polarization. The initial experiment was no more complicated than the problem of measuring individual polarizations with two analyzers. Already in this case, Aspect and his team observed large deviations from Bell's inequality and hence firmly established the non-locality of quantum mechanics. However, nagging suspicions of local influences persisted among the experiment's critics, leading the researchers to devise an ingenious technique that allowed them to select the polarization angle after the photons were already in flight. These experiments continued to agree with quantum mechanics and violate Bell's inequality. Since they delayed the choice of polarization until after the photons were in flight, there was no way for the photons to have shared a local hidden variable when they were created.

The experiments unambiguously proved that *all* hidden variable theories concocted to solve the non-locality problem *are wrong*. None of them will ever give results that agree with quantum theory. The inescapable conclusion is that quantum mechanics is non-local: the instant that one measurement is performed on one member of a pair of twin photons, the other photon's quantum state is immediately known, even if that state is on the other side of the universe. This statement is provably true, as John Bell demonstrated in 1964. Once non-locality is accepted, the next most pressing question is whether this non-locality can be used to communicate faster than the speed of light. We will see that the answer to this question is "no." But we will also see that twin photons are useful for quantum communication and computation, and they provide the basis for quantum teleportation. To understand these points, we need to look closer at the quantum properties of the twins.

ENTANGLED PHOTONS

The photons from the positronium have a redundancy about them. Once Alice makes her measurement, Bob's measurement is redundant. If we know Alice's results, then we can say with certainty what Bob will see if he chooses the same angle for his crystal. Because of this redundancy, the quantum pair of photons are said to be "entangled" in a *single* quantum state. Rather than each particle having its own quantum wavefunction, both particles share a single quantum wavefunction. Performing a single measurement on a single photon already constitutes a measurement of the whole quantum wavefunction, so performing the second measurement on the second particle is not needed. If Alice sees her photon in her V port, then the vertical polarization is shared by both particles, so Bob's particle is immediately known also to have vertical polarization.

There are severe metaphysical problems that entangled pairs of particles present to philosophers. Even if the two entangled particles are separated by the diameter of the universe, they still belong to the same quantum wavefunction. In this sense, the non-locality problem is primarily the problem with a macroscopic quantum wavefunction. It is a challenge to think of a quantum wavefunction, something that is supposed to operate at atomic and subatomic scales, extending over the size of the universe. As we saw, one viewpoint is that the common polarization shared by the two particles is indeterminate until the moment of measurement. At that moment, as one particle assumes a specific property, the entangled twin instantaneously assumes the same property. This viewpoint is known as wavefunction collapse. If the wavefunction is macroscopic, extending over long distances, the common wavefunction shared by both particles collapses at the moment of measurement, regardless of who makes their measurement first.

By taking this view, we can convince ourselves that making a measurement here and now on our side of the universe instantly affects the state of the twin member of an entangled pair on the other side of the universe, regardless of any limits imposed by the speed of light. This interpretation is exactly what Einstein and his friends objected to, and exactly what hidden variable theories had attempted to dispense with. No satisfactory agreement has been reached between the pragmatists, who merrily perform their experiments free from any guilt about philosophical ramifications, and the quantum philosophers, who worry about the "real" meaning of entanglement.

From the pragmatic point of view, the instantaneous nature of wavefunction collapse does not provide a means of sending information faster than the speed of light. It is tempting to try to construct a quantum communication system in which Bob and Alice receive a steady stream of entangled particles from some central source. Bob chooses his crystal angles to be either 0° or 90°, with 0° corresponding to a "0" bit and 90° corresponding to a "1" bit. By making successive measurements on his particle, he collapses the wavefunction instantaneously at Alice's location. If he sees the photon come out of his V port, then she will also see her photon come out of her V port—that is, if she has happened to choose the same crystal angle as Bob. If she chooses a different angle, the results of her measurement are only predictable statistically.

Unfortunately, even if Bob and Alice decide ahead of time to make only 0° and 90° measurements, they cannot send information back and forth instantaneously. The local measurements made by Alice and Bob look completely random. Photons emerge half of the time out the V port and the other half of the time out of the H port. It is only when they meet to compare their results that meaning emerges from their measurements. This is not to say that no information is sent, only that the information cannot be recovered unless they meet. Alternatively, they may send auxiliary information to each other using conventional means (that travels at or below the speed of light). In fact, by sending just two additional (classical) bits of information that describe the results of their quantum measurements, it is possible to transport a whole quantum state from one location to another. This is called quantum teleportation.

QUANTUM TELEPORTATION

"Beam me up, Scotty," has echoed in pop culture since the *Star Trek* TV series first aired in the mid-60s. Captain Kirk of the Starship *Enterprise* is requesting Scotty, his chief engineer, to teleport him out of danger from the surface of some planet where he may have too boldly gone where no man had gone before. On the set of the show, it was cheaper to "beam" a body to and fro with the low budget of the original episodes than to have to animate expensive landing and launch scenes of shuttle craft. But the transporter has become etched in popular culture, and remains one of the lasting icons of science fiction. The question is: What fundamental laws of physics does teleportation violate?

Maybe none, if the teleporting speed is slower than the speed of light. The aspect that makes a teleporter look so far-fetched is the scale of the task—and issues of scale are usually issues of technology rather than fundamental problems. Given enough time, clever engineers can often tackle scale as long as the fundamental physics is allowed. Sending a man to the Moon was a project of immense scale that surely must have seemed like science fiction to writers only a century ago. With many centuries ahead of us (let us hope), perhaps the scale of teleportation will be surmounted.

Nonetheless, the scale of the problem is daunting because the human body contains something around 10^{28} atoms and nuclei, and about fifteen times that many electrons. These would all need to be transported to maintain the complete being. There is furthermore the question of the quantum states of all those particles. Would it be enough to transport the physical electrons and nuclei and place them in identical locations, or would the exact quantum states of the particles need to be preserved in order to preserve the intangible essence of the human soul? This is a point that is hotly argued.

Some say that as long as all the neural synapses are identically configured, it would not matter whether the exact quantum states were reproduced. Others argue that consciousness is a fundamentally quantum phenomenon, which would be destroyed if the quantum states were scrambled during the teleportation.

If the quantum states do matter, there is a fundamental hurdle that must be overcome to measure those quantum states and transmit the quantum information to the destination. Quantum measurement is a violent act that destroys delicate quantum superpositions. It also destroys quantum information because it projects an unknown state, which is in a superposition of states, into only *one* of those states. The "presence" of those other states in the superposition is lost forever to that quantum particle. Quantum measurement is such a disruption of quantum information that theorists were able to prove a quantum non-cloning theorem. This theorem states that it is fundamentally impossible to clone a quantum state because the act of quantum measurement would disrupt the original. This law would seem to place teleportation forever out of the reach of reality.

But there is a small loophole in the law that is just big enough to let teleportation wiggle through. The non-cloning law forbids the cloning of a particle without disrupting the original. But if the original is discarded, the law says nothing about the ability to recreate the original at the same or even a different location, leaving that possibility open. Quantum teleportation is still faced with the conundrum that the process cannot be done by direct quantum measurement. Some alternate approach must be found.

That alternate was proposed in 1993 by Charles Bennett of IBM and Gilles Brassard of the Université de Montréal with their collaborators. They showed that Alice could start with the unknown quantum state that is to be teleported, and then use an entangled pair of particles as a quantum resource. She takes one of the entangled pair, and the other is sent to Bob. Alice makes a quantum measurement of a joint property belonging to both her entangled particle and her unknown quantum state. By doing this joint measurement, the other particle of the entangled pair would assume some of the quantum properties of the original unknown quantum state. Then Alice sends two bits of information through a classical channel to Bob, telling him how to rotate his entangled particle to reconstruct the original unknown state. The beauty of this approach is that the quantum state remains unknown to both Bob and Alice, even after teleportation. Therefore, if it had been in a delicate superposition of states before teleportation, it remains in that superposition after the teleportation. Also, the process of teleportation destroys the original state when the joint properties are measured with the entangled state, thereby obeying the non-cloning theorem.

The key to quantum teleportation is the ability of Alice to perform a measurement that provides Bob with enough information to recreate the original quantum state—but without having Alice actually measure the individual properties of the unknown state. This sleight of hand is performed through a process known as a Bell State measurement, named after John Bell. This is a quantum measurement of an unorthodox kind where the joint properties of two particles are measured relative to each other, but no direct measurement of the individual properties of each particle is needed. Bob's particle collapses at the same time, but knowing this one Bell State does not tell Alice anything about the actual individual properties of the unknown state. On the other hand, this information is all that Bob needs to know to perform the rotation on his entangled particle to get the original unknown quantum state.

The schematic arrangement for quantum teleportation is shown in the Quantum Teleportation figure, p. 220 (between Einstein and Bohr). Particle 1 is the unknown state that is to be teleported to Bohr. Einstein and Bohr share an entangled pair of photons; Einstein has Particle 2 and Bohr has Particle 3. Einstein performs a Bell State measurement on the joint properties of Particles 1 and 2, projecting his unknown quantum state of Particle 1 onto the entangled Particle 2. At the instant of the measurement, Bohr's Particle 3 collapses into the same joint state as Particle 2 and 1. But Particle 3 is not yet in the exact same state as Particle 1. To put Particle 3 into the state of Particle 1, Bohr has to perform one of four possible rotations on his particle. Which rotation to make depends on the results of Einstein's Bell State measurement. Since there are four Bell states, Einstein needs to send two bits of information classically to Bohr ($2^2 = 4$). When Bohr receives whichever Bell State Einstein observed, he then knows which of the four different rotations to perform on his particle. Once he performs the rotation, his Particle 3 is identical to Particle 1 in the unknown quantum state.

After the teleportation, neither Bohr nor Einstein knows what the unknown state is. Neither the Bell State measurement nor Bohr's rotation provides them with any information about the state of the particle. Yet by the laws of quantum mechanics and entangled states, Einstein and Bohr can be certain that the particle has been successfully teleported. Because Bohr needs to know which rotation to perform, and he only gets this information from Einstein through a conventional communication channel, quantum teleportation cannot occur faster than the speed of light. Even though the wavefunction collapse of Bohr's particle is instantaneous with Einstein's Bell State measurement, no information is sent until Einstein and Bohr communicate through classical means. Quantum teleportation therefore satisfies relativity and hence causality. It also satisfies the non-cloning theorem and violates no known physical laws.

The first quantum teleportation experiments were performed in 1997 in Innsbruck, Austria, and in Rome, using non-linear optical crystals to generate entangled pairs of photons and simple beamsplitters and photon detectors to perform the Bell State measurements. In the Innsbruck experiment, the quantum state could be teleported correctly (and verified) only one time out of four. But it was a start. The challenge facing teleportation experiments is the same challenge of the *Star Trek* transporter: one of scale. Teleportation has been accomplished in the laboratory using only one or a few quantum states. Pushing the number of teleported states, and the distances over which they are being teleported, is a severe challenge. Going from one (or a few) teleported states to teleporting 10^{30} quantum states of the human body may be beyond reach. The data rate for such teleportation, even if it took an entire century to transmit all the quantum information of a single human body, would still be a data rate in excess of 10^{20} bits per second. Comparing this data rate to the simple *classical* rate of 10^{12} bits

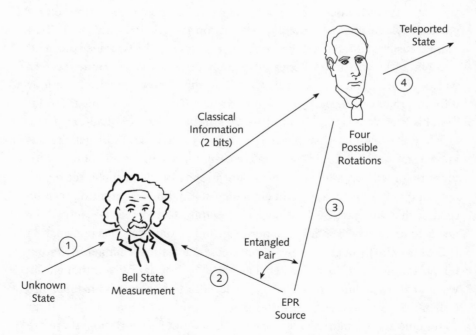

QUANTUM TELEPORTATION

per second we are struggling with today tells us it would take about the age of the universe to teleport a single human. Even with incredible improvements in data rates, teleportation of people does not look promising.

On the other hand, setting our sights on teleporting a human is probably not the best use of the technology. Quantum information contained in small systems of a few particles has potential that goes far beyond classical information. A small ensemble of quantum particles can be in a superposition of hundreds or thousands of quantum states all at the same time. Transporting these states using quantum teleportation therefore becomes an important resource, especially for a quantum computer. Teleportation can become the data bus that ports quantum information from the output of a quantum logic gate to a quantum memory device, where the quantum information is stored until it is needed by another logical operation.

Aside from use in quantum logic gates, there is a much more immediate need for quantum information transmission, especially if the information needs to be unassailably secure, free from any hint of an eavesdropper. Quantum effects guarantee absolute channel security through the simple fact that an eavesdropper must make quantum measurements to extract information, and the act of measurement fundamentally disturbs the information content. The presence of the eavesdropper can therefore be uncovered through simple measurements of the photon statistics, and the channel can be abandoned before any important information is sent.

QUANTUM CLOAK AND DAGGER

Every time you make a purchase over the Internet with your credit card, the pertinent information is scrambled using an encryption scheme that multiplies two large prime numbers together. Multiplying large numbers is easy, but it is very difficult to factor them apart again. See how long it takes you to find the two prime factors of the number $N = 576,603,310,111$. This number takes 40 bits to describe in binary notation, and it takes my old computer (MacIntosh G4 with two processors) about sixteen seconds to factor using a simple sequential search algorithm. The problem is that the time to factor a number increases exponentially. A number with 128 bits would take my machine about 9 million years. Of course, much faster computers and much more efficient algorithms are available. As we will see shortly, 429-bit keys have already been factored, although the technology that is needed to do this is hard to come by.

Therefore, forcing potential eavesdroppers to factor large products of primes is an excellent way to ensure privacy and is the basis of an encryption scheme called RSA (named after Rivest, Shamir, and Adleman, who invented the scheme in 1977) that is used almost universally for the transmission of electronic data. With this scheme, the person (let it be Alice) who wishes to receive a message publishes two public numbers. One is the product of two large prime numbers and the other is any number of choice. Using these public numbers, Bob constructs a message that he sends publicly back to Alice. Because the encryption key is completely public, as is the subsequent coded message, this scheme is known as public key cryptography. Yet the encoded message can only be broken by someone who can succeed in factoring the large key into its prime factors.

As an example of the difficulty factoring large numbers that are the products of primes, Martin Gardner, writing for *Scientific American* in 1977, published the 129-digit number

N = 114381625757888867669235779976146612010218296721242362562561842935706935245733897830597123563958705058989075147599290026879543541.00

plus an additional number M = 9007, and a message encrypted by the original RSA team using these numbers. A cash award of $100 was promised to anyone who could crack the code. This was known as the challenge of RSA-129. A 129-digit number can be represented by 429 bits, and 512-bit encryption was (and still is) commonly being used in commercial RSA schemes.

Over a decade passed before the mathematical and computational tools were available to crack RSA-129, but it finally fell to a sophisticated attack mounted by researchers at the Bellcore research labs in 1994. They mustered a coordinated effort that used 1,600 separate workstation platforms distributed internationally. They succeeded in deciphering the message: THE MAGIC WORDS ARE SQUEAMISH OSIFRAGE. Today, even 512-bit encryption is susceptible to such concentrated attack, which has raised the level of suggested security to 768-bit keys for personal security, 1024-bit keys for corporate security, and 2048-bit keys for ultimate security. Even with the powerful mathematical tools in use today, it would take a time longer than the age of the universe to factor the 2048-bit encryption. Yet these numbers or greater can fail as advances are made in mathematical techniques in number theory. The fundamental problem is that the public key is always susceptible to attack.

On the other hand, quantum cryptography provides a means of sending information that is impervious to eavesdropping. What is needed is a quantum channel, for instance, a fiber carrying single photons, between Alice and Bob. A third person, conventionally named Eve (a play on the word "eavesdrop"), is the suspected eavesdropper. How can quantum effects, especially quantum entanglement, be used to guarantee the security of the communications between Alice and Bob and keep Eve in the dark?

In cryptography by entanglement, Bob and Alice receive entangled photon pairs from a central source. They each perform a long random sequence of polarization measurements along three different directions that they agreed upon publicly in advance. Each makes measurements that are completely random and completely independent of each other. The outcome of each measurement produces a photon in half the cases, just as in the case of the EPR experiment. Afterwards, Bob and Alice publicly send each other the polarization directions they chose for each measurement. They identify cases for which they had each used *different* measurement directions, and they then publicly send the results of only those measurements. If Eve is eavesdropping, the quantum correlations will be perturbed. In that case, Bob and Alice abandon the channel. On the other hand, if the correlations are correct, then they conclude that Eve is not present. In that case they use their remaining data, obtained when they had chosen the same directions, as a random encryption key. Because of entanglement, they each have exactly the same random key. They use this to encrypt a message that they send over a completely classical channel.

This approach to quantum cryptography is virtually immune to attack. Furthermore, once Alice and Bob have their random key, it is almost impossible for the public encrypted message to be decoded because the encoded message has perfectly random statistics based on their random measurements. There is no handle for a codebreaker to grab onto.

Practical implementation of cryptography by entanglement is the closest of all the quantum information technologies to becoming a "real" enterprise. An experiment conducted in Geneva, Switzerland, in 1997 succeeded in sending entangled photons 10 kilometers over a fiber without losing quantum correlations. More recent demonstrations have succeeded in sending quantum information over conventional fibers installed for local area networks, and also through several kilometers in air. In addition, the dense part of the atmosphere near the Earth's surface is only about 10 kilometers thick, which means that quantum communication with satellites is a clear possibility. These recent advances point to the feasibility of quantum communication and cryptography as real-world applications of quantum information. Given the growing importance of information security in a world that is progressively operating on-line, quantum cryptography is poised to become the first commercial quantum technology.

Furthermore, the potential of quantum computing is closely tied to quantum cryptography—for instance, the parallel quantum information contained in superpositions of quantum states can be used to perform calculations that are intractable on any conceivable classical computer. One important problem like this is prime factorization. Quantum parallelism rises exponentially (like the problem of prime factorization) with the number of quantum states, providing an enormously parallel resource. This potential is so vast, and the threat to RSA so great, that research in quantum computing has become one of the fastest-growing fields of science and technology.

10 Quantum Computing the Uncomputable

Spinning Coins and Qubits

QUANTUM COMPUTING IS A QUALITATIVELY NEW WAY OF HARNESSING
NATURE.

David Deutsch, 1997

Quantum logic gates and quantum computers benefit fundamentally from the unique parallelism of quantum superpositions. A single input to a quantum logic gate contains a superposition of all possible input states. The output of the gate operating just once on this input contains all possible answers. Before peeking inside a quantum logic gate, I begin with a classical example to describe one of the basic logic gates called a controlled-NOT gate. As we shall see, classical versions only go so far before we need to turn to the unique features of the quantum world.

COMPUTING WITH SPINNING COINS

Consider a classical coin for which tails represents "0" and heads represents "1." When this coin is flipped and lands, it will end in the "0" state or the "1" state. In other words, the coin is a classical bit. Its value, furthermore, is determined randomly, depending on the outcome of the coin toss. Once the coin lands, it is in a definite state of either "0" or "1." But sometimes this classical coin is both "1" and "0" at the same time, such as the time it is in the air, or if it happens to land momentarily on its side. At the instant it lands, it can tip either way, but which way is impossible to predict. You could say that there is a 50 percent probability that it will fall tails, and an equal probability that it will fall heads.

Yet it is possible to cheat the odds. For instance, if a small additional mass is added to one side, this side will have a slightly higher chance to land down, while the other side has a slightly higher chance to land up. In this case, perhaps there is a 48 percent chance to land tails and a 52 percent chance to land heads. With enough weighting, the odds could be pushed far from 50/50—perhaps as far as 90/10. Even then it is impossible to say with certainty what the coin will do. It can still beat the odds and land tails.

When such a weighted coin is flipped, it is in an indeterminate state while it is in the air. Only the probability of how it will land can be stated. But this changes as soon as you observe the state of the coin. You do this by grabbing the coin in midflight and smacking it on your forearm. The instant you observe the coin, you know exactly what state it is in. With 100 percent probability you will see either a head or a tail. Furthermore, after the observation, the coin will remain in this completely defined state until it is flipped once again into the air.

Now let's think how we might try to do logic with this weighted coin. The simplest type of logic is conditional logic: if the coin lands heads-up, then you do A, otherwise you do B. The action A may be as simple as turning a second coin over, while the action B would be to do nothing. What you have in this case is a two-coin logic gate. There is a control coin that is flipped, and a second coin that is operated on. If the control coin lands heads-up, you flip the second coin over; otherwise you do nothing.

This logic gate is known as a controlled-NOT, also known as C-NOT. The NOT operation by itself is simply the turning of the coin over: NOT HEADS = TAILS and NOT TAILS = HEADS. In our example, whether we apply the NOT operation or not to the data coin is conditional on the value of the control coin. Logic gates are visualized in terms of lines and nodes and are drawn as a diagram. The control bit passes through on its line unaffected, but it connects to the data line where it causes the data bit to switch if the control bit is "1." Let's consider how we might implement the C-NOT logic gate using real coins. Flipping coins is not the best way to do this. When they are in the air, they have a nasty tendency to fall and hit something. And if we tried to maintain the indeterminacy by placing the coins on their sides, this will last for only a short time before they tip over.

On the other hand, we can spin the coin on a flat table. Or if we are concerned with it wandering while it spins, we could place it in a slightly curved bowl. Furthermore, to allow the coin to spin as long as possible, we could make the coin and the bowl out of frictionless material, and we could place the whole thing inside a belljar and evacuate the air. Under these conditions, the coin could continue spinning for a long time—all that time maintaining its indeterminate state. Remember too that the coin can be weighted, giving the control coin uneven probability to land heads-up or down. In spite of the weighted coin, the truth table for the c-NOT does not change. When the indeterminacy of the control coin is removed by the act of observation, it will be either a head or a tail. No other possibility exists. Then the data coin will be turned over or not. The odds of which action is taken depends on the weight on the coin.

It is hard to see how this coin-operated logic switch could do anything useful. But it is not so far-fetched. For instance, it is possible that the weight on the control coin was placed there by some earlier logical operation. And when this coin stops spinning, let's say some weight is added to some later control coin in some subsequent coin-operated logic gate. As these gates are cascaded, complex logic operations can be implemented that go far beyond the capabilities of the single c-NOT gate.

It is important to make the distinction between a single realization compared with a collection of realizations. Let's take a weighted coin that has only a 10 percent chance to land heads-up. The probability for this to happen is low, but it is still one of the allowed outcomes for a single realization. However, if we repeat the experiment 100 times, then even though all possibilities will occur, the cases when the control lands heads-up will be far fewer than when it lands heads-down. Therefore, for a weighted control coin in this classical logic gate, we would need to perform the logic operation many times to get a clear measurement of the weight on the control coin.

The biggest problem is that each calculation by the network of gates is only a single realization. Because this computer operates probabilistically, we would need to run it over and over again. However, the drawback of this computer is not that it is probabilistic, but that it is *classical*. Every single realization is distinct from any earlier or later realization. Each calculation gives only a single answer. The final coin will be either heads-up or tails-up. There are no other classical possibilities.

Now let's make a modification in how we operate this computer. In the way we first described it, it was necessary at each stage to observe the spinning coin before doing the next operation. In a network of such gates, the result of all the previous gates must be made determinant (heads or tails) before taking action on the data coin. But what if we could relax this requirement? What if the output state of the data coin is also indeterminate? In other words, the control coin would operate on the data coin without its ever being made to stop spinning. Since the control coin state is indeterminate, the data coin state is indeterminate as well, but in a special way: the data coin is perfectly correlated with the control coin.

This is where we need to leave our classical coin-operated computer and enter the quantum domain. There is no conceivable classical operation that can do what I just described—to have one indeterminate state operate with a predefined set of rules on another indeterminate state. Qubits, on the other hand, are perfectly happy to operate this way. Qubits, and especially their superpositions, are at the heart of quantum logic gates.

QUBITS

A bit can be constructed from any system that has two states. A light switch can be on or off. A door can be open or closed. For a transistor in an electronic logic gate, the control voltage can be passing current or blocking it. These are all examples of classical bits. Even though light switches can have dimmer knobs, doors can be partly open, and transistors can pass continuous values of current, these possibilities are disallowed explicitly for the expression of binary information. In the decision tree of a binary search (see p. 123), the choice is purely binary. The hidden item is found either in the right-hand branch or the left-hand branch. The number of branches is equal to the number of bits needed to specify the information content of the hidden value. No fuzzy answers are allowed.

Quantum information has similar constraints that are subtly different. A qubit is a quantum entity that has two orthogonal states. For instance, in a two-level atom, the electron can be in the upper state or in the lower state. For a photon, the polarization can be H or V. So far, this sounds like the classical case. But now we can take one step further by considering a 45° photon. This photon is a linear combination of equal amounts of H and V. It is tempting to think of this case as a door half open, but this is where the difference between the classical world and the quantum world is crucial. The half-open door cannot be viewed as a door that is open and closed *at the same time*. For the 45° photon, on the other hand, it is *both* H and V at the same time, just as a photon wave function passes through *both* slits in Young's double slit experiment.

The qubit exists in both states at the same time. A key property of a qubit is that we can always choose a specific direction to rotate our detector which guarantees that we will observe it along that direction. Even though it may be a linear combination of the two possible states for one choice of the detector's coordinates, another set of coordinates can be found for which the photon is in a pure state. This means that the qubit is a single well-defined quantity. Although we cannot predict which port of the calcite crystal it will emerge from *in general,* we can always find some rotation of the axes that will guarantee only one port will emit the photon.

Therefore, when we say that a qubit expresses the answers "yes" and "no" at the same time, we are saying something that must be interpreted very specifically. The qubit is in a coherent superposition of "yes" and "no," just as waves can be in coherent superpositions—as we saw in chapter 2 and again in chapters 6 and 7. The coherence of the superposition allows us to find a rotation that makes the answer a pure "yes" or a pure "no." It is quantum coherence that allows us to see a bomb in the dark. And it is quantum coherence that allows us to use qubits to perform massively parallel computations on quantum information.

The power of qubits arises not from a single qubit, but from collections of qubits. For instance, we can contrast the information content of 2 classical bits with 2 qubits. For a pair of classical bits, there are four possible arrangements of the bits: 00, 01, 10, and 11. However, there is only one possible arrangement *at a time.* Therefore, to enumerate all four possible arrangements, we need to step through the bits four times to produce them all.

On the other hand, for 2 qubits, all four combinations exist at the same time. To enumerate all possibilities, we only need to produce a single quantum superposition. It is important to keep in mind that, because this is a coherent superposition, the qubit is a single entity. To prove this, all we need to do is rotate our axes by the appropriate amount that would make the wavefunction a pure state. Since the wavefunction is a single entity, we only need to express it, or produce it, once. Yet it contains all the possible information of 2 bits. This represents a 4-to-1 savings in effort.

The importance of qubits becomes obvious once we start to increase the number of qubits in our collection. If we have N qubits, we can describe 2^N different configurations *all at the same time.* But a classical system would need to enumerate those configurations one at a time. If $N = 100$, there are $2^{100} = 10^{30}$ distinct configurations. A classical machine would need to define all 10^{30} distinct configurations, while a quantum machine could do it by defining only 100 qubits. The exponential increase of 2^N configurations relative to N qubits becomes a resource of tremendous—literally astronomical—magnitude. Quantum memory systems of only a modest number of qubits have a potential for memory storage that makes our newest and largest classical RAM chips look infinitesimally insignificant. For this reason alone, quantum information sciences have received considerable recent attention.

QUANTUM LOGIC

The quantum controlled-NOT, or C-NOT, gate has the same circuit diagram as the classical diagram. However, its behavior goes beyond classical capabilities, and is one element out of which universal quantum computers can be constructed. The C-NOT gate has two important features that make it fundamental: it is conditional, and it is reversible.

Being conditional means that the qubits on the two lines *interact,* in other words, what comes out of the data line depends on what went into the control line. This interaction among qubits is exactly what causes quantum entanglement of the EPR type. To become correlated, two particles need to interact with each other. The interaction can be the process of creation, as when the positronium decays and creates the two entangled photons. Or two particles that are already in existence can interact with each other. We saw in chapter 6 that photons interact with each other through intermediate electrons, such as electrons on atoms. It is therefore conceivable that a quantum C-NOT gate could be constructed using the quantum states of a single atom to couple the quantum states of two photons.

Being reversible means that the input information of the quantum gate can be reconstructed based on knowledge of the output. Reversibility was shown by Rolf Landauer of IBM in the early 1960s to be a necessary requirement for dissipationless computation. The importance of removing dissipation from classical computers is obvious. For instance, the heat caused by the increasing density of transistors on microprocessor chips is one of the principal obstacles to achieving even higher densities. This is because transistor logic uses voltages and currents that produce heat, just like a resistive heat pad or a thermal electric blanket. What Landauer showed was that dissipation of energy during computation was only necessary if information is destroyed during the computation.

An AND gate is an example of irreversible logic. It has only one output for two inputs. The output is equal to one if and only if both inputs are equal to 1. The output is 0 otherwise. But information is lost here. If the output is equal to 0, that could be because either Line 1 was 0 or Line 2 was 0 or both. Knowing the output therefore does nothing to enable us to reconstruct the input, indicating that 1 bit of information was destroyed by this logic operation, causing the emission of a minute amount of heat in the process. The C-NOT, on the other hand, is completely reversible because the input states can always be reconstructed just by knowing the output states. Therefore, in principle, a C-NOT gate could be constructed that dissipated no energy and hence produced no heat.

Reversibility in a classical logic gate is hard to achieve (although not impossible) because large numbers of electrons need to be transported from one location to another in an electronic device. If superconducting wires are used that have no resistance, it is possible to construct a reversible logic gate that produces no heat, although the engineering involved is highly challenging. On the other hand, reversibility is completely natural for quantum systems. Reversibility in a quantum system is equivalent to rotating coordinate axes. Quantum logic gates like the C-NOT therefore automatically satisfy the requirements of reversible computation to be performed without dissipation of heat. This feature of quantum logic makes it a candidate for the ultra-small scales and high densities that will be needed in computers of the future.

In addition to being conditional and reversible, which can also be satisfied by classical logic gates, quantum C-NOT gates go beyond classical capabilities when coherent superpositions of states are used at the inputs. For instance, the control state can be in a superposition of both 1 and 0. Running the gate therefore performs two controlled-NOT calculations on the input in a single step. In the most general case, the control state and the input state both can be in superpositions of 1 and 0, simultaneously giving all four possible outcomes of the gate. Furthermore, a C-NOT gate is a source of entangled pairs of photons that can be used in quantum teleportation.

More complicated C-NOT gates are obtained in a natural manner by allowing the control line and data line to accept collections of qubits. If the control line has N qubits, and the data line has M qubits, then $N \times M$ combinations of qubits are produced by the operation of the gate. Because these are qubits, and not classical bits, this means that $2^{N \times M}$ combinations of calculations are performed all at once. The values of N and M do not need to be very large before unimaginably immense calculations are performed in a single step by the gate.

The C-NOT gate is as complex a gate as is needed to construct, in the sense of a Turing machine, a universal quantum computer. In 1994, it was realized that by using only a 2-qubit C-NOT gate in combination with a 1-qubit gate that performed a simple rotation, any quantum computation could be performed. Two simple quantum logic gates are therefore all that are required to build a universal quantum computer, much as the AND and XOR gates are sufficient to build a universal classical computer.

QUANTUM COMPUTING

In the description of quantum logic gates, a nagging problem has remained unspoken. Great emphasis has been placed on the ability of the logic gates to calculate all answers at the same time for a single operation of the gate. But there is a problem: How do we read out all those answers? By now, you have gained enough of an understanding of quantum systems to know that an observation on any coherent superposition of states produces only a single answer. It does not matter whether the final quantum superposition contains 2 or 10^{30} answers. When the superposition is observed, only one answer is projected out. This is the essence of wavefunction collapse. To be able to see all 2^N answers in the gate output, we would need to make measurements on at least 2^N identical systems. But this is exactly the number of operations we would need to perform on a classical computer to get the same number of answers!

This seems like a serious problem. It is serious enough to make the potential of quantum computing look like smoke and mirrors. If we can access only one answer from the quantum superposition at a time, what have we gained? What is the value of the vast parallelism of quantum computing if it evaporates as soon as we try to observe it? The value looks completely metaphysical, like the sound of the tree falling in the woods when someone is not there to hear it. Does the information really exist if we cannot read it? And if we cannot read it, who cares whether the information is there or not?

This was the state of quantum computing around 1985. The potential was tantalizing, but it looked beyond our grasp, and hence beyond usefulness. Quantum computing was an interesting exercise practiced by esoteric theoreticians to answer metaphysical questions. Then one of the esoteric theoreticians by the name of David Deutsch working at the Quantum Computation and Cryptography Research Group at Clavendon Laboratory at Oxford University found a way to use all the answers at once before destroying them. The key was not to try to make the quantum computer simply answer questions in parallel, but rather to get all the answers to interfere with one another to produce a single collective answer.

This is something like quantum seeing in the dark, but at a much larger scale. While the separate answers for the bomb are that Path 1 has no bomb and Path 2 has no bomb, the coherent superposition of these two answers produces complete destructive interference at the detector—meaning "no bomb." But when a path *does* contain the bomb, the removal of the interference changes the collective answer to "bomb" (at least some of the time). It is this ability to utilize the coherent interference among all answers to produce a collective single answer that speeds up certain problems that are intractable by classical means. On top of this, Deutsch was able to show that quantum computers could be universal computers.

This was an astounding breakthrough, although his publication in 1985 was largely overlooked—initially. Part of the continuing difficulty was finding the right kind of problems where the quantum parallelism, combined with interference, could be used to produce a single result. In other words, what quantum computing needed to bring it into the big time was a killer application, or "killer app," that was too important to ignore.

That "killer app" was provided in 1994 by a reclusive genius named Peter Shor working at Bell Laboratories in New Jersey. He decided to tackle the problem of finding the factors of the product of two large prime numbers. If such a result could be achieved, then the RSA cryptographic security systems could be broken. This would be catastrophic to world commerce and political stability. Shor found that a quantum computer, using quantum parallelism and interference, could solve the problem. Here was a "killer app" that no one could afford to ignore. What did Shor think up?

Shor realized that a central part of the problem of factorization involved finding repetitive patterns in sequences of numbers. Any time that repetitive patterns are found in a signal, they can be analyzed in terms of waves. And waves interfere. This brought Deutsch's concept of quantum interference into the problem of prime factorization. In a feat of intellectual brawn, Shor was able to apply aspects of quantum parallelism and interference to the problem. In the end, he managed to define a specific quantum algorithm that would be able to break all codes currently in use, and any codes likely to be used in the future. In a single stroke of genius he had toppled the entire world of RSA cryptography—almost.

The problem with quantum algorithms is that they need quantum computers to execute them. And these don't exist yet. For the moment, cryptography and privacy are secure as long as quantum computers remain in the future. But the future has a nasty habit of becoming the present. Quantum computers may still be a long way off, but quantum logic gates have already appeared in selected laboratories around the world, making the first primitive steps toward the third generation of the machines of light.

THE THIRD GENERATION

There comes a time when theoretical speculation must meet reality and be reduced to practice. Qubits need to be more like flesh and blood than spirit. They need a physical existence that can be touched and felt—if not by human hands, then by surrogate means. Not only must qubits be created and supported by physical systems, they must also be protected from outside disturbances that destroy the fragile quantum superpositions. Furthermore, physical operations must be devised to make the qubits entangle themselves. What types of laboratory systems allow qubits to control other qubits? What would these machines be like? More important for our interests, how does light play a role in these prototype quantum logic gates?

Our discussions in chapter 7 of the control of light by light used classical Mach-Zender interferometers to allow one light beam to modify another, using non-linear materials to mediate the interaction. If we let the light beams get progressively weaker, the effects of single photons become more pronounced. In the quantum limit of small numbers there may be only a few photons interacting at a time in the interferometer. To what extent does the interferometer become a quantum optical logic gate?

This question was first asked in 1989 by Gerald Milburn, an Australian theoretical physicist working in quantum optics at the University of Queensland. His device was called a quantum optical Fredkin gate, named after Ed Fredkin of MIT, who was one of the first computer physicists to recognize the importance of reversible gates for computing. A Fredkin gate has three inputs and three outputs. One of the inputs is the control line and carries its bits through unaffected, just as in the c-NOT gate. The information on the other two gates is unaltered if the control is 0, but is swapped if the control is 1. This is just what happens in the Controlled Mach-Zender Interferometer figure on page 161. But that is a classical interferometer that works with strong light beams. What—Milburn wanted to know—happens in the quantum regime? He determined that the idealized quantum optical Fredkin gate could operate as a quantum logic gate, under the right conditions. However, the right conditions were not all that favorable. Milburn discovered that multiple photons would be needed (actually about three), even in the best case, to switch the output.

Here again, as we have seen so often, the control of light by light is a daunting challenge. Photons do not like to interact with each other. Even when we coerce classical light beams into a non-linear medium, we require long interaction lengths to get large effects. In the quantum limit even this ploy fails, and single-photon control of a quantum gate looked fundamentally impossible.

The situation was saved by a timely theoretical discovery in 1995, when Seth Loyd of the Information Sciences Department at MIT was able to show that almost any quantum logic gate is universal, in other words, that almost any quantum gate with two or more inputs is computationally universal, making it possible to produce any desired quantum logic circuit. The question then was whether Milburn's inadequate Fredkin gate could be considered "almost any quantum gate"?

There is a much simpler gate than the Fredkin gate that satisfies Loyd's scheme, one that simply crosses a control beam with a signal beam to induce a mutual phase shift. Because Loyd's scheme does not require a full 180° phase shift in the operation, almost any phase shift would do the trick, as long as it is robust and sizable relative to measurement errors. This type of quantum gate is called a conditional phaseshifter. The phase is shifted only if both photons have the appropriate polarizations, and is not shifted otherwise.

The same year, in one of the first experimental demonstrations of quantum logic, a group at CalTech under the direction of H. J. Kimble constructed a conditional phaseshifter and measured sizable phase shifts that depended on the polarizations of the photons. Furthermore, they operated their logic gate using only single photons. Their apparatus used an atomic beam of cesium atoms as the "non-linear medium." These atoms passed through a very small optical cavity that was much like a miniature laser cavity only 56 microns long. Two laser beams with slightly differing frequencies carried the qubit information in their respective polarizations and were transmitted through the cavity mirrors. The cavity allowed the photons to bounce back and forth many times, letting them interact with the atomic states. The gate was read out by simply measuring the polarizations of the photons that emerged from the cavity.

The performance of the conditional phase shifter was moderate, but sufficient to cause excitement as a real-world demonstration of quantum conditional dynamics. The researchers at CalTech were able to observe a phase shift of 16° per photon. The speed of the operation was also reasonable, clicking along at a rate of 75 megahertz entangling the state of one channel with the other.

However, the experiment also highlighted continuing difficulties with quantum optics as the sole conveyors and processors of quantum information. Kimble described the qubits in the experiment as "flying qubits" because the quantum information encoded on the photons went flying through the apparatus at the speed of light. There was no form of quantum information storage in this configuration, meaning that the entangled photons emerging from the apparatus needed to be used immediately for the next stage of a quantum computation. Also, the small phase shift of 16° was not as big as one might want. Even though larger phase shifts up to 60° would be possible under ideal conditions, the microcavities that could produce this phase shift would slow the interaction down because the photons would need to spend more time in the cavities before being emitted.

An alternative experimental demonstration in the same banner year, 1995, was performed by a group under the direction of D. Wineland at the National Institute of Standards and Technology (NIST) in Boulder, Colorado. It swapped the roles of the photons and the atoms. As opposed to the CalTech experiment, where the photons carried the qubits, and the atomic medium played a passive role as mediator of the interaction, in the NIST experiment, the atoms carried the qubits, and the photons performed the operations on those atomic states. Furthermore, the NIST experiment went farther than the CalTech experiment by actually implementing and demonstrating a C-NOT quantum gate.

Rather than using a beam of atoms that passed through a cavity, the NIST group captured and held a single beryllium atom inside a delicate apparatus known as an ion trap. The two qubits were represented by independent states of the atom. One qubit consisted of an internal electronic state of the atom, while the second qubit consisted of a mechanical (albeit quantum) vibration of the atom in the trap. The input qubits were prepared by a laser pulse that placed the atom in a superposition of internal and vibrational states.

The action of the C-NOT gate on the qubits was performed using laser pulses of specific frequencies and durations. The control pulses did not carry information. All the information in this implementation resides in the quantum states of the atom. The optical control pulses simply provide the physical mechanism that manipulates the qubits and entangles them, producing the output values of the gate. The logic gate performed with high fidelity at a processing rate of 20 kilohertz. Rates as high as 50 megahertz were predicted as plausible.

In the experiment, the qubits in the atoms were prepared in appropriate initial states by photons. The photons carried the qubit to the atoms, which stored the qubits for the duration of the computation. Photons then supplied the quantum "program," changing the internal state of the atom and telling it to perform a C-NOT operation. The subsequent interaction between the qubits was carried out entirely within the atom. Finally, the qubits were read out by photons that pass the information downstream to the next gate. In this way, the photons were used as messenger and programmer, while electrons were used best for interaction. They worked together in a photo-electric quantum network performing quantum logic.

The year 1995 was a watershed year for quantum computing. Loyd simplified the requirements of universal quantum computers, allowing Kimble to perform a conditional phaseshifter as one element of such a computer. At the same time, Wineland demonstrated a two-qubit C-NOT gate using atoms to support the qubits and allow them to interact. By the end of the year, quantum computing had ceased being an exclusively theoretical science and had forged a beachhead in the laboratory.

But much remains to be done. Since 1995, improvements in the experiments have come slowly. The breakthrough experiments were sufficiently difficult that even after five years, few additional experimental groups have had notable impact on the field. A chief obstacle to greatly improved performance of quantum logic gates is the difficulty of increasing the number of qubits enough to be useful or interesting. The recent demonstrations by the NIST group of four trapped ions represents state-of-the-art. It has taken

Herculean efforts to achieve even this low level of parallelism in the number of qubits.

A problem endemic to all quantum computing schemes is something called decoherence. The key element of quantum computing is the linear superposition of quantum states and the coherent interference among the states during computation. Yet the real world is constantly buffeting the quantum system, causing the coherence to decay in time. In the laboratory demonstrations, the computations were completed before the quantum states could decohere; but that was just for a single operation. Quantum computations of interest would require many operations to take place before decoherence could destroy the quantum interference.

Therefore, the best candidates for quantum computing are those that have the longest decoherence times. Single trapped ions are reasonable candidates because the decoherence times are around 1 millisecond. However, as the number of qubits, and hence the number of trapped ions, increases, the decoherence time decreases. This trend goes in the wrong direction and is troubling for the prospects of ion-trap quantum computing schemes.

A recent theoretical breakthrough has made the problem of decoherence a little less severe by allowing quantum computers to make mistakes, yet still arrive at useful answers. This breakthrough is in the area of quantum error correction. New protocols that use entangled states repair the information carried by quantum states that have been damaged by decoherence. These error correction schemes are a life saver for realistic quantum computing because they make real-world implementations (with their unavoidable flaws and dissipation) candidates for realistic quantum computers.

The technological challenges faced by quantum computing are very difficult, just as they are for large-scale integrated electronic circuits based on single-electron transistors, and for holographic computers that use images as the unit of information. The problems that need to be overcome in each of these technologies will take years of concentrated effort by scientists and engineers. The beauty is that we have time. We do not need quantum computers tomorrow. We can live our lives without quantum parallelism. But quantum parallelism is inevitable because the problems that are faced today are chiefly technological and not theoretical. The fundamentals have been hammered out by fifteen years of imaginative search and discovery, which have largely outlined the shape that the quantum Architecture of Light will provide to quantum computing. What remains is the hard work.

IN DEFENSE OF OPTIMISM

In the past hundred years, pundits have generally underestimated techno-logical growth. The history of technology teaches us that what is possible often becomes real. Furthermore, when things become real, demand for performance grows, and the technology grows faster than anyone ex-pected. Just as estimates of the need for bandwidth on the Internet have al-ways underestimated the load, estimates for the uses of quantum communication and computing are likely to be conservative.

Certainly, counterexamples abound. For instance, despite billions of dol-lars spent, nuclear fusion is no nearer to being a source of energy today than it was thirty years ago. The technological difficulties turned out to be more complex than expected. Which points to a trend: that it is easier to work with smaller technology than larger. Feynman's proclamation, "There's plenty of room at the bottom," is encouraging, because we have historically done well with miniaturization. Small scales are intrinsically easier to tackle than large scales because it is easier to work with less and less, than to need more and more to get bigger and bigger. The recent ex-perimental successes driving the burgeoning field of nanotechnology are ample proof of this.

Warp speed and macroscopic teleportation are both probably impossi-ble. But molecular computers that use quantum teleportation for their data buses can become real technologies. When? It is impossible to predict. But many of the germinal ideas are already developing in research labs around the world. In the next few decades, the time of the quantum machines of light, I believe, will be upon us.

Epilogue

The Glass Bead Game in a Stream of Light

... THE SIGN LANGUAGE AND GRAMMAR OF THE GAME ... SHOULD BE
ABLE TO EXPRESS THE MOST COMPLEX MATTERS GRAPHICALLY, WITHOUT
EXCLUDING INDIVIDUAL IMAGINATION AND INVENTIVENESS, IN SUCH A
WAY AS TO BE UNDERSTANDABLE TO ALL THE WORLD.

Hermann Hesse, *The Glass Bead Game*, 1942

Imagine luminous machines of light made from threads of glass and brilliantly colored crystals that glow and shimmer, pulsating to the beat of intelligence. Peer inside and watch as strange symbols condense from amorphous clouds of light, evolving from bright mist into sharp form, then dissolving once more. Sequences of symbols transform themselves into others, at first seemingly at random, but after awhile subtle patterns emerge, mesmerizing in their effects, cryptic in their meaning. Family resemblances are perceived among the patterns as sign begets signs, multiplying beyond comprehension.

Imagine traveling inside the machine with breathtaking speed chasing the symbols through an endless maze of light pipes. The symbolic traffic converges into a resonant ring where the symbols mix their meanings and grow new forms. The circling information presents to the mind a wild ballet of dancing light that radiates in all directions, dispersing beams of energy to other distant rings. Buried in the motion and the patterns, floating barely beyond the edge of consciousness, is a sense of deep meaning, of order within the chaos, of continuity within the endless change.

Imagine you are watching the Glass Bead Game played by intelligent agents in streams of light blanketing the world. The Game evolved with the optical medium as the agents became master players, seeking meaning in the disorder of purported truths. The Game emerged organically after the exponential growth of information on the all-optical Internet exceeded human grasp. With the explosion of information came gridlock and conflict in a virtual world without structure. Truth and meaning had disappeared in the face of a billion fictions that refused to be verified—until the Game crystallized spontaneously out of the luminescent fog. The Game grew and matured, drawing order out of the tangled web, until it emerged as a universal language of light and image to become, finally, Leibniz's elusive tool of discovery.

APPENDIX A. TABLE OF RATES AND MEASURES

Wavelengths

1 millimeter = 10^{-3} meters = one thousandth of a meter

1 micrometer = 10^{-6} meters = one millionth of a meter

1 micron = 1 micrometer

1 nanometer = 10^{-9} meters = one billionth of a meter

Frequencies

1 Hertz = one cycle per second

1 MegaHertz = one million cycles per second

1 GigaHertz = one billion cycles per second

1 TeraHertz = one trillion cycles per second

Times

1 millisecond = 10^{-3} seconds = one thousandth of a second

1 microsecond = 10^{-6} seconds = one millionth of a second

1 nanosecond = 10^{-9} seconds = one billionth of a second

1 picosecond = 10^{-12} seconds = one trillionth of a second

1 femtosecond = 10^{-15} seconds = one thousandth of a trillionth of a second

Bit Rates

1 kilobit per second = 10^{3} bits per second = one thousand bits per second

1 megabit per second = 10^{6} bits per second = one million bits per second

1 gigabit per second = 10^{9} bits per second = one billion bits per second

1 terabit per second = 10^{12} bits per second = one trillion bits per second

1 petabit per second = 10^{15} bits per second = one thousand trillion bits per second

APPENDIX B. OPTICAL R&D COMPANIES

Despite the exponential ups and precipitous downs in the stock prices of information technology (IT) companies, traffic on the optical internet continues to double steadily every six months. Optical technology is advancing practically in step to provide the future bandwidth that this exponential growth entails. The optical revolution is being constructed idea by idea and device by device in companies as large as the behemoths with thousands of PhD scientists and engineers and as small as three-person start-ups with not a single PhD among them.

This list of optical R&D companies supporting the optical revolution are my personal picks. My decision to choose them comes as much from my interest in their technology as from their business potential. For in-depth information on many IT companies, see www.lightreading.com.

Agere (AGR). Formerly Lucent Technologies Microelectronics Group, Agere was spun off in March 2001. It is a strong supplier of integrated circuits and optoelectronic components. They recently announced a 64 × 64 MEMS-based switch module for all-optical routing. "As the world leader in communications components and subsystems, we will enable a new era of connectivity through integrated solutions that address the global demand for bandwidth" (www.lucent.com/micro).

Agilent (A). A spin-off from Hewlett-Packard, this company uses bubble-jet technology in optical routing. Agilent has made 32 × 32- and 32 × 16-port photonic switching subsystems and says that these can be connected together to create larger switch cores. The switch has 10 msec switching speed. The 32 × 32 switch is compact and scalable for wavelength selective crossconnect or multi-tier architectures for wavelength interchange crossconnects with low loss rates. In application as add-drop multiplexers, the switch packages have 128 fiber jumpers each—the highest ever integrated onto a single package, according to Agilent. 32 of these are the input fiber, 32 are for output. The remainder make it possible to add or drop any channel. As the waveguides pass all the way through the chips, they can be linked together in a modular architecture. (www.agilent.com).

Agility. Poised to become the front-runner in the manufacture of tunable semiconductor diode lasers that are needed for DWDM applications. The company is based on the technology of Larry Coldren, the company's chief technical officer who co-founded the firm in October 1998. Coldren has researched lasers, first at AT&T's Bell Laboratories (now part of Lucent Technologies Inc.), and later as director of the Heterogeneous Optical Technology Center at the University of California at Santa Barbara (www.agility.com).

Alcatel (ALA). Engineers at Alcatel recently sent 10.2 Tbit/s of data—comprised of 256 channels, each at 42.7 Gbit/s—over 100 kilometers of TeraLight fiber. It doubled its previous best, set in September 2000, by using polarization multiplexing. In a second experiment, Alcatel sent 3 Tbit/s over 7,380km. This was composed of 300 channels at 11.6 Gbit/s each. It's the highest capacity to be sent over transoceanic distances without electrical regeneration. (www.alcatel.com).

Avanex (AVNX). Avanex is one of the leading R&D companies developing active DWDM components that allow electronic control of wavelengths and routes. This company was championed by George Gilder in early 2000 leading the stock price to skyrocket prior to the IT crash of mid 2000. Despite the stock ups and downs, the company produces truly innovative technology (www.avanex.com).

Ciena (CIEN). In 1996, CIENA Corporation developed and shipped its first dense wavelength division multiplexing (DWDM) system. CIENA's optical networking systems form a core for worldwide telecommunications networks and services. The company offers a portfolio of products, including DWDM optical transport, intelligent switching and distribution technologies that enable carriers to easily deliver multiple services. Ciena recently cited 5,000 unregenerated kilometres for its Multiwave Corestream products.

Corning (GLW). This company is one of my favorites. Corning's long history of inventions won them the National Medal of Technology in 1994. One of those inventions was low-loss optical fiber—created more than 25 years ago. They make steady advances in specialty fibers for components and modules. Corning Photonic Technologies pours 25 percent of sales back into their R&D efforts. A 256-port optical cross-connect is scheduled to hit customer labs in 2001.

Corvis (CORV). Corvis Corp. has a package of optical switching and transmission systems, and says its equipment has carried optical signals over 3,200 kilometers in lab tests. Its Optical Switch switches wavelengths directly through the optical layer, eliminating the intervening electronic layer, while providing 2.4 Tb/s of switching capacity. Corvis has developed the only all-optical switch close to deployment. It's suspected to be a 6-by-6 port switch built around 36 fiber amplifiers that allow light to pass when they're powered up and block light at other times. Each input port is connected to a splitter that divides the light among six of these amplifiers. At the other end of the amplifiers, the reverse happens. The light is collected by six further splitters and steered to the output ports.

InPhase. This small optical storage company was spun off from Lucent Bell Labs on Jan. 30, 2001. The company is pursuing on-disc holographic storage using discs similar in size to DVD and CDs. The storage size would allow a single disc to hold 80 films distributed through the disc in volume holograms that are stored as full "pages" that can each have a million bits.

JDS Uniphase (JDSU). This optical component manufacturer was one of the stellar performers in the exponential IT stock rise of early 2000. It provides basic opto-electronic components (www.jdsuniphase.com).

Kamelian. Kamelian has a variety of products based on semiconductor optical amplifiers (SOA). A recent product is a reconfigurable add/drop multiplexer that adds signals or drops them by combining passive optical components with the SOA by controlling the electronic drive current to the SOAs. The signals remain in the optical domain, but the control is electronic (www.kamelian.com).

Lucent Technologies Bell Labs Innovations (LU). This is also one of my personal favorites. Though they have had stock and financial trouble lately, the innovations coming from their Bell Labs research arm are phenomenal. Their MEMS all-optical router was one of the first into the market (www.lucent.com).

Luxcore. Luxcore demonstrated a working prototype optical switch that incorporated optical wavelength conversion—thought to be a world first. This development promises to reduce carrier costs by eliminating expensive transponders. This was a demo of a small 2×2 switch. Making a larger switch suitable for commercial use still presents an enormous challenge (www.luxcore.com).

Lynx. Lynx demonstrated a working 4x4 switch made in lithium niobate. Insertion loss was around 6dB, remarkably low for this type of material. Its switching speed—less than 5 nanoseconds—means that the device could be used to link together existing high-speed switches and routers to make monster machines, capable of handling many terabits per second of data (www.LynxPN.com).

NEC (NIPNY). Scientists from NEC Corp. managed to transmit nearly 11 Tbit/s of data over a distance of about 115km, using a mid-span amplifier. NEC says it set up 273 channels of 40 Gbit/s each, spaced at 50 GHz, to achieve the rate of 10.92 Tbit/s overall.

Nortel (NT). Nortel Networks Inc. is one of the truly big hitters in the optical communications systems. They blew away Lucent in 1999 when they marketed their 10 Gbps system. Nortel recently announced the key pieces to its strategy for increasing the network's core equipment to speeds of 40 Gbit/s (www.nortelnetworks.com).

Trellis Photonics. This company is developing a holographic 240 × 240 switch based on holograms recorded in transparent crystals. The holograms are "turned on and off" by simply applying an electronic voltage to the crystal. The switching time is a few nanoseconds and can be used for DWDM applications (www.trellisphotonics.com).

Action potential. The electrical signal composed of sequences of voltage spikes conducted along axons by which information is conveyed in the nervous system.

Adaptive optics. Adaptive optical systems adjust themselves to remove changing optical conditions, such as twinkling of starlight caused by atmospheric turbulence. Systems are either active or self-adaptive. Active adaptive optics uses sensors and feedback, while self-adaptive systems, like holograms, respond automatically.

Add/Drop multiplexing. Adding signal packets to a stream of packets on a fiber, or retrieving signal packets from a fiber requires an optical add/drop multiplexer (OADM).

All-Optical. This term is often used when describing fiber-optic technology that keeps the signals in the optical domain without the need to convert to electronics and back again. All-optical switches currently in use keep the signal in the optical domain, but still use electronics for control.

Amacrine cells. Retinal neurons that mediate lateral interactions between bipolar cell terminals and the dendrites of ganglion cells.

American sign language (ASL). ASL is the visual form of communication, primarily expressed by the hands, used by the deaf community in America.

AND gate. And AND gate is a logic gate that has two binary inputs and one binary output. The output is "1" if both intpus are "1," and is "0" otherwise.

Anti-matter. The opposite of matter. The positron is the positive anti-particle to the negative electron.

Arbitrary. A technical term from semiotics that states that the meaning of signs is agreed upon by convention within a communicating community.

Associative memory. A form of memory whereby one member of a class of associated elements elicits the other members of the class.

Bandgap.

PHOTONIC: artificially structured optical materials can be engineered to prevent the propagation of light within a band of frequencies.

SEMICONDUCTOR: a gap of energies between the top of the valence band and the bottom of the conduction band. Laser diodes emit light with a wavelength related to the semiconductor bandgap.

Bandwidth. Bandwidth is a range of continuous frequencies (Δf) used in a communication channel. In the optimal case, the data rate (expressed in bits per second) is equal to the bandwidth of the channel.

Beam clean-up. Holograms perform beam clean-up when the signal beam is passed forwards through the hologram to regenerate the clean reference beam.

Beam-splitter. A 50/50 beamsplitter is a half-silvered mirror that transmits half the light and reflects half the light. Beamsplitters split waves apart and put them back together again in interferometers.

Bell's Inequality. An inequality derived by John Bell in 1964 for any physical system that must satisfy *local realism*. Quantum mechanics, especially two-particle states called EPR pairs, violate the Bell inequality. Many physicists pragmatically interpret this to mean that quantum mechanics in nonlocal, i.e., that quantum influences can occur instantaneously over arbitrarily large distances.

Bell-state measurement (BSM). A measurement of the joint properties of two quantum particles. The measurement provides information on entangled states without actually saying anything about the states individually. Bell state measurements are used in quantum teleportation experiments.

Binary logic. Binary logic entails Boolean logical operations (AND, OR, NOT, etc.) on 0's and 1's. Computer circuits use binary logic.

Binary search. A search of ordered data that eliminates half of the possibilities at each step by asking "greater-than" or "less-than" questions. The search time is proportional to the number of bits needed to code all the possibilities.

Bipolar cell. Retinal neurons that provide a direct link between photoreceptor terminals and ganglion cell dendrites.

Bit. A binary unit of "0" or "1" used in base-2 arithmetic. Bits are also the units of information in Boolean logic and in computers.

Bit error rate (BER). The BER of an information transmission channel is equal to one divided by the average number of bits received correctly before a single error is made.

Black body. A black body is a technical term for an object that emits purely thermal light. The effort to explain the black body spectrum led Max Planck to make his quantum hypothesis in 1900.

Boolean Logic. Logic operations on binary values. Named for George Boole (1815–1864), British mathematician.

Born interpretation. The Born interpretation of the quantum wavefunction states that the probability to detect the state is equal to the squared magnitude of the wavefunction.

Broadband. A term referring to the ability to efficiently use up to the full bandwidth available in a communication system, like an optical fiber. Fibers have a potential bandwidth of 30 Tbps. Field trials have demonstrated broadband performance beyond 10 Tbps.

Broadening.

PULSE: A pulse in a dispersive medium broadens as it propagates because longer wavelengths have a different velocity than shorter wavelengths.

Broca's area. An area in the left frontal lobe specialized for the production of language.

Byte. A Byte is a set of eight bits. Any character or numbers can be expressed in a single Byte ($2^8 = 256$ characters).

Calcite. A crystal of calcium carbonate ($CaCO_3$) has double refraction that splits an image into two, each with a different polarization. When used in optical experiments, the calcite crystals act as a beam polarizer. When viewed quantum mechanically, the crystal "chooses" whether a photon is a V photon or an H photon.

Causality. Causality requires all responses to travel at or below the speed of light. In other words, no response can precede its stimulus.

Cavity. A cavity is composed of two mirrors that reflect light back and forth. The cavity has resonances when the distance between the mirrors equals a half-integer number of wavelengths of light.

Center-surround. The center-surround structure in the retina refers to the most common receptive field of retinal ganglion cells. The signal from the center of the field causes the opposite influence compared to the surrounding field. This structure is fundamentally an edge detector.

Charge coupled device (CCD). A silicon circuit with an array of photodetectors. CCDs are used in digital video cameras.

Chemical vapor deposition (CVD). A material growth process in which a solid grows by accumulating material out of a vapor phase. The CVD growth of silica glass produces ultra-high purity glass fiber preforms.

Chirp. Chirp on a wave pulse describes how different colors arrive at different times. For instance the leading edge of a light pulse can be more red, while the trailing edge can be more blue, or vice versa. If a sound pulse is chirped, low frequencies are heard first, and then higher frequencies, producing a sound like the chirp of a bird.

Choroid layer. The choroid layer is a pigmented vascular layer behind the retina that absorbs light and provides nutrients to the retinal neural cells.

Classical. The phrase "classical physics" is reserved for physics prior to the year 1900, contrasted with "modern physics," which incorporates aspects of Einstein's theory of relativity and quantum theory.

Coherence. Classical coherence refers to multiple waves, such as electromagnetic waves or water waves, that all travel in lock-step with each other. When added together, coherent waves produce classical interference. Quantum coherence refers to well-defined phase relationships among multiple quantum wavefunctions.

Compression. Data compression uses redundancy in a signal to re-express the signal in a format with fewer bits than the original.

Cone. Photoreceptor in the retina that is sensitive to color under high illumination.

Content addressable memory. Content addressable memory is an information memory system that retrieves information by keying on the information content. Many items with the same content can be recalled at the same time in parallel. This is in contrast to random access memory that needs to be searched sequentially.

Context. The surrounding meaning in a text. The context of a message often limits possible meanings of parts of the message.

Correlation.
IMAGE: Image correlators look for matches between a target image and features in a signal image, for instance, looking for the letter "E" in a page of text. Image correlation is a form of parallel content-addressable memory.
STATISTICAL: Statistical correlations refer to the likelihood that measurements on two different variables lead to the same values. Statistical correlations between measurements on entangled quantum states is used to rule out hidden variable theories of quantum mechanics, and to perform secure quantum cryptography.

Coulomb force. The force of electrostatic attraction or repulsion between two charged particles.

Cross talk. Cross-talk occurs when two communication channels should be independent, but part of the information from one contaminates the other. Computers running at higher frequencies suffer more from cross-talk because all the wires start to act like sending and receiving antennas.

Cryptography.
CLASSICAL: Classical cryptography schemes are used to transmit information that cannot be deciphered without a key. Techniques vary from simple substitution of one letter for another, to complex protocols like the RSA protocol for public key cryptography.
QUANTUM: Quantum cryptography uses the unique properties of non-orthogonal quantum measurements to transmit cryptographic codes. If eavesdroppers try to intercept information, their presence is detected through a change in the quantum correlations.

Data bus. A data bus transports information from one logic unit to another in a computer.

Datacom. Shortened form for data communication. Used for short-distance high-data rate communication, usually at wavelengths near 850 nanometers.

Deep structure. Deep structure refers to the underlying tree that represents a sentence. Deep structure is acted upon by transformational rules to produce surface structure.

Decoherence. The process by which fragile quantum superpositions are degraded, usually through interactions with the environment.

Demultiplexing. Demultiplexing is the separation of the individual signals out of communication channels that have interleaved data pulses (TDM) or are using multiple colors (WDM).

Dendrites. A neuronal process that receives synaptic input, usually branches near the cell body, and is typically unable to support an action potential.

Dense Wavelength Division Multiplexing (DWDM). Refers to wavelength-division-multiplexing systems that use tightly spaced frequency channels. In the limit of DWDM it may be possible to pack 1000 channels (different wavelengths) onto a single fiber.

Diffraction. Light that impinges on obstacles scatters off in all directions. The interference of the individual scattered waves constitutes diffraction. Holographic reconstruction occurs through the diffraction of light off the hologram.

Dispersion. Dispersion is the property of all wave media that causes different wavelengths to travel with different speeds. Dispersion of light is caused by the inertia of electrons in matter.

Dura mater. The thick external covering of the brain and spinal cord; one of the three components of the meninges, the other two being the pia mater and the arachnoid mater.

Drift. The slow drift that occurs when the eyes are fixed at a single spot (called a fixation) over a time of about one fifth of a second, which is about 200 milliseconds.

Dynamic holography. Dynamic holography uses materials that respond in real-time to interference fringes. The resulting hologram moves as the optical information on the laser beams changes. Dynamic holography is used in self-adaptive optics to compensate for mechanical vibrations and atmospheric turbulence.

Edge detector. A structure in an optical system that responds maximally to a sharp change in intensity.

Einstein-Podolsky-Rosen (EPR) Paradox. The EPR paradox was presented in 1935 by Albert Einstein, Boris Podolsky and Nathan Rosen to demonstrate that quantum mechanical description was incomplete. The key to the paradox is the concept of entangled states.

Electric field. An electric field is a set of force lines that act on charges.

Electron shell. An electron shell is a way of describing the quantum state of an electron in an atom. Rather than thinking of the electron as being in a specific position around the atom, the electron can occupy any location within a diffuse shell.

Electromagnetic interference (EMI). Electromagnetic interference is caused when electrical currents on one wire transmit noise or information to another wire. EMI becomes stronger at higher computer clock speeds and is beginning to limit the ability of wires to carry information inside computers. This information-carrying role will be taken over eventually by optics.

Electromagnetic wave. Electromagnetic waves are transverse waves of electric and magnetic fields. Electromagnetic waves travel at the speed of light. Light is itself composed of electromagnetic waves, as are microwaves, radio waves, infrared and ultraviolet light and x-rays and gamma rays.

Electro-optic modulator. An optical device that modulates the amplitude or phase of a signal beam through the use of the electro-optic effect where the refractive index of the electro-optic material depends on an applied electric field.

Electron-Volt (eV). The electron volt is a standard unit of energy used in quantum physics. One eV is the energy an electron acquires when it accelerates through a voltage of one volt.

Energy level. Any electron in a confined space has discrete energy levels. The energy values of these levels are governed by quantum theory.

Entanglement. When two or more quantum particles interact, they become part of a single wavefunction for the system. Entangled states have many uses, ranging from experiments on hidden variables to quantum teleportation and computing.

Entropy. Entropy is a measure of randomness. The entropy of a communcation channel is equal to the information content.

Erbium-doped fiber amplifier (EDFA). Fibers that are doped with the element Erbium (Er) can act as optical amplifiers or lasers when they are optically pumped by shorter wavelength light. The amplification occurs for wavelengths around 1.55 microns.

Error backpropagation. Error backpropagation is used in the training of neural networks with hidden layers as an algorithm that sets the correct synaptic weights.

Feature detection. An optical computing process that detects target features in a signal image. Optical correlators are feature detectors that operate in parallel by identifying all the locations of a target feature.

Feed forward. In feed forward neural networks the signals move in only one direction through the network.

Fiber Optics. The field of optical science concerned with the properties of light confined in transparent fibers of glass and other materials.

Fiber-to-the-Box (FTTB). Bringing the optical fiber directly into the internet appliances inside the home.

Fiber-to-the-Curb (FTTC). Bringing fiber optic cables to local distribution boxes at the curb of the street from which the signals are brought into the home electronically.

Fiber-to-the-Home (FTTH). Extending the optical fiber from the curb directly into the home.

Fixation. A fixation is when the eyes rest on a single spot for a time of about one fifth of a second (200 milliseconds).

Flicker Fusion Frequency. The frequency above which a flickering light appears to be constant. The flicker fusion frequency depends on the light intensity, but is nominally in the range of 30 Hz (30 milliseconds).

Fredkin Gate. A Fredkin gate is a quantum gate that uses a control qubit to swap two target qubits.

Free-space interconnects. Interconnections among optical elements that use line-of-sight transmission of laser beams.

Fringes. Fringes are the bright and dark stripes that are created by the constructive and destructive interference of coherent light.

Fovea. An area of the retina specialized for high acuity; contains a high density of cones and rods.

Frontal lobe. One of the four lobes of the brain; includes all the cortex that lies anterior to the central sulcus and superior to the lateral fissure.

Gain.

LASER: Laser gain is achieved through population inversion, allowing amplification through stimulated emission.

CLAMPING: A process in a laser medium when the gain (population inversion) achieves a maximum value but can go no higher.

RAMAN: Amplification of laser light through the Raman effect (excitation of mechanical vibrations in a medium).

Ganglion cell. The cell in the retina that responds to a retinal receptive field. The collection of ganglion cell axons comprise the optic nerve.

Gate.

LOGIC: A classical device that performs Boolean logic on classical bits.

QUANTUM: A quantum logic device that operates on qubits.

Genetic algorithm. A computer algorithm that uses Darwinian selection to allow more "fit" programs to survive at the expense of less fit programs.

Gordon-Haus noise. A fundamental source of noise for solitons in fibers.

Grandmother neuron. A partially hypothetical and partially mythical neuron in the brain that responds when a baby sees its grandmother.

Grating. A diffraction grating is a periodic pattern that diffracts light into specific angles. Holograms are composed of many individual diffraction gratings.

Harmonic generation. Harmonic generation is a nonlinear optical process that takes light of one frequency (color) and generates light with integer multiples of frequencies. Second harmonic generation was the first experimental demonstration of nonlinear optics.

Hertz. A unit of frequency. One Hertz is equal to one wave cycle per second.

Hidden.

LAYER: Neurons in the middle layers of a neural network are called hidden neurons.

VARIABLES: Variables proposed by Einstein, Podolsky and Rosen that explain when a quantum event occurs. Hidden variable theories remove the indeterminacy of quantum measurements.

Hologram. A record of the interference pattern between two or more coherent light beams.

Horizontal Cells. Retinal neurons that mediate lateral interactions between photoreceptor terminals and the dendrites of bipolar cells.

Hydroxide. Hydroxide is the chemical unit OH. Hydroxide impurities in glass limit the distance that light can travel in fiber optics.

Image correlator. An image correlator is a specialized parallel optical computer that simultaneously finds all occurrences of a target image in a signal image.

Incoherent. Light (or more generally a wave) that is incoherent is chaotic and has no phase relationship with later or earlier parts of the wave.

Information. Shannon's information is a measure of all possible messages that can be composed in an information system. The information content of a message is defined as

$$H = - \sum_i p_i \log_2 p_i$$

where p_i is the probability that the letter i occurs in the message.

Information convergence. Information convergence in the retina allows the information from 100 million photoreceptors to be compressed into the signals on a million ganglion cell axons in the optic nerve.

Infrared. Electromagnetic waves that have wavelengths slightly longer than visible light.

Intelligence. Intelligence is defined in three levels: The lowest level is stimulus response. The highest level is consciousness. The middle level contains everything else, including artificial intelligence.

Intelligent agents. Software programs that surf the Internet on behalf of their users. These programs are neural networks that learn what their users want.

Interference.

CLASSICAL: Interference of classical waves occurs when two or more waves add together constructively or destructively. Interference of light leads to bright and dark interference fringes.

QUANTUM: Quantum interference occurs between multiple quantum wavefunctions. Quantum interference makes unintuitive processes possible such as quantum seeing in the dark.

Interferometer. A wide class of optical devices that work on the principle of the interference of coherent light waves.

Ion trap. A physical apparatus that can trap a single ion or a string of ions making them available for quantum operations.

Kerr effect. The non-linear Kerr effect is the change of the refractive index of a material dependent on the incident intensity.

Laser. Laser is an acronym that stands for light amplification through stimulated emission of radiation. Lasers emit coherent light.

Lateral Geniculate Nucleus (LGN). A nucleus in the thalamus that receives the axonal projections of retinal ganglion cells in the primary visual pathway.

Light. Light is electromagnetic radiation in the range of wavelengths from 400 nanometers to 700 nanometers. This term also often refers to infrared light and ultraviolet light.

Light emitting diode (LED). A light emitting diode is a semiconductor device that emits light when a voltage is applied. The light from an LED is not coherent.

Light quantum. Also known as the Lichtquanten, the term was applied by Einstein to describe what later became known as the "photon."

Liquid crystal light valve (LCLV). A liquid crystal light valve is similar to the liquid crystal display on portable computers or a SONY watchman. Pixels are turned on or off by a control light beam.

Logarithm. A logarithm answers the question of how many times a number needs to be multiplied by itself to give a number. For instance $\log_2 (2^N) = N$, where the base is equal to the number 2.

Logic gate. A circuit that takes binary inputs and produces a binary output that depends on the gate function. Logic gates include AND, OR and NOT functions. Logic gates can also be quantum logic gates that operate on qubits.

Mach-Zender interferometer. One of several types of interferometers. A Mach-Zender uses a beam splitter to split a beam into two paths that are superposed again by a second beam splitter. These interferometers are often used for controlling light.

Macroscopic. This term refers to collections of very many atoms or quantum states. Macroscopic systems are generally too large to be described by the individual quantum wavefunctions of their constituents.

Maser. Maser is an acronym standing for microwave amplification through stimulated emission of radiation. Masers were the predecessors of lasers.

Memory register. A set of slots to store bits in memory.

Micro-electromechanical systems (MEMS). Electronically actuated mirrors machined in silicon that are used in all-optical switches.

Mode.

COMPETITION: In a laser with a gain medium above threshold, multiple laser modes compete for the gain. This competition often takes the form of winner-take-all.

FIBER: Light traveling down a fiber does so only in a discrete set of spatial waves called modes. Most telecommunications occur in single-mode fibers that can only support one fiber mode.

LASER: A laser mode in a laser cavity satisfies the condition that the cavity length is equal to a half-integer number of wavelengths. Each mode is a standing wave inside the cavity.

LOCKING: The means of locking together all the modes of a laser in time to produce an ultrashort laser pulse.

Moore's Law. The observation by Gordon Moore, one of the co-founders of Intel, that the doubling time of the number of transistors on a chip is eighteen months.

NAND gate. A NAND gate is a logic gate that stands for NOT AND. It is equivalent to an AND gate followed by a NOT gate.

Neural network. A neural network is a network of neurons. Natural neural networks are brains. Artificial neural networks are idealized models of neurons implemented in software and hardware.

Neuron. A natural neuron is a cell of the nervous system. An artificial neuron is a node that sums its inputs and uses a threshold as a non-linear function to make decisions.

Non-linear Optics. Non-linear optics is concerned with situations when one light beam affects the propagation of another light beam in a medium. Such a medium is said to be non-linear. This is the principal mechanism for the control of light by light.

Nonlocality. Non-locality refers to the EPR paradox. In one interpretation, the measurement of one member of an entangled pair of particles causes the instantaneous collapse of the wavefunction of the other particle regardless of how far away it is.

Non-Return-To-Zero Format (NRZ). A format for optical pulses that places bits in consecutive time slots without guard slots in between. NRZ formats are used for TDM at lower data rates. The advantage of NRZ is that the data rate and the utilized bandwidth are equal. This represents the most efficient use of bandwidth for communication.

Noun phrase. A noun-bearing element of deep structure of a sentence used in descriptions of transformation grammar.

Novelty detector. An optical device that only responds to changes in a scene or image.

Object beam. During holographic recording, the object beam carries the image of interest that interferes with the reference beam.

Occipital lobe. The posterior lobe of the cerebral hemisphere: primarily devoted to vision.

Off-center. A center-surround structure in the retina that has an inhibitory center and an excitatory surround.

On-center. A center-surround structure in the retina that has an excitatory center and an inhibitory surround.

Optical domain. A term referring to devices that keep optical signals as optical signals without converting them to electronics and back again.

Optical modulator. Any of a set of optical devices that modulate the amplitude or phase of a light beam.

Optic Chiasm. The junction of the optic nerves on the ventral aspect of the diencephalon, where axons from the nasal parts of each retina cross the midline.

Optic Nerve. The nerve (cranial nerve II) containing the axons of retinal ganglion cells; extends from the eye to the optic chiasm.

Optic Radiation. The optic radiation is the set of neurons that carry the visual stimulus from the LGN to the visual cortex.

Optoelectronics. Optoelectronics is the hybrid combination of electrons and photons in the same materials or devices.

OR gate. An OR gate is a logic gate that has two binary inputs and one binary output. The output is equal to 1 when either or both of the two inputs is equal to 1, and is zero otherwise.

Orthogonal.
AXES: Directions that are at mutual right angles, such as the x-y-z coordinate axes of space.
POLARIZATION: Two light beams have orthogonal polarization when the electric field vector of one is at a right angle to the field of the other.
WAVEFUNCTIONS: Quantum wavefunctions are orthogonal when neither can be expressed as part of the other.

Packet. Packets are digital data formats used in telecommunication that take a signal and break it down into chunks (packets) that have header addresses that tell where the packet is to go. Packets have been likened to addressed envelopes containing letters. Successive signal packets from the same user can take different paths from source to destination.

Parallel. Any system in which data is stored or transmitted in multiple "channels" is a parallel data system. The channels can be defined by spatial, spectral or temporal variables.

Parietal lobe. The lobe of the brain that lies between the frontal lobe anteriorly, and occipital lobe posteriorly.

Perceptrons. Simple feed-forward neural networks with two or more layers. These were the first neural networks studied and were so-named because they could "perceive" simple patterns.

Phase.
CONJUGATION: A nonlinear optical process that generates a wave that has exactly the opposite phase of an original wave.
OPTICAL: Optical phase is expressed as a fraction of 2 times pi. Examples of points on a wave that have constant phase are the peaks or the troughs.
QUANTUM: The phase of the quantum wavefunction cannot be measured directly, but differences in quantum phase can be measured through interference.

SHIFTER: An optical device, such as an electro-optic modulator, that shifts the phase of a wave that travels through it.

Photodetector. An ideal photodetector takes a photon and turns it into an electron that can be sensed in an external circuit. Typical photodetectors have a quantum efficiency that is less than one, and is typically around 70%.

Photoelectric effect. The emission of electrons from a metal by the absorption of a photon. It was Einstein's prediction of the photoelectric effect that won him the Nobel prize.

Photon. The quantum unit of light energy. The energy of a photon is related to its frequency by the relation $E = h\nu$.

Photonics. The study and engineering of optical devices that generate, manipulate or detect photons.

Photonic router. A router in an optical network that keeps the signal in the optical domain without conversion to electrons. A "true" photonic router would also be able to perform optical control using the optical information of the header.

Photorefractive effect. In the photorefractive effect spatially varying intensity patterns generate refractive index gratings that diffract light. It is one of the highest-sensitivity optical non-linearities.

Pixel. The smallest unit of an image.

Plane wave. A plane wave has wavefronts that are perfectly planar. Plane waves make good reference beams for holography.

Polarization.

ATOMIC: An electric field applied to an atom pulls the electrons slightly away from the atom's nucleus. This displacement is called the atomic polarization.

LIGHT: The direction of the electric field vector in an electromagnetic wave defines its direction of polarization.

Polarizer. An optical device that takes light of any polarization and produces light with only a single polarization.

Population inversion. The condition when there are more atoms in excited states than in the ground state. This is the condition for laser gain.

Positronium. The quantum state of an electron and its antimatter equivalent, the positron. Positronium has a quantum structure much like hydrogen, but decays through self-annihilation in about one-tenth of a microscecond, on average. Two entangled gamma-ray photons are produced in the annihilation.

Probability. Quantum physics is fundamentally probabilistic. It is not possible to know when a quantum event will occur. The occurrence can only be defined through probability. In quantum wave mechanics, the Born interpretation assigns probability to the square of the magnitude of the quantum wavefunction.

Pump rate. The rate at which the atoms in a laser medium are pumped into their excited state, from which light can be stimulated.

Psychophysics. The quantitative study of the physically measurable responses of human subjects to quantitative stimuli.

Quantum physics. The physics of the smallest units of energy and matter.

Quantum State. A quantum state is a discrete physical state. Quantum states can be used to store and transmit information.

Qubit. A qubit is a quantum bit. Any quantum two-state system can store qubits. Qubits are quantum superpositions of 1 and 0. N qubit gates can store 2^N bits of information simultaneously.

RC time. The time it takes an electronic circuit to charge. R and C refer to resistance and capacitance of the the the device, respectively.

Reconstruction. When a reference beam illuminates a hologram the diffracted light reconstructs the original object wavefront. This is called hologram reconstruction.

Redundancy. Redundancy is defined as the difference between the information content of a text and the limiting information content when all orders of statistics are included. The redundancy R of English is given by $R = (H_{max} - H_{lim})/H_{max}$, where H_{max} = 4.71 bits/letter (obtained if all transition probabilities were equal) and H_{lim} = 2.5 for the orthography of the English language on a letter basis.

Reference beam. The reference beam provides the standard in holographic recording to which the phase of the object beam is related. The reference beam is usually a plane wave.

Refractive Index. The refractive index of a material is the ratio of the speed of light in vacuum to the speed of light in the material. Glass has a refractive index of about 1.5.

Resonator.

LASER: A laser resonator is synonymous with laser cavity. The standing waves in a cavity are called resonances.

Retina. The layer of neurons at the back of the eye composed of three layers of specialized neurons that detect light and transmit the signals up the optic nerve.

Return-to-Zero format (RZ). When the optical data bits are represented as pulses with gaps between. This differentiates this format from NRZ (non-return-to-zero) format in which the data pulses fill consecutive time slots without gaps. The data rate of a RZ signal equals half the bandwidth used.

Rhodopsin. The photopigment found in rods.

Rivest-Shamir-Adleman (RSA) Encryption. RSA is a public key cryptography protocol that relies on the difficulty of factoring the product of two large prime numbers. It has become the standard for secure communications.

Rod. Photoreceptor in the retina that responds to intensity and not color. Rods operate at the lowest light illumination.

Ruby laser. The ruby laser was the first laser invented by Theodore Maiman working at Hughes Research Lab in Malibu in 1960.

Saccade. Ballistic, conjugate eye movements that change the point of foveal fixation.

Sclera. The sclera, the white of the eye, is a direct extension of the dura mater, the layer that encases the brain.

Second harmonic. Second harmonic generation is a non-linear optical process that involves the creation of light with a frequency that is equal to two times the frequency of a fundamental pump beam.

Semantic network. A semantic network is a structure for representing knowledge as a pattern of interconnected nodes and arcs. The tree structure for transformational grammar is one example of a semantic network.

Semiconductor. A class of materials whose conductivity can be sensitively controlled with appropriate fabrication. Silicon and GaAs are two common semiconductors used for electronics and optoelectronics, respectively.

Semiconductor Optical Amplifier. A structure similar to a semiconductor laser, but with antireflection coatings that prevent lasing. SOAs are fast and efficient and are making important inroads in all-optical switching that use optical control instead of electronic control.

Serial. Data transmission one bit at a time.

Sign.

    SEMIOTIC: In Pierce's semiotic theory, a sign is either an icon, an index or a symbol according to whether it appears like its referent, has properties of its referent, or is arbitrarily assigned, respectively.

Silica. Silica is a form of silicon dioxide. It can be made very pure to allow optical transmission over large distances in silica fibers.

Single-mode fiber. A fiber optic that allows only a single mode of light to propagate. These fibers eliminate modal dispersion of an optical signal that occurs in multi-mode fibers.

Soliton. A soliton is a solitary wave that travels in non-linear media without broadening. Optical solitons travel in glass fibers without the adverse effects of dispersion.

Spatial light modulator. The liquid crystal display of a portable computer or SONY Watchman is a spatial light modulator. They are used as the image input devices for optical computers.

Speckle. Any time a laser beam strikes an uneven surface, the reflected light is composed of a random pattern of bright and dark interference spots. This is called laser speckle.

Spectral. Pertaining to the color or wavelength components of a signal.

Spontaneous emission. When an atom has an electron in an excited state, the electron can spontaneously make a transition to a lower state with the emission of a photon that carries away an energy equal to the energy difference between the initial and final electron states.

Stimulated emission. An electron in an excited state of an atom can be stimulated by one photon to emit another photon. The emitted photon has identical quantum properties with the first photon. By cascading this effect, laser radiation builds up inside a laser cavity.

Striate cortex. Primary visual cortex in the occipital lobe (also called Brodmann's area 17). So named because the prominence of layer IV in myelin-stained sections gives this region a striped appearance.

Superposition. A quantum superposition means that a particle can be in one of a number of different quantum states—all at the same time. It is expressed mathematically as a sum of wavefunctions with coefficients related to the probability of finding a particle in the specific states.

Surface structure. The physical manifestation of a sentence in sounds or letters or signs.

Susceptibility. The optical susceptibility of an atom or a material is a measure of how easily an electric field can polarize it. Larger susceptibilities lead to larger refractive indexes. Non-linear susceptibility is what allows light to interact with light in all-optical control.

Synapse. Specialized apposition between a neuron and its target cell for transmission of information by release and reception of a chemical transmitter agent.

Synchronous Optical Network (SONET). The physical architecture of current-generation fiber-optic telecommunication systems.

Tachistoscope. A device for projecting images with specific durations and with specific intensities used for psychophysical studies.

Telecom. Shortened form for telecommunication. Used for long-haul and metro-area networks working at wavelengths around 1.3 and 1.5 microns.

Teleportation. Quantum teleportation is the transportation of qubits from one place to another without ever needing (or wanting) to measure the properties of the qubits beforehand.

Temporal lobe. The hemispheric lobe that lies inferior to the lateral fissure.

Thought experiment. This is an idealized experiment that is thought through, using logic and an understanding of physics, leading either to clear conclusions about the meaning of physics, or to paradoxes that can only be resolved through deeper insight. Many of the important discussions between Bohr and Einstein were phrased in terms of thought experiments.

Threshold.

LASER: Lasers require a pumping rate higher than a set threshold before they can begin to oscillate (lase).

NEURON: To fire, neurons need the sum of their inputs to exceed a set threshold.

Time-Division Multiplexing (TDM). Time division multiplexing takes M signals at lower bit rates and interleaves them into a single signal that is at a date rate M times larger.

Time-reversal mirror. A time-reversal mirror takes light waves and sends them back along their original path *as if* the wave had been time-reversed. It is implemented holographically and is useful for beam cleanup.

Transit time. The time for an electron to travel across an electronic device.

Transition.

QUANTUM: When an electron changes its energy level, usually in association with the absorption or emission of a photon.

Transition probability. In a language or a code, the probability that one character will be followed by another character is called a transition probability. A sequence that is governed by transition probabilities is called a Markov chain. Transition probabilities are used to estimate the limiting information content.

Tremor. Motion where the eye oscillates back and forth with small excursions at frequencies in the range of 50–100 times per second (50–100 Hz), with an oscillation period of 10–20 milliseconds.

Trunk line. The central telecommunication line that carries the highest data rates between major distribution stations.

Truth Table. A table of a logic gate that enumerates each output for each possible input value of bits.

Turing.

ALAN: The enigmatic mathematician who is considered the father of computer science.

MACHINE: An idealized algorithm by which any computable problem can be computed, devised by Alan Turing. Elements of the Turing machine, such as a processing unit and a memory unit, later were incorporated in stored-program computers.

TEST: A pragmatic test devised by Alan Turing to determine whether a computer program is intelligent.

Universal computer. Any problem that is computable can be computed on a universal computer. In this sense all universal computers are equivalent.

Visual Cortex. The parts of the occipital lobe involved in vision.

Wavefront. A wavefront is a surface of constant phase of a wave. For instance, a spherical wave has spherical wavefronts, and a plane wave has planar wavefronts. The wavefronts from an object that forms holograms are very complex.

Wavefunction. A wavefunction is the function that describes the mechanics of a quantum particle. The squared amplitude of the wavefunction is proportional to the probability of observing the particle as the result of a measurement.

Wavefunction collapse. If a wavefunction is a superposition of several possible quantum states, then making a measurement of the wavefunction results in only one of those states being observed. This one result from the many possible is called wavefunction collapse because the superposed wavefunction collapses into a single wavefunction. The theoretical aspects of wavefunction collapse are the least certain within quantum theory. Some quantum philosophers have gone so far as to claim that there *is* no satisfactory theory for wavefunction collapse.

Waveguide. A structure that channels waves. A fiber optic is a waveguide for light.

Wavelength. The wavelength of a wave is the distance from crest-to-crest or trough-to-trough. For visible light, the wavelengths vary from 400 nm (in the blue) to 700 nm (in the red).

Wavelength-Division Multiplexing (WDM). Multiple optical signals can be sent simultaneously down the same fiber coded as different colors. This is called wavelength-division-multiplexing.

Wavemechanics. The study of the motion of quantum particles when viewed as waves.

Wave-particle duality. The principle in quantum mechanics that attributes simultaneous wave and particle properties to a quantum state. Measurements that measure wave properties (interference) return wave properties, but measurements that measure particle properties (location and momentum) return particle properties.

Weight. Synaptic: The synaptic weight is the excitatory or inhibitory value associated with the synapse between two neurons.

Wernicke's area. Region of the cortex in the superior and posterior region of the left temporal lobe that helps mediate language comprehension. Named after the nineteenth-century neurologist, Karl Wernicke.

"What" pathway. A neural pathway that is sustained from the retina through the primary visual cortex to higher cortex areas. This pathway deals with color and shape and the identity of an object. It is roughly identified with the P (parvocellular) pathway that constitutes 90% of the retinal ganglions.

"Where" pathway. A neural pathway that is sustained from the retina through the primary visual cortex to higher cortex areas. This pathway deals with spatial information separated into motion and form. It is roughly identified with the M (magnocellular) pathway that constitutes 10% of the retinal ganglions.

XOR gate. An XOR gate is an exclusive OR logic gate that gives a 1 when either of the inputs is equal to 1, but not both, and is 0 otherwise.

BIBLIOGRAPHY

UNIVERSAL AND VISUAL LANGUAGES

Aiton, E. J., *Leibniz: A Biography.* 1985, Bristol: Adam Hilger Ltd.

Arnheim, R., *Visual Thinking.* 1969, London: Faber and Faber.

Baigrie, B. S., ed. *Picturing Knowledge: Historical and Philosophical Problems Concerning the Use of Art in Science.* 1996, Toronto: University of Toronto Press.

Barlow, H., C. Blakemore, and M. Weston-Smith, eds. *Images and Understanding.* 1990, Cambridge: Cambridge University Press.

Boyer, C. B., *The History of the Calculus and its Conceptual Development.* 1959, New York: Dover.

———, *A History of Mathematics.* 1985, Princeton, New Jersey: Princeton University Press.

Cajori, F., *A History of Mathematical Notations.* 1993, New York: Dover.

Dascal, M., *Leibniz: Language, Signs and Thought.* Foundation of Semiotics, ed. A. Eschbach. 1987, Amsterdam: John Benjamins Publishing Co.

Diringer, D., *The Alphabet.* 1968, London: Hutchinson.

Dondis, D. A., *A Primer of Visual Literacy.* 1973, Cambridge, Mass.: MIT University Press.

Eco, U., *The Search for the Perfect Language.* 1997, Oxford: Blackwell.

Ferguson, E. S., *Engineering and the Mind's Eye.* 1992, Cambridge, Mass.: MIT Press.

Field, G. W., *Hermann Hesse.* 1970, New York: Twayne Publishers, Inc.

Ford, B. J., *Images of Science: A History of Scientific Illustration.* 1992, London: British Library.

Friedhoff, R. M. and W. Benzon, *Visualization: The Second Computer Revolution.* 1989, New York: W. H. Freeman and Co.

Gelb, I. J., *A Study of Writing.* 1963, Chicago: University of Chicago Press.

Gombrich, E. H., *Art and Illusion: A Study in the Psychology of Pictoral Representation.* 1968, London: Phaidon Press.

Hagen, M., ed. *The Perception of Pictures.* 1980, New York: Academic Press.

Hall, E. T., *The Silent Language.* 1959, New York: Doubleday.

Hesse, H., *Magister Ludi: The Glass Bead Game*. 1969, New York: Holt, Rinehart and Winston, Inc.

Ishiguro, H., *Leibniz's Philosophy of Logic and Language*. 1972, Ithaca, New York: Cornell University Press.

Jackendoff, R., *Patterns in the Mind*. 1994, New York: Basic Books.

Jensen, H., *Sign, Symbol and Script*. 1970: George Allen and Unwin.

Jung, C. G., *Symbols of Transformation*. Collected Works. 1956, New York: Bollingen-Pantheon.

Kepes, G., *Language of Vision*. 1944, Chicago: Paul Theobald.

Knowlson, J., *Universal Language Schemes in England and France 1600–1800*. 1975, Toronto: University of Toronto Press.

Large, A., *The Artificial Language Movement*. 1985, Oxford: Basil Blackwell.

Mason, W. A., *A History of the Art of Writing*. 1920, New York: The Macmillan Co.

Menninger, K., *Number Words and Number Symbols*. 1969, Cambridge, Mass.: MIT University Press.

Mileck, J., *Hermann Hesse: Life, Work, and Criticism*. 1984, Fredericton, Canada: York Press Ltd.

Miller, A. I., *Imagery in Scientific Thought: Creating Twentieth Century Physics*. 1984, Boston: Birkhauser.

Mitchell, W. J. T., ed. *The Language of Images*. 1974, Chicago: University of Chicago Press.

Myers, J. F., *The Language of Visual Art: Perception as a Basis for Design*. 1989, Fort Worth: Holt, Rinehart and Winston.

Saint-Martin, F., *Semiotics of Visual Language*. Advances in Semiotics, ed. T. A. Sebeok. 1990, Bloomington and Indianapolis: Indiana University Press.

Sampson, G., *Writing Systems*. 1985, Stanford: Stanford University Press.

Tufte, E. R., *The Visual Display of Quantitative Information*. 1983, Cheshire, Conn.: Graphics Press.

Tufte, E. R., *Envisioning Information*. 1990, Cheshire, Conn.: Graphics Press.

INFORMATION THEORY, COMMUNICATION AND LANGUAGE

Attneave, F., *Applications of Information Theory to Psychology*. 1959, New York: Holt, Rinehart and Winston.

Bacon, F., *The Philosophical Works*, ed. J. M. Robertson. 1905, London: Routledge.

Campbell, J., *Grammatical Man: Information, Entropy, Language and Life*. 1982, New York: Simon and Schuster.

Chao, Y.-R., *Language and Symbolic Systems*. 1968, Cambridge: Cambridge University Press.

Cherry, C., *On Human Communication: A Review, a Survey, and a Criticism.* 1982, Boston: MIT University Press.

Chomsky, N., *Aspects of the Theory of Syntax.* 1965, Cambridge: MIT University Press.

————, *Reflections on Language.* 1975, New York: Pantheon.

————, *Language and Mind.* 1972, New York: Harcourt.

Crystal, D., *The Cambridge Encyclopedia of Language.* 1987, Cambridge, Mass.: Cambridge University Press.

Deacon, T. W., *The Symbolic Species.* 1997, New York: Norton.

de Saussure, F., *Course in General Linguistics.* 1959, New York: Philosophic Library.

Locke, J., *An Essay Concerning Human Understanding.* 1995, Amherst, New York: Prometheus Books.

Nöth, W., *Handbook of Semiotics.* 1995, Bloomington: Indiana University Press.

Pierce, J. R., *Symbols, Signals and Noise: The Nature and Process of Comunnication.* 1961, New York: Harper and Row.

————, *An Introduction to Information Theory.* 1980, New York: Dover.

Pinker, S., *The Language Instinct.* 1994: William Morrow.

————, *How the Mind Works.* 1997, New York: Norton.

Shannon, C. E. and W. Weaver, *The Mathematical Theory of Communication.* 1949, Urbana: University of Illinois Press.

ARTIFICIAL INTELLIGENCE AND NEURAL NETWORKS

Bailey, J., *After Thought.* 1996, New York: Basic Books.

Calvin, W. H., *How Brains Think.* 1996, New York: Basic Books.

————, *The Cerebral Code.* 1996, Cambridge, Mass.: MIT Press.

Dreyfus, H., *What Computers Still Can't Do.* 1992, Cambridge, Mass.: MIT Press.

Hofstadter, D., *Gödel, Escher, Bach: An Eternal Golden Braid.* 1979, New York: Vintage Books.

Gödel, K., *On Formally Undecidable Propositions of Principia Mathematica and Related Systems.* 1992, New York: Dover.

Harvey, R. L., *Neural Network Principles.* 1994, Englewood Cliffs: Prentice Hall.

Kurzweil, R., *The Age of Spiritual Machines.* 1999, New York: Penguin.

McCorduck, P., *Machines Who Think.* 1979, San Francisco: W. H. Freeman.

Mendel, J. M., ed. *A Prelude to Neural Networks: Adaptive and Learning Systems.* 1994, Prentice Hall: Englewood Cliffs.

Minsky, M. and S. Papert, *Perceptrons: An Introduction to Computational Geometry.* 1969, Cambridge, Mass.: MIT Press.

Müller, B. and J. Reinhardt, *Neural Networks: An Introduction.* 1990, Berlin: Springer Verlag.

Penrose, R., *The Emperor's New Mind: Concerning Computers, Minds, and the Laws of Physics*. 1989, New York: Penguin Books.

Pratt, V., *Thinking Machines: The Evolution of Artificial Intelligence*. 1987, Oxford: Basil Blackwell.

Quinlan, P. T., *Connectionism and Psychology: A Psychological Perspective on New Connectionist Research*. 1991, Chicago: University of Chicago Press.

Zeidenberg, M., *Neural Network Models in Artificial Intelligence*. 1990, New York: Ellis Horwood.

Zhou, Y.-T. and R. Chellappa, *Artificial Neural Networks for Computer Vision*. 1992, Berlin: Springer-Verlag.

THE EYE AND BRAIN

Dowling, J. E., *The Retina: An Approachable Part of the Brain*. 1987, Cambridge, Mass.: Harvard University Press.

Gregory, R. L., *Eye and Brain*. Princeton Science Library. 1990, Princeton, New Jersey: Princeton University Press.

Keele, K. D., *Leonardo da Vinci's Elements of the Science of Man*. 1983, New York: Academic Press.

Leibovic, K. N., ed. *Science of Vision*. 1990, Springer-Verlag: New York.

Llinas, R. R., *The Biology of the Brain: From Neurons to Networks*. Scientific American Library. 1988, New York: W. H. Freeman and Co.

Marr, D., *Vision*. 1982, New York: W. H. Freeman and Company.

O'Malley, C. D. and J. B. D. Saunders, *Leonardo on the Human Body*. 1983, New York: Dover.

Palmer, S. E., *Vision Science: Photons to Phenomenology*. 1999, Cambridge, Mass.: The MIT Press.

Posner, M. I. and M. E. Raichle, *Images of Mind*. 1994, New York: Scientific American Library.

Rock, I., *The Perceptual World*. Scientific American Library. 1990, New York: W. H. Freeman and Co.

Tovee, M. J., *An Introduction to the Visual System*. 1996, Cambridge: Cambridge University Press.

PSYCHOPHYSICS AND READING

Downing, J. and C. K. Leong, *Psychology of Reading*. 1982: Collier-Macmillan.

Garner, W. R., *The Processing of Information and Structure*. 1974, New York: John Wiley and Sons.

Henderson, L., *Orthography and Word Recognition in Reading*. 1982, New York: Academic Press.

Jensen, A. R., *Individual Differences in the Hick Paradigm*, in *Speed of Information-Processing and Intelligence*, P. A. Vernon, Editor. 1987, Norwood: Ablex Publishing Corp.

Klima, E. and U. Bellugi, *The Signs of Language*. 1979, Cambridge, Mass.: Harvard University Press.

Quastler, H., *Studies of Human Channel Capacities*, in *Information Theory*, C. Cherry, Editor. 1956, London: Butterworths.

Reber, A. S. and D. L. Scarborough, *Toward a Psychology of Reading*. 1977, New York: Wiley.

Smith, F., *Understanding Reading*. 1986, Hillsdale, New Jersey: Lawrence Erlbaum Associates.

LASERS AND FIBER OPTICS

Bromberg, J. L., *The Laser in America, 1950–1970*. 1991, Cambridge, Mass.: MIT Press.

Bloembergen, N., *Nonlinear Optics*. 1996, Singapore: World Scientific.

Chaffee, C. D., *The Rewiring of America: The Fiber Optics Revolution*. 1988, Boston: Academic Press.

Gilder, G., *Telecosm: How infinite Bandwidth will Revolutionize our World*. 2000, New York: Free Press.

Hecht, J., *Laser Pioneers*. 1992, New York: Academic Press.

———, *City of Light: The Story of Fiber Optics*. 1999, Oxford: Oxford University Press.

Townes, C. H., *How the Laser Happened*. 1999, New York: Oxford University Press.

OPTICAL LOGIC AND COMPUTERS

Arsenault, H. H. and Y. Sheng, *Introduction to Optical Computing*. 1992: S P I E-International Society for Optical Engineering.

Karim, M. A. and A. A. Awwal, *Optical Computing: An Introduction*. 1992, New York: John Wiley & Sons.

Li, K., et al., eds. *Parallel Computing Using Optical Interconnections*. 1998, Kluwer.

McAulay, A. D., *Optical Computer Architectures*. 1991, New York: John Wiley & Sons.

Midwinter, J. E., ed. *Photonics in Switching.* 1993, San Diego: Academic Press.

Saleh, B. E. A. and M. C. Teich, *Fundamentals of Photonics.* 1991, New York: John Wiley & Sons.

QUANTUM COMMUNICATION AND COMPUTING

Brown, J., *Minds, Machines and the Multiverse: The Quest for the Quantum Computer.* 2000, New York: Simon & Schuster.

Deutsch, D., *The Fabric of Reality.* 1997, New York: Allen Lane.

Giuluini, D., et al., *Decoherence and the Appearance of a Classical World in Quantum Theory.* 1996, Berlin: Springer-Verlag.

Hey, A. J. G., ed. *Feynman and Computation: Exploring the Limits of Computers.* 1999, Cambridge, Mass.: Perseus Books.

Milburn, G. J., *Schrödinger's Machines: The Quantum Technology Reshaping Everyday Life.* 1997, New York: W. H. Freeman and Co.

————, *The Feynman Processor: Quantum Entanglement and the Computing Revolution.* 1998, Reading, Mass.: Helix Books.

Stachel, J., *Einstein's Miraculous Year: Five Years that Changed the Face of Physics.* 1998, Princeton: Princeton University Press.

Wheeler, J. A. and W. Zurek, eds. *Quantum Theory and Measurement.* 1983, Princeton: Princeton University Press.

Whitaker, A., *Einstein, Bohr and the Quantum Dilemma.* 1996, Cambridge: Cambridge University Press.

Williams, C. P. and S. H. Clearwater, *Explorations in Quantum Computing.* 1998, New York: Springer.

NOTES

1 *This same eternal idea:* H. Hesse, *Magister Ludi: The Glass Bead Game.* New York: Holt, Rinehart & Winston, 1969. p. 7

2 *The parallel data rate on the optic nerve is over a megabyte per second:* The data rate of vision can be estimated by multiplying the number of axons in the optic nerve (approximately 1 million) with the data rate carried by each axon (approximately 1 bit per 30 milliseconds) = 30 million bits per second, or about 4 megabytes per second.

3 *The search for a universal language of visual symbols:* F. Bacon, *The Philosophical Works,* ed. J. M. Robertson. London: Routledge, 1905, p. 122.

3 *The psychologist Carl Jung strove for universality:* See C. G. Jung, *Symbols of Transformation. Collected Works.* New York: Bollingen-Pantheon, 1956.

3 *And in an altogether different sphere:* The purpose of their *Principia Mathematica* was to derive basic mathematical principles from the principles of logic alone. To do this, they developed a detailed and rigorous symbolic notation. It is intriguing that Russell had earlier written "A Critical Exposition of the Philosophy of Leibniz" (1900).

4 *Hesse became acquainted with the theories of Carl Jung:* Hesse underwent psychoanalysis with J. B. Lang, a disciple of Jung.

4 *The narrator tells how the fictitious originator:* Hesse, *Magister Ludi: The Glass Bead Game,* p. 27.

5 *"The true method should furnish us with an Ariadne's thread":* Ariadne, in Greek mythology, was the daughter of Pasiphaë and the Cretan king Minos. She fell in love with the Athenian hero Theseus, and using a thread of glittering jewels helped him escape the Labyrinth after he slew the Minotaur.

5 *Furthermore, it must be admitted that universal language schemes:* U. Eco, *The Search for the Perfect Language.* Oxford: Basil Blackwell, 1997.

5 *James Bailey:* J. Bailey, *After Thought.* New York: Basic Books, 1996.

7 *This stage started with mechanical calculators:* For a complete story on the history of calculators and computers, see V. Pratt, *Thinking Machines: The Evolution of Artificial Intelligence.* Oxford: Basil Blackwell, 1987.

9 *The rudimentary and specialized optical computers built so far:* Notable ex-

amples of optical computers are the digital optical processor developed at
AT&T Bell Labs in the late 1980s, and the optical processors developed at
Rockwell.

9   *Some of the current limitations have been in materials:* New possibilities are
opening up with recent developments in dense arrays of lasers that emit vertically from a semiconductor surface, and with engineered "photonic
bandgap" materials that allow light to turn sharp corners, in seeming defi-
ance of accepted wisdom.

11   *"I can promise you four works"*: Quoted by M. J. Klein in "Einstein's First
Paper on Quanta," D. E. Gershenson and D. A. Greenberg, eds., *The Natural
Philosopher,* Vol. 3. New York: Blaisdell Publishing, 1964, p. 59.

11   *The revolution in fiber-optic telecommunications was a rapid one:* Harnessing Light: *Optical Science and Engineering for the 21st Century.* Washington, DC: Committee on Optical Science & Engineering, ed. National
Academy Press, 1998, p. 33.

12   *This third generation will also harness quantum parallelism:* For instance, a
program that needs to enumerate every single possible configuration for 100
flipped coins (there are $2^{100} = 10^{30}$ configurations) working on a 32-bit computer running at a 1-gigahertz clock speed would take 1 trillion years to finish (the age of the universe is only 20 billion years). This is a problem that a
quantum computer consisting of 100 quantum bits could accomplish in a single operation.

14   *The retina codes this information in a compressed form:* MP3 is short for
MPEG-3, which stands for Motion Pictures Expert Group—Level III, and is a
data compression standard.

15   *Visible light is composed of electromagnetic waves:* The wavelengths of visible light lie between 400 nanometers and 700 nanometers, ranging from violet to red, respectively.

19   *In describing how an atom emits a quantum of light:* quoted by Klein in
"Einstein's First Paper on Quanta," p. 20, 1964.

20   *This means that the electrons in the walls could change their energy only by
jumps or leaps:* The energy difference between initial and final energies was
discovered by Planck to be $E = h\nu$, where h is today called Planck's constant,
and ν is the frequency of the radiation that is emitted or absorbed.

22   *By applying statistics to the problem he was led to the inescapable conclusion:* See A. Einstein, "On a heuristic viewpoint concerning the production
and transformation of light," *Ann. Phys.,* 17 (1905), 132.

22   *"That he may sometimes have missed the target"*: See Klein, "Elinstein's first
paper on quanta," p. 61.

23   *"I shall not attempt to present the basis for such an assumption"*: See ibid.,
p. 62.

23   *When an electron jumps from a higher energy state:* Einstein's light-quantum was renamed in 1926 as a "photon," combining the Greek word for light, φοτος (*fotos*), with the suffix ον by analogy with electron and proton.

26   *The race was won by Theodore H. Maiman:* T. H. Maiman, "Stimulated optical radiation in ruby," *Nature,* 187 (1960), 493.

27   *His discovery was quickly repeated by other groups:* See J. Hecht, *Laser Pioneers.* New York: Academic Press, 1992, pp. 21–26.

27   *Not long after the laser was discovered:* J. Hecht, *City of Light: The Story of Fiber Optics.* Oxford: Oxford University Press, 1999, p. 102.

30   *The first breakthrough came in 1966, with the suggestion by researchers:* K. C. Kao, and G. A. Hockham, "Dielectric-fibre surface waveguides for optical frequencies." Proc. IEE, 113 (1966), 1151–58.

30   *The second breakthrough came in 1970, when researchers at Corning:* F. P. Kapron, D. B. Keck, and R. D. Maurer, "Radiation losses in glass optical waveguides." Appl. Phys. Lett., 17 (1970), 423–25.

31   *The Bell Labs team won the race:* I. Hayashi, et al., "Junction lasers which operate continuously at room temperature." *Appl. Phys. Lett.,* 17 (1970), 109.

31   *The first field trial was conducted by the Bell System:* A comprehensive history of fiber optics can be found in the extensively researched book by Jeff Hecht, *City of Light: The Story of Fiber Optics.*

32   *But electrons, when considered as quantum particle waves:* The de Broglie wavelength of an electron in a semiconductor is typically larger than 10 nanometers, while it is less than 1 nanometer in a metal.

32   *The American physicist Richard Feynman (1918–1988) made the point:* R. P. Feynman, There's Plenty of Room at the Bottom, in Feynman and Computation, A. J. G. Hey, ed., Perseus Books: 1999 Reprinted from the Feb. 1960 issue of Caltech's Engineering and Science. The talk was given on Dec. 29th, 1959 at the annual meeting at the American Physical Society.

35   *In 1961, the American physicist Peter Franken:* P. A. Franken, et al., "Generation of optical harmonics." *Phys. Rev. Lett.,* 7 (1961), 118.

37   *Laser intensities in some applications can be weaker than the intensity of light:* In my research laboratory at Purdue University, my students and I have developed the world's most sensitive non-linear material, called a photorefractive quantum well device. This device allows light to control light at unprecedentedly low intensities. See, for instance, D. D. Nolte, "Semi-insulating semiconductor heterostructures: Optoelectronic properties and applications." *J. Appl. Phys.,* 85 (1999), 6259–89.

41   *All this changed in 1964, when the Irish physicist John Bell:* J. Bell, "On the Einstein-Podolsky-Rosen paradox." *Physics,* 1: (1964), 195.

41   *The measurements were made "on the fly":* A. Aspect, P. Grangier, and G.

Roger, "Experimental tests of realistic local theories via Bell's Theorem." *Phys. Rev. Lett.,* 47 (1981), 460–63.

41　*The same year that Aspect published his paper:* R. P. Feynman, *"Simulating physics with computers."* Int. J. Theoret. Phys., 21 (1982), 467.

43　*"A sign is something which stands to somebody":* in J. Fiske, *Introduction to Communication Studies,* quoted in J. Zeman, "Peirce's Theory of Signs," in *A Perfusion of Signs,* ed. T. Sebeok. Bloomington: Indiana University Press, 1977.

43　*"We can therefore imagine a science":* Fiske, *Introduction to Communication Studies* quoted in F. de Saussure, *Course in General Linguistics.* New York: Philosophic Library, 1959.

44　*It is an open question whether such a computer:* Some physicists, notably Roger Penrose in *Shadows of the Mind,* Oxford University Press, 1994, have attributed consciousness to quantum physics.

46　*In the axon, no laws of physics are violated:* The way a neural pulse travels down the axon is like a chain reaction: when one section of the axon fires, it triggers the next section, which triggers the next section, on and on to the synaptic terminals. The action potential constitutes a pulse that has a duration of approximately 1 millisecond. Before the pulse arrives, the membrane potential is at its resting potential of around -70 millivolts. When the neighboring section fires, it raises the membrane potential to a threshold value of about -60 millivolts, which triggers a rapid rise of the potential as ion channels open in the axon membrane. The potential rises above 0 millivolts, then falls again, undershooting the resting potential. The potential eventually recovers to the resting potential when this segment is ready for another pulse. The recovery period of the membrane, which is called the refractory period, plays two important roles. First, it prevents the pulse from traveling back up the axon to the soma. Second, it limits the maximum firing rate of the neuron.

　　The pulse reaches the terminal button at a synapse, the connection between the signaling neuron and the receiving neuron. The increase in the potential of the terminal button causes vesicles containing specialized neurotransmitters to merge with the cell membrane, releasing the transmitters into a small gap called the synaptic cleft between the axon and the dendrite. The cleft is only 20 nanometers wide, which allows the chemical neurotransmitter to diffuse to the dendrite membrane within milliseconds. The terminology that is used to describe chemical communication across the synaptic cleft is *presynaptic,* for the sending axon, and *postsynaptic,* for the receiving dendrite or cell body. The neurotransmitters activate membrane proteins in the postsynaptic membrane that open and increase the flow of charged ions across the postsynaptic membrane. This flow of charge raises the potential in the dendrite. When enough of the dendrites have received signals that increase the overall potential of the cell body to a threshold value (typically around -60 mV), this triggers the axon hillock that begins the process all over again, on through the myriad interconnections among the neurons.

48 *After the weeding-out period:* This is what limits the ability for a person who was blinded shortly after birth from ever seeing, even if the damage to the individual's eyes was reversible. Once the period of the mind's plasticity has been exceeded, the cortex neurons are simply not configured to receive signals from the retinal neurons.

49 *Nonetheless, these software models have become increasingly adept:* Visual pattern recognition implemented with cameras and neural network software has become highly sophisticated and fast. Face recognition is currently being used by automated bank machines. See R. Kurzweil, *The Age of Spiritual Machines.* New York: Penguin Books, 1999, p. 77.

49 *The seminal paper that launched this field:* W. S. McCulloch, and W. Pitts, "A logical calculus of the ideas immanent in nervous activity." *Bull. Math. Biophys.*, 5 (1943), 115.

49 *However, the budding field was shocked when Marvin Minsky:* M. Minsky, and S. Papert, *Perceptrons: An Introduction to Computational Geometry.* Cambridge, MA: MIT Press, 1969.

49 *However, the exhuberance of the field was dampened when Marvin Minsky:* It has become established in the popular folklore of neural net research that the book *Perceptrons* by Minsky and Papert single-handedly squelched the budding field that had been championed (and arguably over-sold) by Rosenblatt (who originated the concept of the perceptron). In fact, what Minsky strove to show was that simple perceptrons without loops (feed-forward nets) had rigorous limitations. Unfortunately, *Perceptrons* was published at just the moment when the field had gone about as far as it could with the ideas of the time. That the field stalled coincident with the publication of *Perceptrons* was taken as strong evidence that the book killed the field. Furthermore, the heated and very public battles between Minsky and Rosenblatt, and their clash of styles (Minsky's rigor versus Rosenblatt's unbounded enthusiasm), led credence to the theory that Minsky was generally antagonistic to neural networks. To this day, Minsky vigorously denies this, claiming it was never his intent to kill off the field, but rather to bring the sky-high speculations about the abilities of neural nets back to solid ground.

49 *that the perceptron could not implement the exclusive OR (XOR) logic gate:* The inability to perform an XOR operation is not catastrophic if all you want to do is build a universal Turing machine. After all, the perceptrons could implement AND, OR and NOT, and these three gates are universal. All it takes

to make an XOR is to take a combination of two ANDs, one NOT and one OR (you can construct one yourself as an exercise).

49   *Then, in 1986, several groups developed a technique called error back propagation:* D. E. Rumelhart, G. E. Hinton, and R. J. Williams, "Learning representations by back-propagating errors." *Nature,* 323 (1986), 533.

51   *A basic model for learning and adjustment of synaptic weights among neurons:* Neuropsychological Theory, 1949. D. O. Hebb, *The Organization of Behavior.* New York: Wiley, 1949. Hebb is considered by many the father of cognitive psychology. His work (even more than Chomsky's review of Skinner's *Verbal Behavior*) provided the empirical alternative to behaviorism.

53   *The structure of local excitation versus distant inhibition is common:* It is called a center-surround structure because stimulus of the center of the neural group produces a strong output, while stimulus of more distant neurons of the cluster inhibits the output.

54   *Neural networks are currently being etched:* A. Watson, "Neuromorphic engineering: Why can't a computer be more like a brain?" *Science,* 277 (1997), 1934–36.

54   *A silicon-integrated circuit designed by Carver Mead's group:* Carver Mead, *Analog VLSI and Neural Systems.* Reading, MA: Addison-Wesley, 1989. See also www.pcmp.caltech.edu.

54   *For instance, the Advanced Telecommunications Research (ATR) Laboratory:* Kurzweil, *The Age of Spiritual Machines,* p. 80.

54   *In 1957, B. F. Skinner:* B. F. Skinner, *Verbal Behavior.* New York: Appleton-Century-Crofts, 1957.

56   *This book was reviewed in 1959:* N. Chomsky, "A review of Skinner's Verbal Behavior." *Language,* 35 (1959), 26–58.

56   *"the magnitude of the failure":* Attributed to Noam Chomsky in M. H. Ashcraft, *Human Memory and Cognition.* 2nd ed. New York: HarperCollins, 1994, p. 30.

59   *"The third branch [of science] may be called":* J. Locke, *An Essay Concerning Human Understanding.* Amherst, NY: Prometheus Books, 1995, p. 608. Locke's coinage of the term arises from the Greek word Σημειωτικη (*Semeiotike*), used by Greek physicians who viewed medical diagnosis and prognosis as a process of interpreting the signs of the body. The root word comes from the Greek σημειον, meaning "sign," and σημαινειν," "to signify" or "to mean." Other words in English that share a common root include "semantics" and "semaphore."

61   *By this time, the motivated origin of the symbols:* The rotation of cuneiform to facilitate using the new stylus is one of the best examples I have found of the arbitrariness of symbolic representation. Despite the remnant traces of iconicity in the cuneiform symbols at this time, they contributed nothing to

the meaning. The symbols had already become arbitrary. This is why they could be written and viewed on their sides as easily as before they were rotated. The moral of this story is that we do not need iconicity in our symbols. It may help the process of invention, but it quickly becomes conventionalized as an arbitrary symbol.

62   *These two simple questions are answered in physiologically distinct regions:* Interestingly, these same two questions are also answered in related regions of the cortex of non-human primates, and other mammals and birds. Perceiving the external properties of reality is something that humans share in common with almost all advanced animals.

63   *This visual abstraction is purely non-verbal intelligence.:* For instance, see R. Arnheim, *Visual Thinking.* London: Faber & Faber, 1969.

63   *Much of this intelligence draws from spatial and temporal information:* Although not exclusively. For instance, the blind also have mechanical reasoning.

65   *"The visual cortex is perhaps the best-understood":* D. H. Hubel, Eye, Brain, and Vision, Scientific American Library (W. H. Freeman & Co., 1995) pg. 3.

66   *"And though you have a love for such things":* K. D. Keele, *Leonardo da Vinci's Elements of the Science of Man.* New York: Academic Press, 1983, p. 37.

67   *After the hardened mass was removed from the water:* Cf. ibid., p, 204: "In the anatomy of the eye in order to see the inside well without spilling its humour one should place the whole eye in white of egg, make it boil and become solid, cutting the egg and the eye transversely in order that none of the middle portion may be poured out."

71   *Our eyes are quantum photoreceivers:* Rhodopsin is a schizophrenic molecule with two personalities. In its unexcited state, it is composed of two molecules that are bound together. One is a protein called opsin, while the other is a lipid, synthesized from vitamin A, called retinal. Retinal is the light-sensitive component and comes in two forms—a straight chain called all-trans retinal, and a second with a kink in it, called 11-cis-retinal. It is the kinked form that binds to opsin in the unexcited condition. When the retinal absorbs a photon of light, the kink suddenly straightens out in one thousandth of a billionth of a second (known as a picosecond). This form of retinal cannot bind to opsin, so the rhodopsin breaks apart into separate retinal and opsin molecules, and the retinal molecule changes color from rose to pale yellow.

The rhodopsin in the rods and cones is embedded in membranes that resemble microscopic stacked plates. Membranes are extremely important for the functioning of neural cells because they control the flow of charged ions across the membrane by opening or closing specific ion channels in response to chemicals. When the rhodopsin molecules embedded in the membranes are excited by light, they form chemicals that close the appropriate channels which would normally allow positively charged sodium ions Na⁺ to pass through the membrane. This blocking of the sodium increases the electric potential difference across the membrane within milliseconds.

71   *Sufficient light stimulation of many molecules of rhodopsin:* The weakest light the eye can see is about 1 million photons per second.

73   *In addition, there are special neurons that reside:* In the outer synaptic layer, these specialized cells are (somewhat unimaginatively) called horizontal cells. In the inner synaptic layer, they are called amacrine cells. The amacrine cells have considerably more variety than horizontal cells, and make more complicated interconnections among the synapses between the bipolar cells and the ganglion cells.

74   *In addition, there are receptive fields that can respond:* These receptive fields require complicated time-delayed effects in the lateral connections as well as lateral asymmetries. The roles played by the horizontal and amacrine cells are more enigmatic in these cases, and scientists are actively exploring the many ways that these receptive fields may be constructed. See, for instance, W. R. Taylor, et al., "Dendritic computation of direction selectivity by retinal ganglion cells." *Science,* 289 (2000), 2347–50.

74   *The compression ratio of 126:1 of the retina:* It is intriguing that the retinal compression ratio is similar to the MP3 compression ratio. It appears as if nature already solved the optimization problem long before we came on the problem. For virtual reality simulation, the compressed visual information is uncompressed, then fed to the eyes, which compress it again. How much more efficient it would be if the compressed data on the Net could directly stimulate a retinal implant without ever needing uncompression. We could plug our eyes directly into the Net.

81   " . . . *this word information in communication theory"*: C. E. Shannon, and W. Weaver, *The Mathematical Theory of Communication.* Urabana: University of Illinois Press, 1949, pg. 8.

82   *Claude Shannon was the first to put rigorous numbers:* See C. E. Shannon, "Prediction and entropy of printed English." *Bell Systems Technical Journal,* 30 (1951), 50. For earlier work on concepts of information, see R. V. L. Hartley, "Transmission of information." *Bell Syst. Tech. J.,* 7 (1928), 535.

84   *In other words, $2^b = N$, where b equals:* A shorthand way of expressing this is to use something known as a base-2 logarithm. This is defined as the answer to the question: "How many times must I multiply 2 by itself to get a given number?" In mathematical notation, this is

$$\log_2(2^b) = b = \# \text{ of bits}$$

The mathematical symbol $\log_2$, expressed verbally as "log base 2," is just another way of saying "how many factors of 2" go into the number . . . In other words, the number of bits necessary to express one of the choices.

86 *Rather, it suffices to find the probability of occurrence:* In this case, the information can be expressed as an equation

$$H = -\sum_{i=1}^{N} p_i \log_2 (p_i)$$

where p_i is the probability that a letter will occur, and N is the number of signals possible. (The minus sign is needed to make information positive because logarithms of numbers smaller than unity are negative.)

87 *For random sequences of letters from the English alphabet:* For equal letter probabilities the information, H, is

$$H = -\sum_{i=1}^{26} \frac{1}{26} \log_2 \left(\frac{1}{26}\right) = 4.7 \text{ bits per letter}$$

87 *The information content of a series of sentences:* In this example,

$$H = -(0.6 \log_2 (0.6) + 0.24 \log_2 (0.24) + 0.1 \log_2 (0.1) \\ + 0.06 \log_2 (0.06)) = 1.5 \text{ bits}$$

88 *Morse's original code included both long and short dashes:* For Morse's original code, see. C. Cherry, *On Human Communication: A Review, a Survey, and a Criticism.* Cambridge, MA: MIT University Press, 1982, p. 37.

90 *Claude Shannon constructed the following illustrations:* Shannon and Weaver, *The Mathematical Theory of Communication,* p. 43.

92 *The redundancy of English can be quantified:* The redundancy R is given by

$$R = (H_{max} - H_{lim})/H_{max}$$

where H_{max} = 4.71 bits/letter (obtained if all transition probabilities were equal) and H_{lim} = 2.5 for the orthography of the English language on a letter basis.

92 *As a simple experiment to verify this number:* This process may take a while, like deciphering a coded message, but the information content is all there. What is missing, and what makes the decipherment difficult, is redundancy.

94 *The first recorded use of a tachistoscope:* James McKeen Cattell in *Philosophische Studien (Philosophical Studies),* 2 (1885), 635.

99 *In addition, the eye detects about 100 levels of gray scale:* The ganglion axon has a signal-to-noise level of about 128:1, so 128 scales of gray is 7 bits of information.

100 *That number is obtained by taking the 100,000 words in this book:* The in-

formation content of this book is approximately 100,000 words × five letters per word × 2.5 bits per letter of information, using letter statistics. This comes to 1.25 million bits.

101   *At nearly five letters per word:* See F. Smith, *Understanding Reading.* Hillsdale, NJ: Lawrence Erlbaum Associates, 1986, p. 198.

102   *It is this semantic information:* I want to emphasize that the rate of 25 bits per second is merely a rough value. Many studies have noted different values under differing conditions. And practice certainly increases the rate. What is important is not that the rate is exactly 25 or 30 or even 100 bits per second, but that it is not 1 million bits per second. The massive data rate into the eye cannot make it through the Human Comprehension Bottleneck.

104   *A comparison of the rate of speaking and signing was reported:* U. Bellugi, and S. Fischer, "A comparison of sign language and spoken language." *Cognition,* 1 (1972), 173.

105   *The dramatic result of this experiment:* See E. Klima, and U. Bellugi, *The Signs of Language.* Cambridge, MA: Harvard University Press, 1979, chapter 8.

107   *The time between letting up:* A. R. Jensen, "Individual Differences in the Hick Paradigm," in *Speed of Information-Processing and Intelligence,* ed. P. A. Vernon. Norwood: Ablex Publishing Corp:, 1987.

111   *"I have heard a ray of sun":* Quoted in C. D. Chaffee, *The Rewiring of America: The Fiber Optics Revolution.* Boston: Academic Press, 1988.

114   *These two wavelength bands define the working wavelengths:* The absorption band around 1.4 microns is due to water in the silica. New fiber-manufacturing processes from Lucent and Corning have eliminated water from the silica, and hence have eliminated the absorption band at 1.4 microns.

116   *Over the past six years, the doubling time for data rates:* See *Harnessing Light: Optical Science and Engineering for the 21st Century.* National Academy Press: 1998.

118   *What has the frequency bandwidth to do with the data rate:* To build up a square pulse of duration Δt from the addition of waves of slightly different frequency, a frequency bandwidth of $\Delta f = 1/\Delta t$ is required. This leads to the very simple relation $\Delta f\, \Delta t = 1$. A bandwidth of 1 terahertz is needed to generate a single 1-picosecond pulse. A data signal consisting of a sequence of 1 picosecond pulses of "1's" and "0's," with no gaps between them in the NRZ format, constitutes a data rate of 1 terabit per second.

118   *It is the speed limit for this technology:* Different values are quoted for the ultimate bandwidth for communication. Values as large as 50 terahertz are quoted, for instance, for the new fibers that have no absorption band at 1.4 microns. There is no fixed value for the ultimate bandwidth, even for a given fiber. The actual bandwidth depends on what absorption in dB per kilometer

is acceptable for a given system. The value of 30 THz is therefore a rough value, within a factor of 2 of other values typically quoted.

121 *The effect of dispersion on a pulse at the 0.850-micron band:* In a single-mode silica fiber at a wavelength near 0.850 microns, the dispersion is typically 200 psec per km.

124 *An electron traveling at the maximum speed will traverse:* To get a data rate from this transit time, it is necessary to take the inverse of the transit time and then divide by 2π.

A 1-picosecond transit time: When the electric field changes rapidly in space and time, the electron velocity does not saturate, but overshoots the 10 million cm/s "limit" by as much as a factor of 10. People doing high-speed transistor work now are achieving speeds of several hundred GHz and some labs are working on teraHertz transistors. Therefore the upper limit of electronics could approach closer to a THz.

Just as light diffracts off the iris of the eye: Extreme ultra-violet (EUV) is a new development of photolithography that uses reflective optics and is expected to go to line sizes of 25 nm. Even the more conventional deep UV technologies are expected to go somewhat below 0.1 micron. Also, it is important to keep in mind that the physical dimension of the gate on field-effect transistors is smaller than the lithography. For example, the so-called 130 nm technology now going into production has a 65 nm physical gate length.

127 *Time-division multiplexing has been the approach of choice:* Nortel introduced a 10-Gbps system in 1999. The company is developing a 40-Gbps system as of the time of writing.

130 *The duration of an individual pulse depends on:* Active mode-locked semiconductor lasers have pulse widths of 1 picosecond in response to current pulses that are much longer.

136 *Invented in 1961 by Elias Snitzer:* E. Snitzer, "Optical maser action of Nd^{3+} in barium crown glass." *Phys. Rev. Lett.,* 7 (1961), 444.

137 *The success of getting neodymium-doped glass to perform:* C. J. Koester, and E. Snitzer, "Amplification in a glass fiber." *Appl. Opt.,* 3 (10) (1964), 1182–86.

137 *In 1987, researchers at the University of Southampton:* E. A. Mears, "Low-noise erbium-doped fiber amplifier operating at 1.54 microns." *Electronic Letters,* 23 (1987), 1026.

137 *The technology of erbium-doped fiber amplifiers matured:* The twelfth transatlantic telephone cable installed in 1995 was called TAT-12.

140 *These are compression factors of 20 and 40:* See K. C. Pohlmann, *The Compact Disc Handbook.* 2nd ed. Madison, WI: A-R Editions, 1992.

145 *If optical waveguides are used:* The use of waveguides on chips will come much later than the use of fibers or free-space connection between boards.

149   *. . . a knowledge of material properties:* N. Bloembergen, *Nonlinear Optics.* 4th Edition. Singapore: World Scientific, 1996.

150   *As the electric field pulls harder:* In many materials, the forces between the atoms get weaker rather than stronger when the atoms are pulled apart.

151   *The law against photon interaction is lifted:* Non-linear optics is usually expressed in terms of a property known as non-linear optical *susceptibility.* The term *susceptibility* refers to how susceptible an electron is to displacement. There are many ways that the optical susceptibility of a material can change as a function of electric field. For instance, the susceptibility might get stronger when an electron displaces in one direction, but get weaker when it displaces in the opposite direction. This creates an asymmetry in the electron response to the electric field. This type of asymmetric non-linearity is called a second-order non-linear optical susceptibility.

Second-order non-linear susceptibility is the origin of second harmonic generation used in the very first non-linear optical experiment in 1961 by Franken and co-workers. In that experiment, the second-order susceptibility of a quartz crystal converted red ruby light into ultraviolet light. The conversion efficiency was a mere millionth of a percent—the faintest of signals. Since that time, newer materials have been explored and conversion efficiencies now routinely reach 100 percent. This non-linear effect requires a coherent laser beam to generate the second harmonic. Incoherent light (like the chaotic light described in chapter 2) cannot generate the harmonic.

Another type of susceptibility increases (or decreases) with electric field, but is insensitive to the direction of the field. Such third-order susceptibilities can lead to several different types of interactions among light beams. Third-harmonic generation is one example, but this effect is not often used for the control of light by light.

154   *He therefore predicted that optical solitons should be possible:* A. Hasegawa, and Y. Kodama, "Signal Transmission by optical solitons in monomode fiber." *Proc. IEEE,* 69 (1981), 1145.

154   *Seven years later, Linn F. Mollenauer:* L. F. Mollenauer, R. H. Stolen, and J. P. Gordon, "Experimental observation of picosecond pulse narrowing and solitons in optical fiber." *Phys. Rev. Lett.,* 45 (1980), 1095.

158   *Because solitons are non-linear, they are susceptible:* J. P. Gordon, and H. A. Haus, "Random walk of coherently amplified solitons in optical fiber transmission." *Opt. Lett.,* 11 (1986), 665.

159   *These times are easily handled by mechanical switches:* http://www.light reading.com/document.asp?doc_id = 2254.

160   *The interferometer has one input port:* The interferometer can also have two input ports by shining light on both sides of the first beamsplitter.

162   *One type of phaseshifter uses a special material:* This process is related to

non-linear optics, but in this case the driving electric field is provided by electronic circuits, rather than by the oscillating field of a light wave.

163   *At the output beamsplitter, the control beam exits:* D. Cotter, et al., "Nonlinear optics for high-speed digital information processing." *Science,* 286 (1999), 1523.

164   *Though this is only rudimentary logic:* K. L. Hall, and K. A. Rauschenbach, "100-Gbps bitwise logic." *Opt. Lett.,* 23 (1998), 1271.

164   *Using these techniques, switching speeds:* Cotter, et al., "Nonlinear optics for high-speed digital information processing," *Science,* 286 (1999), 1523.

166   *A Turing machine was the conceptual computing machine:* A. Hodges, *Alan Turing: The Enigma:* New York: Vintage Books, 1983.

166   *He presented these at the Second International Congress of Mathematics:* D. Hilbert, "Mathematical problems." *Bull. Amer. Math. Soc.,* 8 (1902), 437.

166   *He anticipated that these problems would be solved:* Roughly half of Hilbert's problems remain unsolved today.

166   *Then, in 1931, a young Austrian immigrant:* K. Gödel, *On Formally Undecidable Propositions of Principia Mathematica and Related Systems.* New York: Dover Books, 1992.

167   *After Gödel's proof, all hope:* Attempts at achieving Leibniz's dream continue in the form of metamathematics that is chiefly concerned with signs and the rules by which they are used.

167   *The foundations of universal computers became even more solid:* Universal computers may also be constructed out of other choices for the simple gates. The important point is that only two or three simple gates are needed to build any universal computer.

169   *At the peak of the project, 500,000 personal computers:* See www.setiathome.ssl.berkeley.edu.

169   *The bottleneck that keeps the nodes:* Propagation times between widely separated nodes also would slow down such a large network. However, using a concept known as small-world networks, it is possible to have very fast communication among closely clumped nodes that are highly connected, and using only a few long-distance connections to other clumps.

169   *He even devised an ingenious test:* A. Turing, "Computing machinery and intelligence." *Mind,* 59 (1950), p. 236.

170   *In the distant future, we may even plug ourselves:* For instance, direct retinal implants might be able to bypass the data uncompression and recompression that we currently use for visual presentation over the Internet.

171   *"it is a subsidiary object of this work":* F. Cajori, *A History of Mathematical Notations.* New York: Dover Books, 1993, p. 306.

171   *For instance, the following propositions:* Ibid., p. 307.

173   *It is quite possible to translate:* D. Gabor, "Holography." 1948–1971. *Science* 177, (1972) p. 299.

177   *In 1994, a research group at Stanford University:* J. F. Heanue, M. C. Bashaw, and L. Hesselink, "Volume holographic storage and retrieval of digital data." *Science,* 265 (1994), 749–52.

177   *In both the "before" and "after" shots:* For an interesting discussion of the visual science behind the ambiguity of the *Mona Lisa's* smile, see M. S. Livingston, "Is it warm? Is it real? Or just low spatial frequency?" *Science,* 290 (2000), 1299.

180   *Given that much time, holographic optical memory:* It is likely that conventional storage technologies will reach the terabit/gigabit-per-second goal before the holographic technology has a chance to mature to that level.

185   *When we want to extract a specific idea:* The Image Correlator figure is at www.physics.purdue.edu/~nolte/mind

189   *It took only a year or two after John Hopfield published:* J. J. Hopfield, "Neural networks and physical systems with emergent collective computational abilities." *Proc. Nat. Acad. Sci: USA,* 79 (1982), 2552.

189   *Dmitri Psaltis, an energetic young physicist:* N. H. Farhat, et al., "Optical implementation of the Hopfield model." *Appl. Opt.,* 24 (1985), 1469.

189   *The holographic neural network of Psaltis's group:* K.-Y. Hsu, H.-Y. Li, and D. Psaltis, "Holographic implementation of a fully connected neural network." *Proc. IEEE,* 78 (1990), 1637.

189   *The experimental arrangement of an iterative feedback loop:* The Optical Neural Net figure is at www.physics.purdue.edu/~nolte/mind

192   *The path lengths are kept fixed by the dynamic hologram:* In my research lab at Purdue University, we are developing sensitive adaptive interferometers for applications as diverse as laser-based ultrasound detection and processing ultra-fast laser pulses. The dynamic holographic medium we use is a special semiconductor film with quantum enhancements called photorefractive quantum wells. See, for instance, D. D. Nolte, "Semi-insulating semiconductor heterostructures: Optoelectronic properties and applications." *J. Appl. Phys.,* 85 (1999), 6259–89, and D. D. Nolte et al., "Adaptive beam combining and interferometry with photorefractive quantum wells." *J. Opt. Soc. Amer. B,* 18 (2001), 195.

193   *Appropriate changes in the hologram occur:* However, there are practical obstacles that need to be overcome before time-reversal mirrors can be used for astronomy or communication satellites. For instance, time-reversal mirrors require coherent light (not available from stars) and highly sensitive non-linear crystals.

193   *He constructed a ring resonator:* D. Z. Anderson, "Coherent optical eigenstate memory." *Opt. Lett.,* 11 (1986), 56.

194   *Second, it moved optical neural networks:* The injected information in the experiment is provided by a spatial modulator driven by an electronic computer. But it could in principle have been the output of an upstream optical machine without any need to translate into the electronic domain.

199   " . . . *because nature isn't classical, dammit*": R. P. Feynman, "Simulating Physics with Computers." Int. J. Theor. Phys. 21 (1982) p. 486.

207   *One ways is to replace Young's apparatus with a simple interferometer:* The Quantum Society in the Dark figure is at www.physics.purdue.edu/~nolte/mind

208   *These are much better odds than for Young's apparatus:* See P. Kwiat, H. Weinfurter, and A. Zeiliger, "Quantum seeing in the dark." *Scientific American* (Nov. 1996), and P. Kwiat, et al., "Interaction-free measurement." *Phys. Rev. Lett,* 74 (1995), 4763–66.

209   *Nature has provided us with an ideal method:* The Calcite figure is at www.physics.purdue.edu/~nolte/mind

212   *These are about the best odds you are going to get:* You can do even better with a slightly more sophisticated experimental arrangement. See P. G. Kwiat et al., "High-efficiency quantum interrogation measurements via the quantum Zeno effect." *Phys. Rev. Lett.,* 83 (1999), 4725–28.

212   *When the positronium is initially at rest:* Angular momentum is associated with any rotating mass, like the rotation of a bicycle wheel or a spinning top.

212   *In Bohm's thought experiment:* Calcite cannot be used to analyze the polarization of gamma rays emitted from the annihilation of positronium. In most tabletop experiments that study the EPR paradox, visible or near-infrared photons are generated by calcium atoms or by special non-linear crystals called down-conversion crystals.

213   *He proved, using arguments about probabilities:* J. Bell, "On the Einstein-Podolsky-Rosen paradox." *Physics,* 1 (1964), 195.

214   *However, nagging suspicions of local influences:* A. Aspect, J. Dalibard, and G. Roger, "Experimental test of Bell's inequalities using time-varying analyzers." *Phys. Rev. Lett.,* 49 (1982), 1804.

218   *This theorem states that it is fundamentally impossible:* The quantum non-cloning theorem is more rigorously a theorem that states it is impossible to clone two or more general quantum states. It is always possible to clone at least one state, but this would not be very useful.

218   *That alternate was proposed in 1993:* C. H. Bennett, et al., "Teleporting an unknown quantum state via dual classical and Einstein-Podolsky-Rosen channels." *Phys. Rev. Lett.,* 70 (1993), 1895.

220   *The first quantum teleportation experiments were performed in 1997:* D. Bouwmeester, et al., "Experimental quantum teleportation." *Nature,* 390 (1997), 575–79.

220   *and in Rome:* D. Boschi, et al., "Experimental realization of teleporting an unknown pure quantum state via dual classical and Einstein-Podolsky-Rosen channels." *Phys. Rev. Lett.,* 80 (1998), 1121–25.

221   *See how long it takes you:* 576,603,310,111 = 759359 × 759329.

221   *This number takes 40 bits to describe in binary notation:* In binary notation, the number 576,603,310,111 = 1000011001000000001111000100100000 011111.

221   *it takes my old computer (MacIntosh G4 with two processors):* A brute-force Matlab program to do this is given by

```
function y = prime(n)
        tic
        i = 2;
    sqrtn = sqrt(n);
while ((i<sqrtn) & (rem(n,i) ~ = 0))
        i = i+1;
    end
    if (rem(n,i) == 0)
        i
    y = 0;
    else
    y = 1;
    end
    toc
```

221   *The problem is that the time to factor a number:* The time to factor a product of primes increases as $2^B/2$, where B is the number of bits needed to express the number.

222   *Therefore, forcing potential eavesdroppers to factor:* R. L. Rivest, A. Shamir, and L. M. Adleman, "A method of obtaining digital signatures and public-key cryptosystems." *Commun. ACM,* 21 (2) (1978), 120–26.

222   *As an example of the difficulty factoring large numbers:* M. Gardner, "Mathematical games." *Scientific American,* (August 1977), 120–24.

222   *They mustered a coordinated effort:* G. Taubes, "Small army of code-breakers conquers a 129-digit giant." *Science,* 264 (1994), 312–16.

222   *Today, even 512-bit encryption is susceptible:* See J. Brown, *Minds, Machines and the Multiverse: The Quest for the Quantum Computer.* New York: Simon & Schuster, 2000, p. 170.

223   *An experiment conducted in Geneva, Switzerland, in 1997:* W. Tittel, et al., "Violation of Bell inequalities by photons more than 10 km apart." *Phys. Rev. Lett.,* 81 (1998), 3563–66.

223   *More recent demonstrations have succeeded in sending:* R. Hughes, and J.

Nordholt, *"Quantum cryptography takes to the air."* *Physics World,* 12 (1999), 31–35.

225   *"Quantum computing is a qualitatively new way":* D. Deutsch, *The Fabric of Reality.* New York: Allen Lane, 1997, p. 221.

228   *No fuzzy answers are allowed.:* Fuzzy logic is an alternative logic system that allows mixtures of answers.

230   *Reversibility was shown by Rolf Landauer:* R. Landauer, "Irreversibility and heat generation in the computing process." *IBM J. Res. Dev.,* 3 (1961) 181–91.

231   *Furthermore, a c-NOT gate is a source of entangled pairs:* The control state can be in a superposition of both 1 and 0 in the coherent state $\Psi_c = \psi_0 + \psi_1$. The output is then also a coherent state. If the input data state is 0, then the output of the c-NOT is $\Psi_{out} = \psi_{00} + \psi_{11}$. Notice that there are two subscripts for the output functions. The first subscript stands for the control-out value, which is just the control-in value. The second subscript stands for the data-out value. Since the data input was 0, it remains 0 when the control is 0, and it flips to 1 when the control is 1. The quantum c-NOT has therefore performed two controlled-NOT calculations in a single step. The output $\Psi_{out} = \psi_{00} + \psi_{11}$ is also an entangled state between the control line and the signal line. It does not matter that the control bit goes through unchanged. The interaction between the qubits correlates their values.

232   *In 1994, it was realized that by using:* S. Loyd, "Almost any quantum logic gate is universal." *Phys. Rev. Lett.,* 75 (1995), 346–49.

233   *This was an astounding breakthrough:* D. Deutsch, "Quantum theory, the Church-Turing principle and the universal quantum computer." *Proc. Roy. Soc. Lond.,* 400 (1985), 97.

233   *He decided to tackle the problem of finding the factors:* P. W. Shor, *"Algorithms for Quantum Computation: Discrete Logarithms and Factoring,":* *35th Annual Symposium on Foundations of Computer Science.* Santa Fe, NM IEEE Computer Society Press, 1994.

234   *This question was first asked in 1989 by Gerald Milburn:* G. Milburn, "Quantum optical Fredkin gate." *Phys. Rev. Lett.,* 62 (1989), 2124.

235   *The situation was saved by a timely theoretical discovery:* Loyd, "Almost any quantum logic gate is universal." 346–49.

235   *The same year, in one of the first experimental demonstrations:* Q. A. Turchette, et al., "Measurement of conditional phase shifts for quantum logic." *Phys. Rev. Lett.,* 75 (1995) 4710–13.

236   *Furthermore, the NIST experiment went farther:* C. Monroe, et al., "Demonstration of a fundamental quantum logic gate." *Phys. Rev. Lett.,* 75 (1995), 4714–17.

237   *The recent demonstrations by the NIST group:* C. Sackett, et al., "Experimental entanglement of four particles." *Nature,* 404 (2000), 256–59.

241   *" . . . the sign language and grammar":* Hesse, *Magister Ludi: Game,* p. 27.

ACKNOWLEDGEMENTS

Just as this book is a journey, beginning with the human eye and ending by exploring quantum optical computers of the future, it is also a personal journey. I started down this path shortly after leaving Eugene Haller's group at the University of California at Berkeley in 1988 when I arrived at AT&T Bell Laboratories to work with Alastair Glass, then Head of the Optical Materials Department. The Holmdel lab was Mecca for optical science. Never before, or since, have I experienced such critical intellectual mass. Ideas flew up and down hallways and around lunch tables, and many of those ideas, whose birth I witnessed, became the basis of the optical revolution that is now supplying the ever-increasing demand for bandwidth. When I left Bell Labs in 1989 to accept a faculty position in physics at Purdue University, I carried away with me intense memories of the power of optics and the concept, that evolved through frequent discussions with Alastair, of the parallel communication advantages of light and image. I owe him, and Bell Labs, a great debt for planting that seed.

The conception of the book evolved over the years, crystallizing into its final form with the astute suggestions of my editor, Stephen Morrow of The Free Press, who encouraged me to make a foray into current advances in quantum optics and quantum computing. The research for those chapters turned into the first course offered on the topic at Purdue, a course designed for daring undergraduates who had never had quantum mechanics or modern physics.

During the writing of the manuscript I received valuable insights from friends and family. I thank: Arthur Pyrak and my brother James Nolte for reading the manuscript early in the process; Yi Ding, Mihaela Dinu, Mark Lundstrom and Ephraim Fischbach for technical remarks; Nancy Nolte for her editorial work on the manuscript; my graphic artist, Krista Buuck for her fine artistic sense that vastly improved my original illustrations. Above all, I thank my wife Laura for her patience and help over the many days, months and years to bring this book to fruition. Her unwavering belief in me made this project possible.

INDEX

ABOUT THE AUTHOR

David D. Nolte teaches physics at Purdue University in West Lafayette, Indiana. As a leading researcher of the physics of optical materials and devices, he is the author of over 130 journal papers, has several US patents on adaptive holographic films, and has edited two books on optical properties of semiconductors. A popular lecturer on the Purdue campus, he has been recognized both for his teaching and for his distinguished research. In 1997 he was elected a Fellow of the Optical Society of America for his pioneering work on dynamic holography in semiconductor nanostructures.